What People Are Saying About
Chicken Soup for the Baseball Fan's Soul . . .

"Any book that has baseball *and* Lasorda has got to be great!"
Bobby Valentine
manager, New York Mets

"From the neighborhood dugouts to Yankee Stadium, the stories in *Chicken Soup for the Baseball Fan's Soul* capture the All-American sport on every level. The memories these writers have chosen to share make time stand still."
Dave Dravecky
former San Francisco Giants pitcher
and president, Outreach of Hope

"These colorful and heartwarming tales elevate baseball's place in our hearts and solidify it as our national pastime."
Mike Conte
head baseball coach
California University of Pennsylvania

"*Chicken Soup for the Baseball Fan's Soul* reminded me that this game has so many similarities to business. I have no doubt baseball's lessons about teamwork, practice, and hard work have helped me throughout my business career. As a catcher, I also had to deal with plenty of pitchers with unique personalities and temperaments. This experience is invaluable in business relationships today."
Rick Rayson
managing partner
Arizona practice, Deloitte & Touche LLP

"This book is very well done and really great for the fans."
Sparky Anderson
Hall of Fame baseball manager

"You've seen the T-shirt, 'Baseball Is Life.' If that's true, then this book about baseball is really about life—the victories, the tragedies, the work, the strategies, the disciplines, the rewards, the camaraderie and the fun. Since I've lived most of my life inside this wonderful game, I know it's true that baseball is life. And this book delivers so many of these good things for you to enjoy. This is more than just chicken soup. This is good medicine."

Orel Hershiser
baseball veteran and author of the bestseller, *Between the Lines: Nine Principles to Live By*

"This book provides insight into the life lessons that can be learned from competing in the great game of baseball. Reading *Chicken Soup for the Baseball Fan's Soul* will revitalize old memories and create new excitement for baseball players and fans."

Jeff Weins
athletic director, Reynolds High School

"The inspirational memories created by the family of baseball's past and present have been captured in *Chicken Soup for the Baseball Fan's Soul*. May the passion and power of this book bless and inspire."

Jack and Mary Cain
former owners of the Portland Rockies Baseball Club

"Reading *Chicken Soup for the Baseball Fan's Soul* is like spending time with good friends."

Robin Roberts
Hall of Fame pitcher

CHICKEN SOUP FOR THE BASEBALL FAN'S SOUL

Inspirational Stories of Baseball,
Big-League Dreams and the
Game of Life

Jack Canfield
Mark Victor Hansen
Mark Donnelly & Chrissy Donnelly
and
Tommy Lasorda

Health Communications, Inc.
Deerfield Beach, Florida

www.hci-online.com
www.chickensoup.com

We would like to acknowledge the following publishers and individuals for permission to reprint the following material. (Note: The stories that are in the public domain, or that were written by Jack Canfield, Mark Victor Hansen, Mark Donnelly, Chrissy Donnelly and Tommy Lasorda are not included in this listing.)

A Baseball for Dad. Reprinted by permission of Patrick Thomson. ©1985 Patrick Thomson.

No Crying in Baseball. Excerpted from *Sermon on the Mound* by Michael O'Connor. ©2001 Bethany House Publishers. Reprinted with permission.

Batter Up, Dad. Reprinted by permission of Anne E. Carter. ©2001 Anne E. Carter.

The Only Way I Know. Excerpted from *The Only Way I Know* by Cal Ripken Jr. and Mike Ryan. ©1997, 1998 Cal Ripken Jr. Reprinted by permission of Tufton Sports & Management, his agents.

The Lost Ball. Reprinted by permission of Dan Connolly. ©2001 Dan Connolly.

(Continued on page 382)

Library of Congress Cataloging-in-Publication Data
Chicken soup for the baseball fan's soul : from the world of baseball / [edited by] Jack Canfield . . . [et al.].

    p.   cm.
    ISBN 1-55874-965-9 (tradepaper) — ISBN 1-55874-966-7 (hard)
    1. Baseball—Anecdotes. 2. Baseball fans—Conduct of life. I. Canfield, Jack, 1944-

GV873 .C53 2001
796.357—dc21

                       2001039648

©2001 Jack Canfield and Mark Victor Hansen

ISBN 1-55874-965-9 (trade paper) — ISBN 1-55874-966-7 (hardcover)

Publisher: Health Communications, Inc.
                3201 S.W. 15th Street
                Deerfield Beach, FL 33442-8190

Cover design by Larissa Hise Henoch
Inside book formatting by Lawna Patterson Oldfield and Dawn Grove
Cover graphics by ALLSPORT Photography

With love, Tommy Lasorda
dedicates this book to
Emily Tess,
the apple of her family's eye.

We also dedicate this book to the fans
who love the game, and to baseball writers
and sportscasters, whose passion and eloquence
bring this game to life for those
who can't get to the ballpark.

Contents

3. DEFINING MOMENTS

4. HEROES

5. FROM THE DUGOUT

6. HEADING FOR HOME

7. FIELD OF DREAMS

8. WISDOM OF THE GAME

9. BOTTOM OF THE NINTH

Acknowledgments

It's been and honor and a privilege to write, compile and edit *Chicken Soup for the Baseball Fan's Soul.* At times it's been a home run and at times it's been a base on balls, but as a whole, it's been an incredible season. As with all projects of this magnitude, we received important help from many caring people. We would like to thank the following people:

First and foremost, we thank our families for all of their love and support on this project: It all begins and ends at home.

We are grateful to the following people who read and scored nearly two hundred stories and helped make the final selections: Fred Angelis, Sabrina D. Black, Veronica Cire, D'ette Corona, Dominic Dale, William Dent, Chris Garman, Kelly Garman, Donald Gurley, David R. Hamilton, Melanie Johnson, Mike Johnson, Tim Johnson, Tom Krause, Dan Kyburz, Dennis Lewis, Barbara LoMonaco, Jack Lowe, Jonathon Martin, Aly McKenzie, Heather McNamara, Louise A. Mehr, Linda Mitchell, Bob Neale, Jeanne Neale, Lydia Nelson, John Newman, Ron Nielsen, Kevin Radford, Rick Rayson, Vickie Rayson, Amy Lynn Reifsnyder, Chad Sayban, Victoria Smith, Tom Varitek, Jeff Wiens and Jim Williamson.

Bill Goldberg, thank you for your belief in us and your passion for this project. You helped us stretch a triple into a home run.

Thanks to Bob Elliott of the *Toronto Sun* for your help and support.

Patty and Jeff Aubery, a special thanks for your friendship, moral support and guidance. You are true friends.

Kelly Garman, thanks for becoming a baseball expert. Without you our batting average would be just that— average. Debbie Merkle, Paul Van Dyke and Greg Ottersbach, thanks for your help and encouragement along the way.

Heather McNamara and D'ette Corona, thanks for your expert editing and guidance. As usual, you've enhanced the quality of the final product.

Mark Victor Hansen's team: Patty Hansen, Trudy Marshall, Maria Nickless, Laurie Hartman, Michelle Adams, Tracy Smith, Dee Dee Romanello, Dawn Henshall, Lisa Williams, Kristi Knoppe, David Coleman, Laura Rush, Paula Childers, Tayna Jones, Faith Fuata and Shanna Vieryra.

And Jack Canfield's team: Deborah Hatchell, Nancy Autio, Veronica Romero, Cindy Holland, Leslie Riskin, Robin Yerian, Vince Wong, Teresa Esparza and Geneva Lee.

The entire Health Communications team, your professionalism, dedication and teamwork are an inspiration and make all of our jobs easier.

Peter Vegso, it's truly a pleasure to work with a publisher and friend who shares our desire to make a difference in the world.

Terry Burke, it's always a home run working with you. We also thank the entire sales and marketing team for their enthusiasm. Oh, and of course a big New York thank you to the most loyal Yankees fan of them all, Kelly Maragni.

Christine Belleris, Lisa Drucker, Allison Janse, Susan Tobias and Kathy Grant, thanks for the expert editing and support.

To Larissa Hise, Lawna Oldfield, Andrea Brower, Lisa Camp, Anthony Clausi and Dawn Grove, thanks for your creative design work.

Kim Weiss and Paola Fernandez, thanks for helping us reach all those baseball fans.

We also thank those who made the heartfelt effort to submit the thousands of stories, letters, poems and quotes we reviewed for possible inclusion in the book. While we weren't able to use them all, we were touched by each one. Your stories provided us with constant encouragement and reinforcement that we were in the ballpark. Thank you all!

Introduction

For millions of fans worldwide, baseball is much more than a sport. It is a filter, a backdrop, a canvas against and through which we experience and live our lives. Nowhere is this more evident than in the movies. No sport has had more movies (or books for that matter) produced about it. More interesting though are the type of movies that rate as the classics of the sport. Movies like *Field of Dreams, The Natural, Bull Durham, A League of Their Own, For Love of the Game,* and for you vintage film buffs, *The Pride of the Yankees* (in which Babe Ruth has a cameo), are included in almost any Baseball Top Ten List out there. These movies celebrate all that is good about baseball, along with some of the bad for contrast. They portray baseball as a search for meaning, as a sport for the everyman, as a mirror of how we evolve as a culture, as the continual struggle to overcome, as a place where relationships are forged and as an experience that forms the strongest of character traits. They portray baseball as something more than just the American pastime. They portray it as something more like the game of life. This is what inspired us to begin work on *Chicken Soup for the Baseball Fan's Soul.*

The stories in this book celebrate the full spectrum of the baseball experience. From George Brett's valiant end-of-season pursuit of his milestone three thousandth hit to an unknown high school baseball coach making his first major-league pitching start—eighteen years after being drafted; from the exuberant innocence of a T-baller's first game to a sportswriter's self-described perfect-game-journey back from the depths of cynicism; from a celebration of the bigger-than-life legend of Babe Ruth to the story of the birth and life of the world's most losing player, Charlie Brown; from a Little Leaguer's first hilarious, unconventional inside-the-park home run to the unexpected pre- and post-catch adventures of the man snagging Mark McGwire's seventieth round-tripper; and from the story of a mother who remembers the transitional stages in her son's life through their shared baseball experiences to the father and son engaged in that timeless, never-ending, full-circle experience called having a catch.

These stories will inspire you, make you laugh out loud, bring a tear to your eye and perhaps cause you to reflect on the things that really matter in life. Within these stories you will find many of the finer qualities of the human spirit. You will find courage, strength, passion, persistence, integrity, love, compassion and a whole host of others. And you will find them not just in the superstars of the game, but in the unsung bit players and everyday heroes that make up the soul of the game. Because what we found as we neared the completion of this heartfelt project is that baseball is indeed more than a game. Or, as Annie Savoy, the self-proclaimed "high priestess of the church of baseball" from the movie *Bull Durham* might have said, "Baseball isn't a sport; it's a religion."

Share with Us

We would love to hear your reactions to the stories in this book. Please let us know what your favorite stories were and how they affected you.

We also invite you to send us stories you would like to see published in future editions of *Chicken Soup for the Baseball Fan's Soul.* You can send us stories you have written or stories written by others you like.

Send submissions to:

Chicken Soup for the Baseball Fan's Soul
P.O. Box 30880
Santa Barbara, CA 93130
Fax: 805-563-2945
Web site: *www.chickensoup.com*

You can also access our e-mail or find a current list of planned books at *www.chickensoup.com* or *www.clubchickensoup.com.*

We hope you enjoy reading this book as much as we enjoyed compiling, editing and writing it.

1

FOR LOVE OF THE GAME

*This field, this game, is a part of our past.
It reminds us of all that was good and
could be good again.*

*James Earl Jones
as Terrance Mann, in*
Field of Dreams

A Baseball for Dad

Many hot summers ago, when I was in elementary school in California, I fell in love with an idea, a game, a dream. I fell madly in love with baseball.

I soaked in baseball. I threw, hit, ran, read, felt baseball. I would throw without a ball, hit home runs in my head, be a hero, be a bum. I loved it all.

For a while, baseball was bigger than even my dad. I saw that he had a hero. How could my hero have a hero?

My dad's hero was Stan the Man. Stan Musial from Donora, Pennsylvania, who played for the St. Louis Cardinals. At the time, St. Louis was the closest major-league team to Los Angeles. All major-league players were heroes in my eyes, but Dad told me that Stan was the greatest of his time.

There were others who could hit the ball harder, run faster, field better or even put on a better show than Stan the Man. But Dad said that Stan was special.

God had given Stan the tools and he used them well. But that was only a small portion of what made him great. He was all the things that my father valued. He was the embodiment of all that life stood for.

I wanted to be like Dad and I felt that Dad wanted to be

like Stan Musial. I knew I couldn't go wrong trying to fit into those shoes.

This particular summer was special because my dad and I were going to the place where my father grew up— St. Louis. Just the two of us. It was hot and humid in what seemed like a foreign land where the people were pale and talked slightly off English.

In California, everything was new. In St. Louis, everything was old. Only the people were young.

Our mission was to meet Stan the Man. I almost didn't believe it. There was a part of me that didn't really think that these idols were real people. To me, they only came to life as legend, like Paul Bunyan or Robin Hood. But the closer I came to the meeting, the more obvious it was that Mr. Musial was a real man. Newspapers said so, all my relatives said so, and most important, Dad reassured me.

Through some good fortune, I got a ball autographed by Musial. An injured rookie was at the hospital where my grandmother worked. She told him my story and he got Stan's autograph on the ball. The ball was living proof that Stan was for real.

That night, the Cardinals were playing the Brooklyn Dodgers and we went. I held onto my ball so tightly that I elicited an inquiry from the guy next to me.

"New ball?" he asked.

"Yep, with an autograph," I teased him.

"Who?" he prodded.

"The Man," I bragged.

"No."

"Yes."

"I don't believe you."

"Here," I handed him the ball.

"Wow! I'll give you $20 for it right now!" Twenty dollars to a ten-year-old boy in 1955 was a pot of gold.

"Nope, let me have it back," I demanded.

"You've got a dream in the form of a baseball," he said. "Take good care of it!"

I shoved it deep into my pocket and resolved that the ball was the most important thing in my life.

The next day was the big day. We would be meeting the Man. As Dad and I walked up the walk to the door, I was in a state of shock. "He'll be here," Dad said, knocking.

Sure enough, the door swung open, and there stood Stan the Man in his robe and slippers. My dad introduced himself then me to Stan, and explained that the ball he had signed earlier was for me.

He was just as I had imagined him: sincere, kind, strong. He looked at me in a way that only a few adults look at kids, and we knew that we had a common bond— baseball.

He inquired about my baseball playing. I bragged. Next to Stan, I felt that it was necessary. I thought that I was some great baseball player. He understood.

Getting back to Los Angeles couldn't happen fast enough. When I told everyone about my experience in St. Louis with Stan Musial, nobody believed me. Such a reality didn't exist, my friends insisted. I knew that it had happened, though, and that the ball, the meeting, the feeling would always be mine. The older I became, the less I revealed my treasure.

The seasons paraded by. Teams won, players got traded. There were retirements, rookies, home runs, other kids and other idols. My father died. As in life, he wished to carry on in death. His last request was that in his casket there be a deck of cards, a bottle of Jack Daniel's and, most important, a baseball. He knew that, wherever he was going, he ought not be ill equipped.

On the day he was buried, the whiskey and the cards were ready. The last item was a baseball. I decided it should be my twenty-year-old autographed treasure.

Since my father had been responsible for me meeting Stan Musial, I felt it most appropriate that it should be with my dad. I would miss it, but it belonged with him. Some people thought that it was a sacrifice. I did my best to assure them that it was not. The ball was where it belonged.

Spring trainings, long hot Julys and thousands of extra innings later, my sister, Kathie, asked me to stand in for Dad at her wedding. I was flattered. I was honored to give my sister away, to stand in the shoes of my dad.

On the eve of my sister's big day, we went to an elegant French restaurant for the rehearsal dinner. As the evening went on, the impact of the occasion seemed to build to an emotional crescendo. The speeches were many. I became aware that something special was happening.

My sister is an airline stewardess and had flown with the Los Angeles Dodgers for part of the 1984 season. After dinner, she thanked my younger brother for his participation in her wedding by giving him a baseball autographed by all of the Dodgers and dedicated to him by Tommy Lasorda.

I was next for a gift.

She told all of us about flying with Lasorda, about how, on the way to spring training, she had told him the story of my Stan Musial baseball.

She said she'd had a difficult time completing the story, stopping again and again to recapture her composure. She said she had been amazed to learn that Tommy Lasorda knew exactly what she meant.

"I'll get that baseball back for you," he told her.

Later during the flight, Lasorda told my sister that he, too, had had a magical relationship with his father, and that when his father had been laid to rest, a baseball accompanied him.

Lasorda told my sister that his life in baseball, his

success in baseball and his love of baseball, had all come from his father.

Being a friend of Stan Musial, Lasorda called and told him the story of the baseball. Musial responded with a new autographed baseball and sent it to Lasorda. The ball was then mailed to my sister.

I looked up to see her holding the ball. "I got you another one," she said, throwing it to me.

I was a child again, coming home. I heard the distant crack of bat on ball and the roar of a crowd. I heard that man sitting next to me in St. Louis in 1955. "New ball?" he asked.

"Yep, with an autograph," I teased him.

"Who?" he prodded.

"The Man," I bragged.

"No."

"Yes."

And then: "You've got a dream in the form of a baseball," he said. "Take good care of it!"

And so I will.

Patrick Thomson

No Crying in Baseball

Had the pitcher noticed my right foot twitching nervously on the bag he would have easily surmised my criminal intent. Sweat soaked the upper portion of my uniform, the back of which proclaimed the virtues of Brown's Hardware. Two batters had come and gone, fastball victims now reposing in the statistical morgue of the official scorekeeper. But still I remained anchored after my lead-off single.

So long had I been on first base that it had become like a second home to me. I was getting mail there. Social Security checks would be arriving soon. Yet no sign from Mr. Barclay in the third-base coach's box. Second base, the promised land, was sixty feet away, but I may as well have been standing on Alcatraz.

Maybe it was the heat. It must have been ninety-five degrees that day and the sweltering valley sun surely extracted all reason from my brain. Perhaps it was boredom. A fellow can go stir crazy waiting around for a jailbreak. It might have been a rare polar event as the magnetic pull between myself and that square-shaped flour sack could not have been stronger. Does it really matter why? Looking back, I see I had no choice. I was as helpless as a sailor succumbing to the call of the Sirens.

History records that on the first pitch to the inning's fourth batter, as the baseball hit the center of the catcher's glove, the sound of horsehide kissing cowhide conspired to simulate a starter's pistol. At least this is how I remember it. I do know it was an electrifying sound that startled me into action. Never mind that I had gotten a late jump. Never mind I had no plan. I bolted for my destination like a turkey being chased on Thanksgiving.

Surely the well-known fact that I was the league's slowest runner would only shock and fluster the catcher into stupefying inaction. Surely as my quest was noble and my heart was true the ball would sail over the shortstop's reach into center field. Surely I had not counted on a quick release and the straight throw that was awaiting me as I reached the midway point of my incredible journey.

My eyes grew wide. I had not considered this possibility. I was about to feel the sting of baseball mortality. In an instant I experienced the entire spectrum of Dr. Kübler-Ross's five stages of death: denial, anger, bargaining, depression and, finally, acceptance. As I strolled into second with the force of a train half an hour after the coal is depleted, I felt a dysfunctional obligation to slide, though it was merely a formality. Denial had decided to step back into the box and take some extra cuts.

To my discredit and lasting embarrassment, I tried a last-minute trick slide, which led me to dance out of the base path and into shallow centerfield where, from my opponent's flank, I then threw my body at the base in a final desperate, twisted, flailing motion that nearly inspired spectators to throw a telethon on my behalf.

The umpire was generous. He could have made one of those huge arm-motion calls that looks like a pitcher winding up and throwing the ball straight into the ground with raw, brutal force. For indeed, I had been shot down from Austin to Dallas and deserved as much. Instead, he looked at me with compassion, clenched his meaty fist gently and muttered, "Yer out, Son."

The shame of it all. Oh, the humanity! I laid on my back wondering, *What should I do now?* If a game show had somehow magically broken out right there on the diamond, the final *Jeopardy* question would have been, "What is get up, dust yourself off and look as good as you can jogging back to the dugout?" Instead I panicked and chose a regrettable course.

I started crying.

I had been found guilty of hubris and was sentenced to the spectacle of public humiliation. If tears could have melted me as the bucket of water did Margaret Hamilton in *The Wizard of Oz,* I would have been grateful for the escape.

Instead, I was led off the field by Mr. Barclay, bawling my eyes out. But, hey, I was ten years old that day. Nobody had ever warned me about the taboo I had broken, nor the cardinal rule I would be encouraged to follow the rest of my days.

My moment of searing clarity came, as so many universal moments do, in the movies. The film was *A League of Their Own,* the true story of the women's baseball league that entertained Americans during World War II. In one scene, a blond young woman had just made an egregious fielding error. Approaching the dugout after the inning, her manager, played by Tom Hanks, gave her a scathing earful of advice on the merits of hitting the cutoff girl. In an instant, she was reduced to tears. Hanks was stunned. He, a veteran manager and grizzled former major leaguer, had, apparently, never witnessed such an event on a ball field.

"Are you crying?" he inquired, dumbfounded. "There's no crying. There's no crying in baseball!"

No crying in baseball?

Sez who? Tom Hanks? My dad? Mr. Barclay? I want to know. Who fed us this line of propaganda?

Baseball not only brings out, but encourages, the humanity in us. The game is a festival of emotional excess. When so much in life tells us to keep our feelings close to the vest, baseball has always been a signed permission slip to let go of whatever needs releasing. You name it, baseball invites it. Joy, pity, anger, regret, envy, jubilation, despair, euphoria, amazement, hatred, respect, laughter—all these emotions are played out on the field and in the stands, inning after inning, game after game, season after season.

And crying.

Sometimes when I go back to my hometown, I retrace those ill-fated steps taken on the diamond of my youth. I remember a ten-year-old boy in a baseball uniform. Maybe he wasn't looking for that extra base. Maybe his mind was really on home—the warmth, the safety—and he just couldn't wait to get there. Maybe he just wanted someone to say, "Well done . . . well done, good and faithful Little Leaguer."

I think about him laying there in the dust as I stand at the exact spot some thirty-five years later. I want to reach down and tell him everything will be okay, that one day he will be safe at home, that there will be no more tears, no more embarrassing moments, and I know the way if only he will follow. But the years are a one-way mirror. I can see him, but he cannot communicate with me. So he's going to have to learn his lessons through trials of fire and journeys of joy.

How clearly I see him wiping the dirt from his uniform, preparing for that looooonnnggg walk back to the dugout. There is so much life, so much joy, so many tears before him. And despite all the well-intentioned advice and sound training I have received through the years, when I picture him walking back from second base with that affected limp, I cry.

Michael O'Connor

Batter Up, Dad

My father was an avid baseball fan. I grew up in New York City and was able to see the greats play at the Polo Grounds, Ebbets Field and Yankee Stadium. Many a Saturday was spent with my dad cheering on our favorite team. As much as I loved the game of baseball, alas, I was born female at a time when girls watched more than they played. Whenever he could, Dad took me out to the park where the neighborhood Little League played and pitched balls for me to hit. We played together for hours, and baseball became a big part of my life.

One day at the park, a woman pushing a young boy in a wheelchair stopped to watch us play. My dad was over to them in a flash to ask if the child could join our game. The woman explained that the boy was her son and that he had polio and wouldn't be able to get out of the chair. That didn't stop my dad. He placed the bat in the youngster's hand, pushed him out to home plate and assisted him in holding the bat. Then he yelled out to me on the mound, "Anne, pitch one in to us."

I was nervous that I might hit the child but could see the delight in the boy's eyes, so I aimed at the bat and let the ball fly. The ball made contact with the bat with an assist from my dad and the child screamed with joy. The ball flew over my head and headed for right field. I ran to catch up with it and, as I turned, I heard my dad singing "Take Me Out to the Ball Game" while he pushed the wheelchair around the bases. The mother clapped and the boy begged to be allowed to continue the game.

An hour later we all left the field, very tired but very happy. The boy's mother had tears in her eyes when she thanked my father for making it such a special day for her son. Dad smiled that wonderful grin that I loved so much and told the mother to bring the boy back next Saturday and we would play another game.

Dad and I were at the field the next Saturday but the mother and son never came. I felt sad and wondered what had happened to change their mind about joining us. Dad and I played many more games of baseball but never saw the two again.

Twenty years passed and my beloved father died at the tender age of fifty-nine. With my dad gone, things changed so much that the family decided to move to Long Island. I had very mixed emotions about leaving the neighborhood where I had grown up.

I decided to take one last walk around the park where Dad and I had spent so many happy moments. I stopped at the baseball field where we played our Saturday games. Two Little League teams were on the field just about to start a game. I sat down to watch for awhile. I felt the sting of tears in my eyes as I watched the children play the game that I loved. I missed my dad so much.

"Jeff, protect your base," one coach yelled. I cheered the runner on when the ball was hit far into the outfield. One coach turned and smiled and said, "The kids sure love a rooting section, Miss." He continued, "I never thought I'd ever be a coach playing on this field. You see, I had polio as a child and was confined to a wheelchair. One day my mother pushed me to the park and a man was playing baseball with his daughter. He stopped when he saw us watching and asked my mother if I could join them in their game. He helped me to hold the bat and his daughter pitched to me. I was able to hit the ball with the man's assistance and he ran me around the bases in my wheelchair singing the song 'Take Me Out to the Ball Game.' I went home happier that night than I had been in years. I believe that experience gave me the desire to walk again. We moved to New Jersey the next day—that's why my mother had taken me to the park, so I could say good-bye to my friends. I never forgot that man and his daughter or that day. I dreamed about running around the bases on my own two feet and the dream, with a lot of hard work, came true. I moved back here last year, and I've been coaching Little League since then. I guess I hope that some day I'll look up in the stands and see that man and his daughter again. Who knows, I might find him on one of the fields pitching to one of his grandkids—a lot of years have come and gone. I sure would like to thank him."

As the tears ran down my face I knew that my dad had just been thanked and even more I knew every time I heard "Batter up!" my dad would be right beside me, no matter where life took me and the family. That simple act of kindness that spring day had changed a life forever, and now twenty years later the memory of that day had changed my life forever. "Batter up, Dad," I said as I left the field, "I know you're still playing the game we love— baseball!"

Anne Carter

The Only Way I Know

Am I proud of him? Well, sure, I'm proud of him as my son. But as a ballplayer, ask in fifteen years.

Cal Ripken Sr. on Cal Ripken Jr. at age twenty-two

I sat on the bench for the first time in my life when I was called to the big leagues with the Baltimore Orioles. This wasn't what I had in mind for my career. So as I chewed more sunflower seeds in two months in 1981 than in three and a half years in the minors, I wondered, *How can I break into this line-up and, if I do, stay there?*

I came up with two answers: Play well and play every day. If I do get the opportunity, don't give anyone else the same opportunity. I didn't want the organization to have any reasonable option but to play me. That may sound cold, but it's mostly old-school.

Some people will never understand why I go about things the way I do, and that's okay. But I'll keep going about them the same way until it's proven that there's a better way. To this day, the old-school "Oriole way" is the only way I know. And the person who taught me most about it, and about life, is that former Orioles coach and manager—my dad, Cal Ripken Sr.

My father started out as a promising ballplayer. I don't claim any credit, but 1960—the year I was born—did turn out to be his greatest as a hitter. He was playing in the Three-I League in Appleton, Wisconsin. Dad was a catcher with a respectable batting average. But that year he hit his personal best, .281, with nine homers and seventy-four runs batted in.

Then, the following spring training, he injured his throwing shoulder. To stay in the game he shifted with typical practicality from playing to coaching and managing in the Orioles organization. He worked his way up through the minors and finally to the big leagues.

Years later I was to see firsthand the way Dad dealt with a major setback. On opening day 1988 I was having fun in the Orioles starting line-up as shortstop. My brother, Billy, was at second base. And our father was the manager. A father managing two sons on a team—a baseball first.

But just a week later, on April 12, I was driving to Memorial Stadium and heard on the radio that Senior—as I sometimes called him—had been fired just six games into the regular season. Six games!

When I came into the clubhouse, Dad had already left. I was deeply hurt for my father. I couldn't imagine how painful this must have been for him, after being so loyal to the franchise for thirty-one years. He must have been angry and hurt beyond words. But he conducted himself with great, dignity. The harshest thing he said publicly was, "I wasn't happy about the thing."

Later, Senior agreed to return the following year as third-base coach for the new manager, Frank Robinson. By way of explanation, Dad said with his usual dry understatement, "I guess you know I'm an Oriole."

My father is, by nature, a hard-working man. During the

summers when I was growing up, he was at the ballpark by early afternoon—weekends included, of course—not returning until late at night. Half the time he was off on a road trip with his team.

In the winters back home in Aberdeen, Maryland, Dad worked about as hard as in summer. Even now there's not much money in minor-league baseball, and there was less when we were growing up. He managed a pharmacy, drove a delivery truck, worked at a local hardware store and lumberyard. He was out the door at dawn and then fell asleep on the couch after supper almost every night, dog-tired.

I can't see myself as a manager after I retire because I'm adamant about spending time at home with my wife, Kelly, and our two kids. One reason is that I didn't have much time with my own father. I missed him when he was gone, though he was always there in ways that counted.

Some of my best memories of Dad are from 1969 and '70, when we were living in Rochester, New York, where my father managed the Red Wings. He'd come into my bedroom on Saturday mornings and shake me awake to see if I wanted to go to an early clinic he held with a couple of his players.

I usually went along, but not for the baseball. It was my chance to have Dad to myself on the rides, and I knew he enjoyed having me with him. I was nine years old.

For my tenth birthday, I took my first plane ride, joining Dad on the road for games against the Tidewater Tides and Richmond Braves—a real grown-up thing to do. I was with him all the time and wore a full uniform. It was the ultimate baseball field trip.

With Dad, everything was instructional. One snowy day he decided to help our neighbors by plowing the nearby streets, since the city crews were slow to get to us. He took me and my brother Fred to get the tractor.

Dad explained the right way to crank the engine and then warned against doing it wrong—windmilling the crank 360 degrees—because if the engine backfired it might throw the crank off. Meanwhile, I wondered, *When am I ever going to have to crank a tractor?* Maybe I even made a sarcastic remark.

After no luck cranking the right way, Dad said, "Now don't you do this, but I'm going to windmill it." Sure enough, the engine backfired, and the crank flew off and cracked Dad right on the forehead. Blood spurted out as he reached for a rag. I thought we would go to the hospital, but Dad just drove home, got a bandage and came back to plow the streets.

My father had his mottos and pronouncements. He'd tell his baseball players, "It's like a bank, men. You can't take out more than you put in." I'm sure he still says this at the summer camp he runs.

Another favorite saying—"Do two million little things right, and the big things take care of themselves"—is the essence of the Oriole Way: pride in the fundamentals.

Yet Dad's bluntness sometimes frustrates my mother. When I was in high school and Dad told reporters he looked on me as "just another prospect," my mother was annoyed. Later when he announced the likelihood that I'd be drafted, she replied sarcastically, "I'm glad you noticed."

When I was called to the majors, reporters asked my father if this was a dream come true. I knew what Senior would say, and he didn't disappoint me: "I don't dream. People say you have to have dreams, but what's the use of dreaming if you can't do the job?"

The father-son relationship is not a factor in the big leagues, as I learned the hard way. One day I called Dad just that—"Dad"—within earshot of some players, who then had a mocking refrain of their own every time the two of us were together. "Dad! Oh, Dad!"

They teased me pretty hard, and after that Dad became "Senior" or "No. 47" to me.

My father is a classic case of the guy with the tough exterior but melting inside. He's one of those men who has strong feelings about hiding their feelings. Imagine my surprise when he finally let loose with emotion when the Orioles clinched the division title against Milwaukee in 1983. Dad, third-base coach at the time, poured a beer over my head. "I guess the father in me finally came out," he told reporters.

Among the Ripken kids there's even a theory that our father softened up in recent years. Asked in the old days about his greatest experience, Dad always said it hadn't happened. After September 6, 1995, when I broke Lou Gehrig's Iron Man record—playing 2,131 consecutive games—he said that now it probably had.

Maybe my father could have been a successful major-league catcher if he hadn't injured his shoulder. We'll never know. Coming up through the minors I heard a lot of stories about frustrated fathers pushing their sons to achieve something they never did. But Senior wasn't that way at all. One of his strongest beliefs is that you should do in life what you enjoy doing.

The pressure he did exert on his children was this: Whatever we did we should do correctly and to the best of our abilities. He always said, "Be yourself and prove yourself." He hates anything shoddy or lazy. My brother Billy says I broke Lou Gehrig's record because I could. I might add, on behalf of my father, and because I could, I should.

Senior was inducted into the Orioles' Hall of Fame during the 1996 season. At the banquet he was funny, direct and foursquare in his remarks. In conclusion, he said that he accepted the honor on behalf of all the equally dedicated men he had worked with in the minor leagues for all those years.

Then it was my turn. It was difficult. I wasn't certain I could say what I wanted about my father and what he means to me. So I told a little story about my two children, Rachel, six at the time, and Ryan, then three. They'd been bickering for weeks, and I explained how one day I heard Rachel taunt Ryan, "You're just trying to be like Daddy."

After a few moments of indecision, I asked Rachel, "What's wrong with trying to be like Dad?"

When I finished telling the story, I looked at my father and added, "That's what I've always tried to do."

Cal Ripken Jr. and Mike Bryan

The Lost Ball

This story is about a little kid and an autographed baseball. It's a story about that awful feeling in your stomach when you lose your prized possession.

This story is also about rediscovering the joy of childhood, no matter how old you are, and this story is about brotherhood.

The story starts around Christmastime 1954.

My oldest brother, Jerry, was less than a month old. My parents wanted to buy him something special, and they learned about a promotion at a local department store. Bob Turley, a pitcher with the first-year Baltimore Orioles of the American League, was signing baseballs one afternoon. An autographed baseball seemed like a perfect, inexpensive keepsake so my parents waited in line for Turley's autograph.

When it was time for Turley to sign my parents' ball, my mother mentioned that it was for her newborn. Turley responded that he, too, had a new baby.

That was enough for my mother, who could make small talk with a brick wall. For the next few minutes, Turley and my mother talked about newborns while my father rolled his eyes and the rest of the line waited.

My mother will never forget that encounter, always remembering what a nice man Turley was, but that's only part of this story.

Now it's 1965.

Jerry is ten and his younger brother, Chuck, is about eight. They want to play catch in the back alley, but they can't find an old ball to use. So they make a mistake that thousands of little boys and girls have made over the years.

"Let's use the autographed ball."

They promise not to drop it. But, eventually, the inevitable happens. One overthrows the other, and the baseball skips down the steep alley. The two boys run after it as fast as they can. When they reach the end of the alley, though, the ball has disappeared. Two older boys say they saw the ball hit the sewer grate and fall down into the sewer.

Jerry and Chuck check out the scene. They find nothing except that sick feeling in their stomachs.

Flash forward to Thanksgiving 1991. My family has eaten turkey and stuffing and watched football.

Now it's time to sit in the living room and talk—our favorite pastime. As it always does, the conversation eventually turns to baseball. And to the Baltimore Orioles.

Six weeks before, the team had hosted its last game in venerable Memorial Stadium, which was being replaced by Oriole Park at Camden Yards. Many former Orioles had been invited back to say good-bye to the old ballpark, including Turley, the man who threw the first pitch for the Orioles in their first game in Memorial.

The mention of Turley's name brings the old stories rushing back. First, my mother and the tale of the department store line. And then the sigh from Jerry Jr.

"Are you going to cry again about how you lost that ball?" I chide my brother.

"I didn't lose it," he responds with the high-pitched

voice of a ten-year-old. "Those older kids—they stole it. I know it didn't go down the sewer."

My family burst into laughter.

Twenty-eight years had passed, but the memory still pains my brother. He's a successful businessman with a wonderful wife and two beautiful daughters. He can buy as many autographed baseballs as he wants.

But that's not the point. He'll never forget the ball that got away.

"Do you know how silly you sound?" I ask him.

A slight smile crosses his lips.

"You don't understand," he says in an anguished voice. "Those older kids stole my ball."

We laugh for a few more minutes at Jerry's expense before the subject changes to something else, but his anguish stays with me. He is my big brother, after all.

Two weeks later, I devise a plan. It seems like a long shot, but it is worth a try. I make some phone calls. And some more phone calls.

Finally, I find the man I am looking for. He laughs when I tell him the story of the old ball. He graciously agrees to help me out.

On December 24, the package arrives. And, on Christmas Day, we all meet at my brother's house.

After opening all of the other presents, I hand Jerry a small box. Our mother readies her camera. His wife giggles.

"What is this?" he asks as he lifts a baseball out of the box. "Is this for real?"

I nod.

"This is unbelievable," Jerry says, laughing as his face turns red.

"Well," our mother says, "read it aloud."

My brother clears his throat.

"To Jerry. Don't lose this one. Your friend, Bob Turley."

Dan Connolly

IN THE BLEACHERS   By Steve Moore

"Gee Dad, it was the only ball I could find
in the house. . . . Is Babe Ruth someone famous?"

Special Delivery from Michigan

The older you get, the more you realize that kindness is synonymous with happiness.

Lionel Barrymore

The kid in the picture was holding up a ball. It looked like a baseball without its cover, with just the string wrapped around the core. From my childhood, I remembered the kind of buzzing sound those uncovered baseballs made as they sailed past, trailing two feet of string.

The picture was taken in San Pedro de Macoris, a city of 130,000 in the Dominican Republic; it was part of a series written by Glen Macnow, then a *Detroit Free Press* sportswriter, on winter baseball in the Dominican Republic. "For youngsters in San Pedro," Macnow wrote, "baseball is one of the dominant things in life. Another is poverty." He talked about watching twenty shoeless kids play ball on a mud street called Calle de Restauracion.

"The ball was actually a woman's nylon stocking wound tightly with rubber bands," he said, "and the bat was a broken table leg that still had nails in it, and the bases were paint-can lids. None of the kids had gloves. They tied pieces of cardboard on their hands and shaped them so they could catch the ball." San Pedro is a long way from the vacant lots of Detroit, but there's a world-shrinking sameness about kids playing baseball with a coverless ball.

Pedro Gonzalez, an Atlanta Braves coach and a former major-league infielder, lives in San Pedro. So do Pedro Guerrero of the Los Angeles Dodgers and Joaquin Andujar of the Oakland A's. Last year, in fact, fifteen men from San Pedro, which calls itself the Baseball Capital of the World, played in the American Major Leagues. "American parents want their children to become doctors or lawyers," Gonzalez told Macnow. "But here, the way to get rich is to be a baseball player. That's the way out."

I soon found myself thinking about all the major-league dreams in my old neighborhood. No matter how far-fetched those dreams were, they were an important part of growing up. And regardless of how tight the money was in those years, if there wasn't a glove for everybody, there were always enough to share.

Then a plan started forming in my mind. I thought about all the old gloves sitting in attics, closets and basements, their days of glory just distant memories. I asked readers to get out those gloves, dust them off and send them to me at the *Free Press*. We'd ship them to San Pedro and distribute them to the kids there. I said to look at it this way: The old glove never got you a tryout with the Tigers. Why not give it another chance?

Peter Gavrilovich, another *Free Press* writer, wandered into my office just before the first gloves arrived. "You don't understand the depth of a relationship between a man and his baseball," he told me. "Do you seriously expect people to send you their old gloves? Ask them for money, but not for their old gloves." He predicted we'd receive fewer than two dozen.

What if he's right? I thought. It just might not be possible to separate people from baseball gloves that carry so many rich memories. Would I send my first glove, even if I still had it, to some kids on a Caribbean island? I wasn't sure.

Later that morning a box arrived in the mail. It was from Tom Kolinsky in Watersmeet, a town in Michigan's Upper Peninsula. "Enclosed are three baseball gloves," he wrote. "The catcher's mitt was my brother Bob's. He passed away eleven years ago at the age of twenty-eight, and I kept his mitt as a memento. We enjoyed many good years of ball together (I was the pitcher, he was the catcher) and I am sure he's got a big grin on his face knowing that the glove is going to a kid who will probably sleep with it the first week or so, the way he did."

That day in February 1986 was only the beginning. Gloves soon arrived from all over the state, and they spanned the history of the game—from fat-fingered antiques to bright new peach-basket models designed to snare anything batted in their direction. They carried worn autographs of stars like Bob Feller, Ted Williams, Stan Musial, Phil Rizzuto, and even players like Jim Greengrass, Wally Bunker and Bump Hadley, a pitcher who played in the majors in 1926.

Casimer Rejent, a retired engineer who lives in Grosse Pointe Farms, sent the glove he got from his parents when he graduated from Toledo Catholic Central High School in 1940.

Teacher Bill Brown collected one hundred gloves at Ferndale High School. Dorian Rowland, a student at St. Joan of Arc Elementary School in St. Claire Shores, put up a poster and a box there.

The two gloves sent by Donald R. Hein of Battle Creek had tags tied to them with his address and phone number and a request, "Write me when you make the big leagues." The pile of gloves grew, each one with a special memory.

John Walls, a *Free Press* engineer, came in one evening to tell me there was no way I was going to get his glove: "It's part of me. I still use it. Wouldn't think of giving it away, even for a good cause." Then he picked up a glove from the pile, put it on and punched the pocket a couple of times.

"It belonged to a kid in Berkley named David Barber," I told him, and showed him a picture of a smiling ninth-grader. The picture came in a letter with the glove David's father had sent them.

"This first baseman's glove was my son's," Ron Barber wrote. "He passed away from cancer at age fourteen. I hope some young man from San Pedro will enjoy the mitt as much as he did."

John Walls put the letter down and left. In a few minutes he was back, carrying his glove. "I had it in my locker," he explained. "I can always buy another one. See if you can find a kid named Juan to give it to." He put it on the pile—next to David Barber's glove.

As soon as we saw the three little boys in San Pedro de Macoris, we decided they probably were on their way to play baseball. One of them gripped a stick with two hands, taking swings at an imaginary ball as he walked with his friends. We stopped our van and asked if they were ballplayers.

In San Pedro, the question is purely rhetorical. All the kids there play baseball. Sugar may be the region's most profitable export and cane fields may be the reality of these children's lives—but Dodger Stadium is the dream.

So I sat on the curb with Jose Antonio, Daniel Ottavio and Teofilo Rosario, and told them that in the United States, in a place called Detroit, there are people who believe that proper ballplayers should have proper equipment. I gave each of them a baseball glove, a ball and a bat, and told them the people who had donated the gloves expected great things from them.

They weren't entirely convinced the gloves were theirs to keep. They walked away, looking back until they got to the corner, where they raised their gloves over their heads and broke into a run. We could hear them laughing long after they were out of sight.

Gloves had come in by the hundreds, and the previous Sunday, with the help and cooperation of the folks at the airport in Santo Domingo, we had unloaded thirty cartons of baseball equipment. Included were 1,062 gloves, waiting to work old magic with new kids. From Michigan, with love.

Photographer John Collier and I had then loaded the van with gloves, bats, balls, T-shirts and caps, and headed for San Pedro. There we picked up the Reverend John Breslin at his church. At his suggestion, we took the first load of gloves to a desperately poor part of the city called Barrio Blanco.

It was shortly after 10 A.M., but there was already a ball game in progress on a field that had been reclaimed from a dump. A smoldering trash fire sent a haze across the outfield. The excitement and the large number of kids made it impossible to distribute the gloves in any orderly manner. Amid a lot of pushing, I simply put a glove in every outstretched hand I could reach until the box was empty. The only disappointing feeling was driving away from the barrio knowing that for every kid who got a glove, there were a dozen or more who didn't.

In the middle of San Pedro is an old green-and-white hospital. The children's ward is on the fourth floor. We went through the ward, talking to the youngsters and their parents, and passing out gloves and hats to children with malaria, hepatitis and dysentery. There were more smiles in the ward when we left than when we arrived. Some of them were ours.

At 4 P.M. we went to San Pedro's Tetelo Varga baseball

stadium for a ceremony with representatives of San Pedro's twenty-one baseball leagues. The cartons from Detroit were placed along the third-base line. About four hundred kids from San Pedro filled the seats between home plate and third base.

Juan Francisco Mateo, the regional commissioner for sports in San Pedro, asked me why Americans had sent their gloves to the children of San Pedro. I told him the people in Michigan love baseball and that the children of San Pedro love baseball; when two groups of people care so much for the same thing, it brings them very close together.

He repeated that to the crowd, adding that the people of San Pedro love the people of Michigan. Then a representative from each league carried off a box of gloves to distribute to his team.

Two hours later, with the sun going down behind the stands, kids were chasing fly balls with gloves that, a short time before, had belonged to people in a part of the world these children didn't know: the glove that Cas Rejent got when he graduated from high school in 1940; the catcher's mitt Tom Kolinsky sent, the one that had belonged to his dead brother; the one hundred gloves from the kids at Ferndale High School; the first baseman's mitt that had been David Barber's until he died at fourteen.

As we drove away from the stadium, we could still hear the kids playing. The magic had passed. The old dreams were now a part of new dreams.

Neal Shine

A Binding Contract

Reputation is what you have when you come to a new community; character is what you have when you go away.

William Hersey Davis

He didn't know me and I didn't know him, but this was about to change. It would change with the simple act of a major-league player rolling a beautiful grass-stained official American League baseball across the top of a dugout to a ten-year-old boy.

The year was 1971. I was that ten-year-old boy, and Vada Pinson was that major-league player. I had taken up my position behind the visitor's dugout at Kansas City's old Municipal Stadium. It was two hours before game time and the Cleveland Indians were a bad team taking batting practice. But Vada was not a bad player; no, he was once a great player. In his younger days with the Cincinnati Reds, when he played alongside Frank Robinson, Vada had been a star in his own right. Twice, he led the National League in hits. Once, he won a Gold Glove for his shining play as a center fielder.

Honestly, though, when Vada came jogging toward the dugout that day, I didn't know all that. I only knew the name and had this vague sense in the back of my young mind that he had enjoyed more glorious days in another time and place. Not that it mattered, because he was a big-leaguer and that was more than enough. I simply wanted—needed—a baseball from a real big-league ball-player so I summoned my courage, and asked No. 28 as politely as I knew how, "Vada? Could I have a baseball?"

His eyes met mine, but he didn't say a word. He just disappeared into the dugout.

I sighed, my shoulders slumped, and I decided I was a fool for even asking. And that's when Vada popped up the steps and rolled that gorgeous baseball into my waiting hands.

"Hey, Vada, can you sign it?" I yelled as he started to turn away.

"You want me to sign it, too?" he said with a smile.

He signed it like this: "To Donald 'Always' Vada Pinson."

Vada didn't realize it, of course, but with those five words he had signed a binding contract between player and fan, friend and friend.

I started checking the Cleveland box score every morning, sure, but I wasn't content with that. I kept in touch. I wrote him letters. I called him at the team hotel.

When Vada was traded to the California Angels, I tossed my big inflatable Cleveland Indians beach ball into a closet and bought one of those plastic batting helmets with a halo on it. I was loyal. But here's the too-good-to-be-true part: So was he.

As luck would have it Vada would be traded from the Angels to the Kansas City Royals, and would play his last two seasons in my hometown. On the team scorecard, he was listed as another outfielder. But his true position? Personal hero.

Vada gave us free tickets to all the games, and for two summers I had the prestige of being recognized on sight by all the middle-aged ladies who worked the will call window and all the ushers who cleaned off the seats behind home plate. Every night we'd get to the ballpark right when the gates opened, I'd sprint for the Royals dugout and chat Vada up for a few minutes. Sometimes, he'd give me another baseball—which I always had him sign and which I never would have dared to use in a game of catch. Always, he would look up to where my mom and dad were sitting and wave.

Vada could have tired of talking to me about baseball—he probably did—but instead included me. He admitted he wished he were playing more, explained why his manager sometimes drove him crazy, let me know that even when you're in the majors you're human and get frustrated like anybody else. Though I'm not sure either of us was consciously aware of it at the time, he came to trust me as much as I idolized him.

Now, I suppose, in that day and time, the color of our skin could have been enough to make one, or both of us, uncomfortable. But to me, he was always a ballplayer, not a black ballplayer. And to him, I was always that young fan, not that young white fan.

At the end of his first season with the Royals, we invited Vada over to our house for dinner. He understood it was important that he come. Not just for me, but for my mom and dad, who had no other way to show their appreciation. For years, the underneath side of one of our dining-room chairs bore the words, "Vada sat here."

But as fantastic as his visit to my house was, at least I was expecting it. I wasn't prepared at all the next summer when I was deep into a game of Strat-O-Matic tabletop baseball, and the telephone rang.

"Donald," the smooth voice said, "this is Vada. I couldn't

remember if you needed two tickets tonight or three?"

I couldn't believe it. He took the time to make sure he left enough tickets. Actually kept my phone number and then used it. I was scared to leave the house the rest of the summer. It was the best summer of my life.

Unfortunately, Vada's baseball-filled summers would end way too soon. He died in October 1995, at age fifty-seven, following a stroke. We had last seen each other in the summer of 1994 in St. Louis. He was a coach for the Florida Marlins and I was a sports columnist who'd come to town to write about the Cardinals. And so we sat in front of Vada's locker and talked about old times and present times. Among other things, Vada said he had been visiting a young boy in a Florida hospital, and I smiled and thought to myself, *Vada hasn't changed a bit.*

I also figured we would talk again the next season. Maybe I'd come to a game off-duty, as a fan, and introduce my oldest son, Stephen, to him. That never happened, of course, but every time I walk into a ballpark, I check to see who's wearing No. 28.

I still see Vada, still hear his voice over the telephone, still see that baseball rolling across the top of the dugout.

Always.

Don Wade

The Sermon on the Mound

My heart sank. The last person I wanted to see right then was Tommy Lasorda. What could he want? I wasn't sure I wanted to know. In fact, with a 2-2 record and a 6.20 earned run average, I was pretty sure I didn't.

But Ron Perranoski was the boss. When the pitching coach tells you the skipper wants to see you in his office, you don't stand around wondering what to do. "What does Tommy want, Perry?" I asked. I hoped against hope it didn't mean a trip back to the minor leagues.

"He'll let you know."

Uh-oh. "You goin' with me?"

"I'm invited, just like you. That's how Tommy works, you know. He wouldn't tell you anything without me there."

"Well, that's good. I guess. I hope."

It was early May 1984, during my first full year in the big leagues, and I was a Los Angeles Dodger relief pitcher trying to hang on for dear life. I couldn't get anything going, couldn't maintain any consistency. I might get a guy or even two guys out, then I'd get too fine, too careful, and walk somebody. Tommy hated two-out walks. Almost as much as he hated two-out runs. And two-out runs too often followed my two-out walks.

I'd get even more careful, and before you knew it, someone had doubled up the alley. I'd be yanked, aired out for not doing what I was paid to do, and then I'd sit, wondering what was happening to my brief career.

As a rookie I was pretty much a non-entity with the Dodgers. I didn't have that casual relationship with the coaches that the veterans did. I wasn't consulted about strategy. Nobody cared what I thought was the right pitch in a specific situation. If I offered an opinion, it might just as likely be ignored as disputed. I was proving on the mound that I couldn't execute the pitches, even if I knew what they should be. Everyone said I had potential, the most frustrating label any player can have. I'd been hearing that since the day I signed.

Because I was young and looked younger, and because I was thin and wore glasses, and because I was known as a Christian athlete, I got the feeling people assumed I had no guts. Hershiser was too passive, too nice, too mellow to get the job done.

I was intimidated by Tommy Lasorda. Loud and brash and a real veteran baseball man, he was a manager any player would want behind him. He could be an encourager, but I didn't know where I stood. I feared I was on the bubble. There had to be guys in triple-A who could do better than I was doing.

And now he wanted to see me and my pitching coach. What could that mean? What could he want? Perry wasn't saying much. Did that mean he didn't know? Or worse, that he did know? Though the walk to Tommy's office seemed to take forever, I wished we hadn't arrived so soon. This was like being sent to the principal's office, but the stakes were much higher. I'd sure rather stay after school than be shipped back to Albuquerque.

Perry knocked, and Tommy waved us in. My mouth was dry, and I noticed Tommy wasn't smiling. He pointed to a couple of chairs, and Perry and I sat down. Tommy sat on the edge of his desk and looked down at me. I didn't take my eyes off him, and if I blinked I wasn't aware of it. I was prepared to agree with whatever he said, no matter what. I wondered if he could hear my heart.

"I invited you here with Ronnie because I never talk to a player without his individual coach present."

"Yes, sir, I know. I appreciate—"

He continued as if I hadn't said anything. "I wanted to talk to you about your game, the use of your ability, your mental approach to pitching."

I nodded.

"You remember how mad I was about how you pitched to Cruz the other day against Houston . . ."

I nodded again. Did I ever. It was one of those two-out situations with two men on. Jose Cruz was a great contact hitter, a dangerous RBI (runs batted in) man.

". . . You throw low and away, ball one. Low and away, ball two. Low and away, ball three. He's takin' and you finally get a strike over, luckily, 'cause that one could'a been called low or outside, either one. He knows you can't afford to walk him, so he's sittin' on your three and one pitch, and what do you do?"

I didn't want to think about it, and I sure didn't want to talk about it. The worst thing was, Tommy was getting himself upset all over again just rehashing it. He grew louder. His face reddened. He leaned closer.

"You laid the ball in for him! Boom! Double and two runs! Hershiser, you're givin' these hitters too much credit! You're tellin' yourself, 'If I throw this ball over the plate, they're gonna hit it out.' That is a negative approach to pitching!"

I knew. I felt small and young and stupid. Sitting there

nodding, I finally knew what he thought of me. My worst fears had been confirmed. I was hopeless. And, if it was possible, Tommy was getting louder. He was in my face now, those eyes bulging, his cheeks crimson. Sweat broke out on my forehead and the back of my neck. I didn't dare move even to wipe it off.

"You don't believe in yourself! You're scared to pitch in the big leagues! Who do you think these hitters are, Babe Ruth? Ruth's dead! You've got good stuff. If you didn't, I wouldn't have brought you up. Quit bein' so careful! Go after the hitter! Get ahead in the count! Don't be so fine with him and then find yourself forced to lay one in!"

As he sped on, louder and louder, something registered with me. Was that more than an airing out I just heard? Did a compliment slip by, disguised as a tongue lashing? I've got good stuff? He believes that?

Tommy continued, "If I could get a heart surgeon in here, I'd have him open my chest and take out my heart, open your chest and take out your heart, and then I'd have him give you my heart! You'd be in the Hall of Fame! If I had your stuff, I'd a been in the Hall of Fame!

"I've seen guys come and go, son, and you've got it! You gotta go out there and do it on the mound! Take charge! Make 'em hit your best stuff! Be aggressive. Be a bulldog out there. That's gonna be your new name: Bulldog. You know, when we bring you in in the ninth to face Dale Murphy and he hears, 'Now pitching, Orel Hershiser,' man, he can't wait till you get there! But if he hears, 'Now pitching, Bulldog Hershiser,' he's thinkin', *Oh, no, who's that!?* Murphy's gonna be scared to death!"

We're nose to nose now, and I could use a towel on my face, but I don't even swallow, let alone move. "I want you, starting today, to believe you are the best pitcher in baseball. I want you to look at that hitter and say, 'There's no way you can ever hit me.' You gotta believe you are superior to the hitter and that you can get anybody out who walks up there. Quit givin' the hitter so much credit. You're better than these guys."

Part of me resented anyone thinking that I needed a nickname to make me tough and aggressive. No question I had not learned a proper approach to pitching. But I didn't think I needed a new name to make me stronger. Still, I couldn't get over that Tommy Lasorda felt I was worth this much time and effort. It hurt to hear him say what he said, but beneath it there had been a foundation of confidence in me. He believed I had more than potential. He believed I had big league stuff.

He was right that I had been treating big-league hitters in a special way. I believed they had special ability. Which they did. What Tommy was telling me was that so did I. I wasn't some minor-leaguer who had lucked his way up to the big club because it was a thin year for pitchers. I belonged on that mound just as much as the hitter belonged in the box.

Two days later against the San Francisco Giants the Dodgers needed a reliever in a difficult situation. The bullpen was full of tired, sore-armed pitchers, me included. The call came, "Can anybody down there pitch?"

I volunteered, despite a tender elbow and an arm weak from overwork. I strode to the mound reminding myself what a pleasant surprise it had been to learn that Tommy believed in me, thought I was special, needed me, thought I would be successful with an adjustment in my approach. I didn't know what I could do with my arm and elbow in the shape they were in, but my attitude was finally right.

From the dugout Tommy hollered, "C'mon, Bulldog! You can do it, Bulldog! You're my man, Bulldog!"

I challenged the hitters, kept the ball low, got ahead in the count on nearly every batter. In three innings, my arm feeling like a rag, I gave up only one run. Tommy's talk had worked. (He calls it his "Sermon on the Mound" and says he wishes he had taped it. "It'd sell a million, Bulldog!")

With my performance against San Francisco, I became a believer. I told myself that if I could do that when my arm felt terrible, think what I could do when I felt great. I still didn't like the nickname (I still don't), and I was still chagrined that anyone thought I needed it. But that day I became a big-league pitcher. My attitude was revolutionized. I believed I deserved to be there, competing with big leaguers because I was a big leaguer. (The legendary Branch Rickey once said, "A big-leaguer is a minor-leaguer with a chance to play there.")

I learned years later that assigning a nickname to a player was Tommy's unofficial way of welcoming him to the big leagues. Until you showed him you could compete at that level, you were called by your given name. Franklin Stubbs was just Stubbs until Tommy decided he was worthy of a nickname. Then he became Cadillac. Mike Marshall was just Marshall until Tommy christened him Moose. Neither Tommy nor I knew then that he was right and that I could succeed at this level. But within two months, we had more to go on.

An injury to Jerry Reuss thrust me into a start on May 26. I joined the starting rotation for good June 29 against the Chicago Cubs, when I began the longest consecutive scoreless inning streak in the National League that year (332/3 innings). I pitched four shutouts in July alone (and was named Pitcher of the Month), tied for the league lead in shutouts for the year, and finished third in ERA (earned run average), sixth in complete games, and eighth in strikeouts. I was third in Rookie of the Year voting.

My game had become focused. And the concentration motivated by the confidence Tommy instilled in me remains a key to my success today. Do you wonder how a pitcher could have had a 1988 like I had? Do you wonder how we Dodgers could have been motivated to maintain our intensity all through the season and the post-season, in spite of injuries and setbacks? We owe a lot of it to Tommy, of course, because he is a true motivator, encourager, cheerleader.

Knowing he believed in us allowed us to focus our energy, to eliminate distractions, to major on the fundamentals that outweigh everything, no matter what the task or pursuit. I benefited from realizing that there was too much to think about, too many variables, too many distractions if a pitcher tried to stay on top of every nuance of the game all the time. In my mind I narrowed my emphasis and priority to one thing and one thing only: the pitch.

Orel Hershiser

It's Baseball Season

The team members' attention spans stretch barely the length of a cartoon. Their eyes are invisible beneath oversized batting helmets. They wear T-shirts with messages like "Critter Ridders Pest Control: 30 Years of Service in Roaches."

All across the country, it's T-ball season.

I became a T-ball mom when my seven-year-old son signed up to be a Giant (an obvious misnomer for a team where no one can bench press a Nerf ball). I should have been prepared. We limped through flag football last fall.

I still remember that day when the youngest kid on the football field kept interrupting the game squealing, "Coach, are we winning yet?"

It's a significant question.

In T-ball, no one even keeps score. That's good. It makes me think of Megan, a little girl I met before I moved to Idaho. Megan could neither hit nor throw a ball, but she wanted to play T-ball. I saw a few of her games.

Megan's parents and coaches practiced with her, encouraged her and never once considered calling her a klutz. But when the last game of the season rolled around, Megan still hadn't connected with the ball.

When she finally did, she hit an easy pop fly and her team lost. But the people in the bleachers stood up and cheered for Megan. Because, by that time, everyone knew she was a winner.

I moved away before Megan grew up, but I'm sure she grew up successful. Not because she had any more talent than the boy whose dad yelled at him whenever he didn't get a hit. In fact, she probably had much less. But Megan had something else. She had people around her who cared, not about her batting average, but about her.

Not long ago, I sat listening to a speaker who insisted that we are living in the midst of a generation of kids who see themselves as potential failures.

Among the causative factors, she said, parental influence is the greatest. I'm determined to be the right kind of T-ball mom. My husband may do a better job with practice sessions, but I'm pretty good at screaming, "Way to go, slugger!" Even when (and all of this has happened this season) . . .

The second baseman is turning cartwheels when he's supposed to be fielding the ball.

A child is lying flat on the ground refusing to budge after he's been thrown out—and the other kids are trampling over him.

A batter is rounding the bases because the right fielder doesn't want to give up the ball.

The coach is yelling, "Take your base, Son," but the kid is standing there pointing toward center field. His mother yells from the stands, "That means he has to go to the bathroom."

In spite of it all, these children are making their first stabs at growing up. They're taking their first steps toward life in the major leagues. They may be chewing bubble gum instead of tobacco and they may not have learned how to scratch themselves yet, but they take their base hits seriously.

I'm glad they haven't yet "arrived." I'd hate to give up being a T-ball mom, because I think I really like the game.

After all, anything that ends with Reese's Pieces and Kool-Aid Kool Bursts can't be all bad.

Denise Turner

Watching the Next Mark McGwire?

It is not flesh and blood but the heart that makes us fathers and sons.

Friedrich von Schiller

It could have been any vacant lot, any playground, any open field. It just happened to be the park two blocks from my house, the park where I took my two-year-old daughter on sunny afternoons when I manage to ditch out of work early and on weekends.

Surely you know the scene, fresh off a Norman Rockwell canvas—a young boy and father playing catch. It is a rite of youth, a rite of fatherhood and always a rite of spring.

Thus it was that I witnessed my first father-and-son baseball game of the new year—a sighting equal in magnitude, and goosebumps, of spotting one's first butterfly of spring or one's first robin. Long days and warm nights, double-scoop ice cream cones, swimming in a lake and sunburned noses cannot be too far off.

The boy, his head only barely peeking up into Ken Griffey Jr.'s strike zone, looked to be about four years old. As with puppies, guesstimating the exact age of these little fellows of boundless energy is sometimes difficult. To be certain, when he swung the bat it was like the tail wagging the puppy.

The block from which the little blond chip had been chopped was tall and lanky and bespectacled. He also looked a little worn out and weary, probably from a hard day at the office. His short sidekick, on the other hand, was bursting at the inseams with energy.

After a few compulsory minutes of fielding practice—pop-ups mostly, with a few worm-burner grounders mixed in—the boy flung his mitt to the ground and picked up a bat, a huge oversized plastic job. Blue. It was a Prince tennis racket of a baseball bat. Probably a King Kong autograph model. Or at least a Mark McGwire "Power Stick."

As the small boy took his big cuts, the park magically transformed into Dodger Stadium, or so the boy's L.A. baseball cap suggested. Probably got it at "cap nite" last year, I reckoned.

Two trees, a sweatshirt and the boy's discarded mitt became the four bases. And unbeknownst to the two players, an SRO (sitting room only) crowd of two watched from the upper deck of the jungle gym. For the record, no pop fouls came the spectators' way.

Surprisingly, the small boy wielded the big bat with deft control. His hand-eye coordination was excellent. The Dodgers could use a lead-off man—er, boy—like him. *Whack! Whack! Whack!* The sound of the white plastic ball meeting the blue plastic bat echoed through the air far more often than did *Whoosh!* or *Whiff!*

Laughter, too, filled the late afternoon air after each successful swing of the lumber—er, plastic—as the batter giggled and tried to outrace the pitcher to the first-base tree. And then to the second-base sweatshirt and the third-base tree and the home-plate mitt.

More than once the fleet-footed giggling boy turned a

swinging bunt into an inside-the-park home run.

After a while, the dad took his swings in the invisible batter's box. Between pitches that bounced on their flight to the home-plate mitt or sailed wildly over the batter's head, the dad connected with a 1-2-3 inning of easy ground outs, which the boy fielded like a Hall of Famer.

And, of course, the future Joe DiMaggio—or Mark McGwire, perhaps, because the boy surely doesn't know who Joltin' Joe is—giggled as he chased his father from tree to sweatshirt to tree to mitt.

And the dad, who always got caught and tagged out just short of scoring, laughed even louder.

If any sight is more pleasing and heartwarming than a smiling father and his giggling son piled in a ta ngled heap together on the grass in a park under the late afternoon sunshine, it escapes me at the moment. Unless, perhaps, a father playing on a jungle gym with his daughter.

And so the two fellows played—the four-year-old dreaming of being a man and the man magically trans-formed to four years old again. For a moment, at least, life's problems and worries were put on hold.

Watching the father and son laugh and play and run and hug and roll around on the grass, you could not help but think this was baseball in its purest form. Sport at its best, even life at its best. Play ball!

Woody Woodburn

My Finest Hour

It's all part of the psychology of baseball. But the saddest words of all to a pitcher are three—take him out.

                                        Christy Mathewson

Ever since that first game with my dad, baseball had been my life. And my life as a ballplayer was wrapped up in my arm. The more strikes that my arm could throw, the more I was worth. The more games that arm won, the more managers wanted me on their teams.

"How's the arm today, Dave?" "Is your arm ready for tonight?" "Better get some ice on that arm; don't want it to swell."

My arm was to me what hands are to a pianist, what legs are to a ballerina. It's what fans cheered for, what they paid hard-earned money to see. It was what gave me worth—at least in the eyes of the world.

January 1990, my wife Jan and I left for Memorial Sloan-Kettering Cancer Center in New York, where Dr. Murray Brennan found that the tumor in my pitching arm had returned. He removed the rest of my deltoid muscle plus

10 percent of my triceps and isolated me for five days of treatment with iridium pellets. God had stood by me before, but now he seemed to be withdrawing. It scared me.

By May the cancer had wrapped itself around my radial nerve. Dr. Brennan scraped the nerve of cancerous cells, but the prognosis wasn't good. My doubleheader with cancer was going into extra innings.

In July and August, I underwent further radiation treatment. Shortly afterward I began to run a low-grade fever, and my doctor discovered a staph infection in my arm. I fought the pain and the persistent infection until one day when Jan and I visited an elementary school. I spoke to some sixty kids and showed them a video of my comeback game and the game in Montreal where I broke my arm. Then the kids flocked around with scraps of paper and baseball cards. As I pushed it through the loops and curves of my name, my arm was almost immobile. I finally realized: It was time.

I met with Dr. Brennan and told him I was ready for the arm to come off. On June 18, 1991, I went back into surgery. The first thing I saw after I woke up were two hazy figures. Then my eyes came into focus, and I recognized Jan and my mom. I blinked again, and Dad was there, too. Jan came alongside the bed and put her hand on my forehead. Her fingers felt soothing as they brushed across my brow.

The next day I got out of bed. I went into the bathroom, where I saw myself for the first time. The image that stared back from the mirror horrified me. An incision started at my neck and went to my underarm. My arm was gone. My shoulder was gone. The left side of my collarbone was gone.

"Okay, God. This is what I've got to live with. Please help me put this behind me," I prayed. "Let me go forward."

When the one-armed man stared back at me, there was peace in his eyes.

I felt relieved to have the arm amputated, for I had been in such pain. But I also felt apprehensive. I wondered how my son would react. *Would he keep his distance? And what about my daughter? Would she be embarrassed? And Jan?*

When I came home, I realized that all they wanted was to have me back. As important as my left arm had been to my boyhood, and later to my livelihood, it meant nothing to them. It was enough that I was alive.

Everything I do now I do with my right hand, and I can do pretty much everything I did before; it just takes longer. Instead of wearing a coat and tie, I wear an open shirt. And when I fly I carry just one bag.

I miss doing things with my own two hands, and—of course—I really miss baseball. There is a scene in the movie *Field of Dreams* where "Shoeless" Joe Jackson—one of the eight Chicago White Sox players banned from baseball for conspiring to lose the 1919 World Series, said, "Getting thrown out of baseball was like having part of me amputated. I'd wake up at night with the smell of the ballpark in my nose, the cool of the grass on my feet. Man, I did love this game. I'd have played for food money. It was a game. The sounds, the smells. I'd have played for nuthin'."

That scene had a powerful effect on me. I missed those feelings, too. The feel of stitched seams as you cradle a new ball in your hand. The smell of seasoned leather as you bring the glove to your face. The sound of a bat cracking out a base hit.

I'd have played for food money. I'd have played for nuthin'.

On October 5, 1991, the Giants invited me to San Francisco for Dave Dravecky Day. When I left the clubhouse and looked out across the stadium, the finely manicured grass was almost an iridescent green. The bright orange seats were starting to fill. Flags rippled in the breeze. I felt like a seven-year-old kid, seeing it all for the first time.

People in the stands stood and clapped. High over their heads, they carried banners and placards:
DRAVECKY #43
THANKS FOR THE HOPE
GOOD LUCK, DAVE
GOD BLESS U

For one last time in a Giants uniform, I walked onto the field. A few yards in front of the mound, I wrapped my fingers around a ball, felt its stitched seams. Then, in front of 42,712 fans, I threw out the opening pitch—and one final cheer arose for No. 43.

It was my last hurrah, my shining moment. I had come to Candlestick Park to say good-bye to the fans and to the game I loved.

A convertible drove Jan, my son and daughter, and me around the perimeter of the park, and I lifted my cap to the crowd. Then we took our seats in the stands. I was a fan now, and it felt good.

Other fans at Candlestick that day were saddened by what cancer had done to my life. They didn't say it in so many words, but I could see it in their eyes and hear it in their voices. They thought it was a tragedy.

I don't feel that way. I used to see everything in black and white; now I see the shades of gray in between. I used to think there was an answer for everything; now I realize many questions don't have answers. I used to be preoccupied with my own needs; now I am learning compassion for others. I used to depend on myself; now I lean more on God. I used to think I could put God in a box; now I know his ways are too deep for any box to contain.

In another scene from *Field of Dreams*, the hero, Ray Kinsella, tracks down an old ballplayer named "Moonlight" Graham, whose career in the majors was so short it wasn't even a flash in the pan. Graham was an old man now. He had become a doctor and had dedicated his life to alleviating suffering in the small town where he lived. Kinsella could not get over how short Graham's career had been.

"For five minutes you were that close," Kinsella marveled. "It would kill some men to get that close to their dream and not touch it; they'd consider it a tragedy."

Graham looked him in the eye and with a wistful smile said, "Son, if I'd only got to be a doctor for five minutes, now that would have been a tragedy."

When I look back over the past four years and see all I've learned from other people who have suffered, all I've experienced of their love and all God has shown me of his mercy, I think, *If I'd have continued as a ballplayer and missed that, now that would have been a tragedy.*

Dave and Jan Dravecky with Ken Gire

2

A DAY AT THE BALLPARK

I see great things in baseball. It's our game—the American game. It will take our people out-of-doors, fill them with oxygen, give them a larger physical stoicism. Tend to relieve us from being a nervous, dyspeptic set. Repair these losses, and be a blessing to us.

Walt Whitman

My Quest for a Baseball

To the fierce, ardent, leather-lunged professional fan, baseball is life itself, a motive for breathing, the yeast that helps his spirit, as well as his gorge, rise.

Jim Bouton

While attending the hundred or so major league baseball games that make up the better parts of my childhood memory bank, souvenirs of all kinds were gathered in earnest. Pennants and programs and tickets stubs and autograph after autograph—including one of Philadelphia Phillies star Mike Schmidt that was corralled after a parking lot sprint and is little more than an indecipherable wiggle, wave and dash of a pen.

But there was never a baseball—not a real live baseball. And a foul ball or home-run ball or batting-practice ball—any kind of ball from a major league baseball game was all I wanted.

As the years passed, near-misses accumulated along with my ticket stubs. At a sparsely attended minor-league game, I watched each pitch with eagle eyes, figuring nearly empty stands quadrupled my chances. I turned my back for one sip of a Coke and only heard—never even saw—the ball that thwacked the seat next to mine and was gobbled up by a more nimble adversary.

Lower deck seats and an uninteresting game at one Phillies contest emptied the stands and again increased my chances. But when a high pop foul was lofted my way, I froze in fear of its height and in awe at my dream coming true. It hit a few rows over and hopped over my head. My uncle called me "Gluefoot."

Friends of my parents finagled third-base line seats for one game, and invited me to join them and borrow their fishing net in an attempt to snag batting practice grounders. Instead, stadium security snagged the net.

As time went by, and I grew from chubby ten-year-old to a chubby and awkward thirteen-year-old, my foul ball lust only increased. But so did my knowledge that I was no longer cute, and no player or kindly nearby fan was going to toss me a free ball at this point. That was reserved for gap-toothed eight-year-olds waiting for the tooth fairy—and high school girls who were anything but awkward.

This was reinforced on a family trip to California the summer after my eighth-grade year. An unplanned trip to a California Angels game left my typically upper-deck family with front-row seats, again down third base. My glove was home in Pennsylvania. So when a batting practice grounder caromed toward me, I had only my hat with which to snag it. The cap gathered the ball in—and the force ripped them both out of my hand. A Milwaukee Brewers outfielder came over, picked up the ball and tossed it to me in the stands.

I nearly fainted in my moment of ecstasy—until the player pointed at me.

"No," he said. "For him."

He then pointed to the adorable six-year-old next to me. I looked down and handed over *my* ball. I went home to deface the player's baseball card—which I then carried in my wallet until college.

At Northwestern University outside Chicago, I planned my spring class schedule around the afternoon games at Wrigley Field. Not just Chicago Cubs games, but Chicago Cubs batting practices. I'd hop the subway with my glove, knowing that this day in the left-field bleachers would reward me with my first real baseball. But for two and a half years, it was nothing but misjudgments and missed opportunities.

Until one series when the Phillies were in town. Over time, I had grown loyal to the Cubs, turning my attention from catching baseballs to taunting the opposing left fielder once the game started. And of course, there was the time-honored ritual of chanting "Throw it back" whenever an opposing player hit a home-run ball into the bleachers. Whoever grabbed the ball had little choice but to fire it back onto the field.

But when the Phillies were in town, I didn't taunt the opponents. I cheered for them. I wore my Phillies jersey and Phillies cap and rooted against the Cubs.

And for a ball.

The Cubs were ahead by several runs in the third inning. I sat in my usual seat in the second row, the girl-friend who would later become my wife beside me.

Darren Daulton, the Phillies catcher and best hitter, was at the plate. His left-handed swing produced a slicing opposite-field line drive that looked to be headed for the left field wall.

But it cleared the wall, smacking into the crowd just to my left. Bodies flew as fans dove for the home-run ball, hands grasping at air. I reached my hand into a teeming mass of flesh and grabbed.

All ball.

I pulled Daulton's homer from the chaos and raised my arm triumphantly in the air. I finally had my real live baseball.

And I was wearing a Phillies jersey in the Wrigley Field bleachers, the enemy's home run in my hand.

I did the only thing I could: ducked and covered.

I pulled down my arm and curled up in the fetal position as the hands suddenly started reaching for me. As the "Throw it back" chant started, the hands became more aggressive in their efforts to pry the ball from me.

I stayed curled, the strength from twenty years of futility keeping my fingers firmly clasped around my ball.

Finally, the hands stopped and the negotiations began. As the chant died, the bleacher leader that night began to reason with me.

"It's a Phillie homer, you have to throw it back."

But I would not be reasoned with. Soon a compromise was reached—rather, thrust on me. The Bleacher Bum pulled the Phillies cap off my head and offered a choice.

Something was going on the field—the hat or the ball.

Away went my hat.

It didn't end. The crowd started a new chant that would continue between every half-inning for the next six innings—a chant that can't be printed here. I took off my Phillies jersey and shoved it in my backpack, hoping to eventually fade into the crowd.

It didn't work.

As other fans continued to harass me, two strangers in front of me told the others to leave me alone. A minor scuffle ensued and my defenders were kicked out of the game.

Then from behind me, a fan dumped half a cup of water on my back and was also ejected. All the while, the Phillies were rallying to take the lead, causing the between-innings chant to grow more intense. Finally, as random fans decided to make more diving grabs for my baseball, a security guard came by and suggested that he take the ball and stash it in a security room under the stands.

I readily agreed, and was left to smile as I endured the chants for the rest of game, knowing the Phillies were winning and my ball was safe. Even the fact that my girlfriend was pretending not to know me didn't deter my joy.

When the game ended in a Phillies win and she and I stood to leave, a Wrigley regular stopped us.

"You took everything we did and handled it okay," he said, shaking my hand. "You're alright."

Of course I was. I had my baseball.

That's all I cared about as my girlfriend and I walked back to the subway—escorted by a security guard, just in case a Cubs fan still wanted to kill me.

Doug Lesmerises

CLOSE TO HOME JOHN McPHERSON

"Management says they are fed up
with losing foul balls and homers to the fans."

Get Lost, Kid!

It was June 1991, and Clement J. Keshorek—his once lithe body weakened by bone marrow disease—gripped the baseball with thin, pale fingers, then reached across the rumpled bedsheets for a pen and started writing. C... L ... E ... the former Pittsburgh Pirate began, each new letter on the leather bringing him a step closer to mending a heart he'd unwittingly broken forty-one summers before.

That was 1950, and Clem "Scooter" Keshorek was the smallest, scrappiest, most popular player on the Flint Arrows, a Detroit Tigers farm team. Scooter, who stood 5-foot 4-inches tall and weighed 140, was on his way to being named the Central League's most valuable player, and whenever the Arrows were in town, the diminutive shortstop was besieged with autograph seekers.

When I was eleven he was my hero, too, and on that July evening my heart was thumping as I sat there in the stands clutching a scuffed baseball and watching the players take their pregame warm-ups.

When they were done, I ran to the railing and shouted, "Hey, Scooter, can I have your autograph?"

Instead of taking the ball, he shot me a disdainful look,

snarled, "Get lost, kid!" and disappeared into the dugout.

I saw Keshorek play several more times, but I never again asked him for his autograph.

He left Flint before the 1951 season and even though I often thought about looking him up, I never did because other things always seemed to get in the way.

Then in the spring of 1991, after reading that several major-league baseball players had refused to sign autographs for youngsters, I went looking for Scooter. I found him in the Detroit suburb of Royal Oak, where he was born on June 20, 1926.

When I phoned, Scooter's wife Marilyn answered. I sketched my story for her and when I was done, I said, "So, you see, your husband owes me an autograph . . . and I'd like to collect."

She laughed softly. "Clem would like that." Then she added, "But if you're coming, do it soon because he's very ill and we never know what tomorrow will bring."

Two days later, I was ringing Keshorek's doorbell. Scooter, wearing pajamas, let me in.

"So you're the guy who says I cheated him out of an autograph, huh?" he said. "When was it? '50? That would have been Flint. Had me a heckuva season that year. Hit .270-something and made league MVP."

He scratched his head. "Y'know, I don't remember ever turning down a kid who wanted an autograph. But I could have done it, I suppose. Maybe I was having a bad night or something."

He walked away, motioning me to follow.

"Sorry I move so slow, but I've got myelofibrosis and it knocks me for a loop. Has something to do with the bone marrow. I get regular blood transfusions. Doctors don't know what causes or cures it. But, hey, you didn't come here to hear me talk about that, did you? Sit. We'll talk baseball."

Scooter plucked a fistful of faded photographs from a cardboard box and spread them on the bed.

"That's me sliding into second under Jackie Robinson's tag," he recalled, lifting one picture.

"And there I am with Gil Hodges," he said, pointing to another.

For the next six hours we talked baseball as Scooter, laughing one minute, misty-eyed the next, talked about his career that reached its peak in 1952 when he had his one and only shot at the "bigs."

He appeared in ninety-eight games for the Pittsburgh Pirates that year, collecting eighty-four hits in 322 at-bats for a .261 average. Playing shortstop, second and third, he had seventeen doubles, scored twenty-seven runs, knocked in fifteen and stole four bases.

The next year, however, he batted only once—as a pinch hitter—then was shipped to Hollywood of the Pacific Coast League. Scooter quit baseball after the 1959 season and returned to Royal Oak where he took a job selling sporting goods.

Then, too soon, or so it seemed to me anyway, the afternoon was curving toward twilight and it was time to go.

Scooter finished signing the baseball. O . . . R . . . E . . . K, he wrote. Then he leaned back on his pillow and said, "Still can't figure out why I didn't do this back in '50. I mean, I really hate ballplayers who ignore their fans."

He handed me the baseball. "Sorry you had to wait so long," he said.

"No problem," I replied.

"Am I still your boyhood hero?" he asked.

"Always and forever," I answered, shaking his hand.

I started out of the room, then turned back to face him. "Scooter?"

"Yeah."

"Will you say it again?"

"Say what again?"

"What you said that evening in 1950 when I asked you for your autograph."

He sat up in bed. "I told you I don't remember ever telling a youngster to . . . oh, what the heck. Okay . . . just this once . . . um . . . Get lost, kid!"

It sounded just like it had forty-one years before.

Except for one thing.

This time Scooter was smiling.

Bob Batz

The Mad Hungarian's Fastball

When I was a boy, playing Little League baseball, I dreamed—as most boys did back then—of someday getting a call from the major leagues.

"Son," I dreamed the major leagues would tell me, "you stink. We're kicking you out of Little League."

I would have been grateful. I was a terrible player. I was afraid of the ball and fell down a lot, sometimes during the National Anthem. So in 1960, I hung up my Little League uniform for good (it immediately fell down), and I had no contact with organized baseball for the next forty years.

Then, recently, I was asked to participate in the Joe DiMaggio Legends Game, which raises money for the Joe DiMaggio Children's Hospital in Hollywood, Florida. I said yes, because (a) it's a good cause, and (b) since they were asking ME to play, I figured it would be a relaxed, low-key event, like those company-picnic softball games where beer is available in the outfield and as many as six people play shortstop simultaneously.

Imagine my horror when I found myself at a real stadium, with thousands of spectators in the grandstands. Imagine my further horror when I found myself in a locker room containing several dozen former major league baseball players. Some were older guys, such as Minnie Minoso of the White Sox, who I believe once caught a fly ball hit by Magellan. But there were also some guys who had played big-league ball recently and still looked capable of hitting a baseball all the way through a human body.

I expressed concern about this to one of my teammates, the great Orioles third baseman Brooks Robinson, who gave me some reassuring advice.

"Don't play in the infield," he said. "You'll get killed."

I was on the American League team, managed by former Yankee John Blanchard. He gave me a nice little pregame pep talk, which I will reproduce here verbatim:

BLANCHARD: You should see how these guys hit the ball.
ME: Hard?
BLANCHARD: Oh, Lord God. Are you wearing a cup?
ME: I don't own a cup.
BLANCHARD: Oh, Lord God.

I did pretty well for the first few innings. This is because I was not in the game. Then Blanchard sent me out to left field to replace Mickey Rivers, which is like replacing Dom Perignon with weasel spit.

I trotted out of the dugout wearing the stiff new glove I'd bought that afternoon. When I brought it home, I removed the price tag and spent a few minutes fielding grounders thrown to me by my wife, who was nine months pregnant and thus could not put a ton of mustard on the ball, which dribbled my way at the velocity of luggage on an airport conveyor belt. That was my preparation for this moment, for standing alone in deep left field, with vivid Little League memories swarming in my brain—memories of praying for the ball not to come to me, and memories of falling down when it did.

So I'm standing out there, and for almost two innings, nothing comes my way. Then it happens: George Foster, five-time All-Star slugger for the Cincinnati Reds, rips a ground ball between second and short. I get a good break on the ball, going to my left, running hard. Foster is rounding first, trying for a double, and the crowd is roaring, and suddenly I realize, with a sense of elation, that I'm actually going to get to the ball. Yes! I can see it clearly, and I have the angle, and I'm closing fast and I'm going to make it! I'm almost there! And now I'm there! And now OH NO I RAN PAST THE BALL. THE BALL IS BACK OVER THERE. OH NOOOOOOO.

And of course I fall down. I've seen a video replay; I look like a man whose lower and upper body halves are being operated by two unrelated nervous systems. I make a pathetic, longing gesture toward the ball as it zips past to the outfield wall, where center fielder Dave Henderson retrieves it. After he throws it in, he puts his arm on my shoulders and says, "You're supposed to catch the ball in your glove."

I also got to display my batting prowess. The pitcher I faced was Al "The Mad Hungarian" Hrabosky, who still looks as though he has just been kicked out of the Institute for the Criminally Insane for being a little too insane, and who can still throw pretty hard (by which I mean "faster than light"). He struck me out on three pitches. I was still swinging at the last one when Hrabosky was in the showers.

So it was a pretty humiliating experience. But mark my words: I'll be back next year, and that's going to be a different story. Because next time, I'll be ready to "play with the big boys." That's right: I'm going to be wearing a cup. TWO cups, in fact. Because I'm assuming you need one for each knee.

Dave Barry

CLOSE TO HOME   JOHN McPHERSON

A good indication that the softball team
you joined isn't overly competitive.

The Impossible Dream

*Those who dream by day are cognizant of
many things that escape those who dream only
by night.*

Edgar Allen Poe

In 1968 my daughter, Carrie, was in fifth grade, and her
teacher was Mr. Kennedy, the most avid Cleveland Indian
fan in Tucson, the winter home of the team. Every year Mr.
Kennedy took a class field trip to see the Indians play, and
this year's game was sure to be special. Willie Mays and
the San Francisco Giants were coming to town.

Carrie was absolutely sure, as only a ten-year-old can
be, that she would catch a fly ball—maybe even a home
run—and get all the Cleveland players to sign it. "And I'm
gonna get Willie's autograph, too," she announced.

How does a parent prepare a child for inevitable failure
and disappointment without destroying the faith that
spawned the dream? We tried. "That'd be wonderful,
Honey, but well, there'll be hundreds of kids, maybe even
thousands, at Hi Corbett Field."

"That's okay," she answered, totally undeterred.

But her dad and I knew that every kid there would be scrambling for autographs. Willie Mays would be swamped—maybe even surrounded by a police escort. We assured her that we'd be proud of her if she brought home a signature or two on her game program.

"Nope!" she told us. "Mr. Kennedy says the only sure way to get autographs is to catch a ball. The players will autograph that, but they mostly ignore the programs. So I'm going to catch a ball."

We suggested that fly balls were traveling so fast that even grown-ups had trouble landing one. We told her there wouldn't be many pop-ups and maybe no home runs, and such big stands spread out all over. She didn't hesitate. "One of those flies will find me," she said confidently. "Where's Dad's old mitt? I want to practice."

So, in the three days we had before the big game, her dad and I took turns hitting easy pop-ups and shaking our heads. It was hopeless. Carrie had never been interested in baseball and had only played softball in the once-a-week P.E. classes at her elementary school. Every time a ball headed toward her, she held out the mitt and closed her eyes.

At least we could help her with that. I yelled at her to keep her eyes open. Her dad kept telling her, "Watch the ball. Eyes on the ball!"

On the day of the game, she stood poised at the door—a bright-eyed little girl with a Cleveland Indians cap on her curls and her dad's old mitt in her hands. I wanted to hold her, to warn her about the real world, to tell her there would be no pop ball, no autographs—certainly not Willie Mays'! Instead, I said, "Give it your best shot, Honey!"

Her dad added, "Go, girl!"

All day I stewed and fretted, until around lunchtime when I decided worrying was useless. I couldn't fly over the field and drop a baseball into my daughter's hands. I could do nothing except . . . "Please, dear God," I prayed, "give me the words to comfort her, to help her understand that wanting and getting don't always go together, that there are many things in life that we can't control."

When she got off the school bus that afternoon, I could see she had had a wonderful time. She was a blur of leaping, bouncing motion. Obviously, the other kids were excited, too. They yelled and cheered and waved at Carrie, and she waved back before jumping into the car.

"I caught one, Mom!" she announced breathlessly. "Willie popped one up, and it came right at me, and I held up my mitt and kept my eyes open, and it just plopped right in!"

In her outstretched hands lay a baseball—a baseball covered with scrawled signatures. I took it tenderly and turned it slowly. Most of the autographs were unrecognizable, but there was one in large, bold letters that stood out from the rest—Willie Mays!

"How . . . ?" I began.

"It was the ball, Mom, like Mr. Kennedy said. All the kids were pushing and shoving, holding out their programs, but Willie stopped signing those. Then he looked up and saw me hanging over the fence, holding out the ball I caught. He walked right over and grinned at me. Mom, Willie Mays grinned at me and took my baseball and signed it right across the middle."

Carrie still has that ball and the game program, keepsakes of a truly special time in her life. For me, there was an intangible lesson in my daughter's unlikely catch—You gotta believe.

Peggy Spence

A Proud Father

A boy wants something very special from his father. You hear it said that fathers want their sons to be what they feel they cannot themselves be, but I tell you it also works the other way.

Sherwood Anderson

My dad still isn't a hug-first kind of guy.

That's not to say he doesn't love his kids. It's just that, at age thirty-eight, I've long since learned to demand an embrace, to detect, I think, a bit of gratitude when he relents and grumbles something about me being "the sensitive one."

I must have learned it at the ballpark. The only ballpark that counted, really.

Old Comiskey was Dad's park when he was a kid growing up on Chicago's south side, and he made it ours after moving out to the south suburbs.

When he got out to Comiskey, something about my old man melted, something opened up—the same way it did when we were playing catch in the backyard and he'd tell me I didn't need to learn a curve because my fastball had "natural movement." It's like he was letting me in on a secret every time he pulled on his mitt to flag down my heaters, and every time we headed out to Comiskey.

Man, those trips were an adventure, especially for a kid from a subdivision not much older than he. Just walking through dank city viaducts and across crushed gravel parking lots strewn with broken glass to get to the park marked a Comiskey excursion as something different, something exciting, something just a little scary.

We could always count on Bat Day as our annual trip. There might be more if my brother or either of my two sisters scored free tickets at school for getting straight As, or if I managed the miracle of perfect attendance (straight As being completely out of the question). But Bat Day was a sure thing.

We were there in '73, among Comiskey's all-time record crowd of 55,555, to collect our bats and watch a doubleheader with the Twins. We were there at least four years running, because the bats—far worse for the wear—are still in a barrel in Dad's garage.

Well, three years' worth, anyway. There are a couple of Dick Allen models, a Bill Melton—dipped in a weird yellowish paint one year, red another and blue a third, but still bats you could use in a game instead of the mini-souvenirs they hand out these days.

I don't remember whose autograph was on the missing year. But those bats are the ones I'll always remember best.

My sisters, too old and too cool to hang out at the ballpark with their jerky little brothers, stayed home with Mom. So, it was just the men—and a buddy of my dad's from work and his sons, both much younger than me and my brother.

We were old pros by then, Comiskey veterans. We were ready to show these rookies the wonders of Comiskey— the gaping window at the back of the outfield stands that bathed you in a cool breeze and let you look down on the handball courts below; the picnic bunker beneath the left field stands where, if you yelled loud enough, an outfielder might wave at you; the ramp in center where you could look right down into the bullpen.

But even before the game started, it happened. The coworker's kids went off to find a bathroom, only to come back in tears.

Some older kids stopped them. The crowd, as usual for a Bat Day, was huge, and there weren't enough bats to go around. Taking in the story between stifled sobs, we gathered that the big kids asked if they could see the bats, grabbed them, then ran off, blending into the crowd.

My brother and I looked at each other. We looked at our dad. We handed the two crestfallen kids our bats.

A few innings later, after his buddy and the kids went off in search of a hot dog or something, my dad stunned me.

"I've never been prouder of you boys," he said.

For some reason, I remember being in the left-field stands, beneath the rusting, girdered canopy that was Comiskey's upper deck. But I don't remember asking for the hug my dad gave us that day.

Phil Arvia

The Whistle Story

When people find out I represent Tommy Lasorda, they usually want to hear a good baseball story. One of my favorites goes back to my graduate-student days, which were filled with complex classes, long nights of study in the law library and midnight treks home to my cramped apartment on Sunset Boulevard. There was very little free time compared to my carefree high-school days back in the Bronx, where schoolwork was broken up by leisurely summers of life guarding at the Castle Hill Community Pool.

The year was 1977 and I had just turned twenty-four. I hadn't even known Tommy Lasorda then, but under his wing the Los Angeles Dodgers won the National League Pennant that would take them to the World Series. I recall watching the play-off game on TV with the Red Sox and the Yankees, wondering who would get to play against the Dodgers. I still remember the thrill of watching Bucky Dent hit the home run that would take my home team to the World Series.

One night after a particularly grueling day at law school and the usual six hours at the library, I came home, tossed my books on the counter, opened a cold drink and sat down in time to catch the sports on the 11 o'clock news. The announcer was explaining that because of a lack of hotel space near the stadium, the Yankees had checked into a hotel on Sunset Boulevard. Though tired, I grasped this news much as a struggling swimmer grabs onto a pole to be pulled out of the water. As great as school was, sometimes I felt as though I were drowning in work. *The Yankees? In my neighborhood?* Someone had just tossed me a lifeline.

On impulse, I decided that somehow, I was going to get to that World Series. I was determined. I came up with a plan that I thought was pretty good. I called the hotel where the players were staying and asked to speak to Brian Doyle, one of the more conservative players. They actually put me through to his room and when he answered the phone, I had to talk fast. "I'm a law student, originally from New York," I said. "I'd like to interview you for the newspaper." The next thing you know, I was in the hotel lobby waiting for Brian, who had agreed to meet me for an interview.

I waited and watched as players milled around the lobby, giving autographs and trying to get their rooms squared away. I think I saw every team member except Brian Doyle. Dejected, I sat down, resigned to returning to my apartment. All of a sudden I heard my name. "Billy Goldberg," a young man said, reaching to shake my hand.

"Do I know you?" I asked, certain this was not Brian Doyle.

"It's Jimmy," he replied. "You remember me? . . . I know I'll never forget you. You were the lifeguard at Castle Hill. I remember you were the only one who would stop and talk to us younger kids. You even gave me your whistle to wear. I thought that was the coolest thing."

"What are you doing here in California?" I asked.

"I'm the bat boy for the Yankees," he explained. "Say, let me introduce you to some of the team."

He took me around then, and told the whistle story to one Yankee after another. He made it sound as though I was the nicest guy in the world.

Well, one thing led to another and before you know it, center fielder Mickey Rivers offered me a ticket to the World Series if I would drive him to the ballpark the next day. He ended up giving me tickets for all of the games and I also got invited to a party where they honored the most valuable player—who turned out to be Brian Doyle. I never did get to interview him, but I got my tickets!

I have told this story many times throughout my career as an agent and representative. And for as often as I've repeated it, I always thought the main point was the persistence it took to get those tickets. But now as I've grown older and have learned a bit more about life, I realize that the real point of my baseball adventure began not with some late night news announcement, but long, long before that, with the small act of sharing a whistle with a little kid.

Bill Goldberg
As told to Anita Gogno

A Three-Million-Dollar Grab

I mean, it's slightly unheard of for somebody to hit seventy home runs. I'm slightly in awe of myself.

Mark McGwire

When the 1998 baseball season drew to its close, the staggering home-run totals of St. Louis Cardinal Mark McGwire and Chicago Cub Sammy Sosa were at the center of attention. Major-league officials began marking and tracking the balls pitched to McGwire and Sosa.

On September 7, McGwire tied Roger Maris's single-season home-run record of sixty-one, once thought untouchable. The very next day McGwire hit his sixty-second home run of the season.

By the Cardinals' last game of the season on September 27, McGwire had sixty-eight home runs and had eased ahead of Sosa.

Present at the St. Louis game that day was Philip Ozersky, a twenty-six-year-old research scientist at Washington University School of Medicine. He and his colleagues were occupying a private party room in the left-field stands.

In the middle of the third inning, McGwire came up to bat. There was a crack and a whoosh, and everyone stood as McGwire hit his sixty-ninth home-run ball.

Ozersky watched it, thinking how incredible it was to be seeing baseball history in the making. In the seventh inning, McGwire came to the plate for what would likely be his last at bat of the season.

As McGwire sent a line drive toward the left-field fence, the young research scientist rose—and got that thrilling stomach drop even major-league outfielders admit to feeling when they see the ball coming their way.

The ball sailed into the open front of the small room and ricocheted off the back wall.

Ozersky looked, and there it was: Mark McGwire's seventieth home-run ball, resting wondrously beneath one of the metal bleachers.

Ozersky dove toward the ball and swallowed it in his grip, just an inch or two ahead of another young colleague. Ozersky was not sure if he was speaking or if maybe his thoughts were simply careening around in his head, *Oh, my God. Oh, my God.* Over and over.

Later, at the postgame press conference, Ozersky sat in the front row as McGwire talked to reporters.

Afterward, Cardinals media-relations manager Steve Zesch offered Ozersky their standard trade for the ball: a signed bat, ball and jersey—and a brief meeting with McGwire.

"I want to hold on to it for a while," Ozersky said, unsure of his plans except that it would be nice to show the ball to his family and friends. "I'd love to be able to congratulate him," he added.

"Mark can't negotiate over this," Zesch said. There was a time when McGwire met everyone who caught one of his home runs, until the guy who caught the sixty-third ball presented the player with a list of demands.

Still, Ozersky was stunned by the response. He turned to his girlfriend, Amanda Abbott, saying, "All I wanted was to shake his hand."

Phil Ozersky got a lot of calls in the days following his lucky grab. A $1 million offer was already on the table from three memorabilia dealers. This was followed by a proposal from an entrepreneur who had sold seventeen tons of the Berlin Wall to market images of the ball as holograms.

Perhaps the strangest proposal came from a Detroit-based collectibles marketer. His thought was to make a half-million baseballs, each containing a single thread extracted from inside home-run number seventy, and sell them for $29.95. He would resew the original covers around new windings and offer the ersatz ball to the National Baseball Hall of Fame. He withdrew his proposal when other offers reached $1.5 million.

To Phil Ozersky, all this carried an enormous responsibility. It left him thinking that whatever he did with the ball should be for the greater good. He kept coming back to that phrase "the greater good." But what it meant, exactly, he wasn't yet sure.

He considered if he should donate the ball to the Hall of Fame, whether the enjoyment of the relatively few visitors to Cooperstown, New York, was enough.

Ultimately, Ozersky accepted a proposal from Guernsey's, a New York City auction house, to conduct a sale at Madison Square Garden. Internet bids were also accepted via eBay. The sale took place on January 12, 1999, at 7 P.M. After about ten minutes, the auctioneer awarded the ball to a telephone bidder, comic-book publisher and entertainment entrepreneur Todd McFarlane, for more than $3 million.

Less than two weeks after the sale of the ball, Philip Ozersky was invited to the annual dinner of the St. Louis chapter of the Baseball Writers Association of America as a guest of the Cardinals' community charity, Cardinals Care.

During the evening, NBC sportscaster Bob Costas auctioned a caricature of McGwire, with the proceeds to benefit the slugger's charitable foundation. When the bidding began to slow, McGwire offered to sign the picture with a personalized message. "This is worth more than the ball," he joked. "I touched this."

Ozersky joined in on the bidding as a gesture to the people who had invited him and because he wanted to help McGwire's foundation. And he still hadn't met McGwire. When the auction stopped, he held the winning offer, eleven thousand dollars.

As Ozersky was making his way to the dais, the main thing on his mind was that he would finally get to shake Mark McGwire's hand.

The man was positively enormous. The two men chatted. Then McGwire whispered to Ozersky, off-mike. He asked if he should sign the picture Philip or Phil, wanting to get it right. McGwire held the signed picture up for all to see: "To Philip, Great Catch!"

Later it occurred to Ozersky how he'd built it up in his head that meeting McGwire was going to be much larger than life, but now he realized it wasn't. It was exactly the right size.

On February 15, 1999, Philip Ozersky sat down to map out how he was going to use his money. He planned to donate to the Leukemia Society of America in memory of the brother-in-law of Nancy Miller, his former boss, who had arranged for the tickets to the game, and to the American Cancer Society. He was also developing an ongoing giving plan with Cardinals Care.

But mostly he wanted to combine his love of sports with Mark McGwire's well-known dedication to disadvantaged and abused children. All along, his sister had been talking with him about his postball life, and they agreed that as a gesture to the home-run hitter he'd help causes McGwire cared about.

A summer sports camp for kids—he thought that might be a way to go. It would be done under the umbrella of a foundation. It could be his legacy, at least as far as catching Mark McGwire's seventieth home-run ball was concerned. He realized that the chance to help so many people was the greater good he had been thinking about. This was the reason the ball had landed in his hands.

Daniel Paisner

A Magical Moment

My fatherhood made me understand my parents and honor them more for the love they gave.
Kent Nerburn

I sit gazing idly from the front porch, as the brilliant January sun streaks against the soft virgin snow on the Connecticut hillside. Yet somehow, even now, while nature rests, my thoughts turn to baseball. I'm brought back to a time when heroes loomed, tall and strong, in a child's eyes.

In June 1964, my father brought me to Shea Stadium for the first time to see my beloved Mets. Living in Brooklyn, it wasn't easy being a Mets fan in those days, with the twilight of the Mantle–Maris Yankees still lingering. My father had been a Giants fan, but gave up on them when they left. When the Mets were created, he naturally took them up, and I, a blooming sports fan, followed. It was a bond we would share forever.

Shea was brand-new then, as was the World's Fair across the highway. It was a time of "All the Way with LBJ." Few Americans of the time could place Vietnam on a map. The Mets may have been perennial losers, but they were fun, and more importantly, they were mine.

I had never seen a color television, and was therefore shocked, walking through the tunnel, as the vibrant expanse of incredibly green grass exploded in front of me. In those days, they allowed you to watch batting practice. And in that era, before card shows and cynicism set in, players actually signed autographs for kids.

Everyone would gather behind the first-base dugout. The players would take their swings, warm up, stretch and prepare for yet another game as they always have. But this wasn't just another game. I was at this one. My father yelled out something about the receding hairline of Wes Westrum, a Mets coach and future manager and an old Giant, and I was amazed when Westrum laughingly acknowledged by tipping his cap and showing off his bald pate, as if he and my dad were old friends.

Players from both the Mets and Cubs were signing autographs. In another five years, these same two teams would stage one of the classic pennant races. But that year they were both the doormats of the league. These were the Cubs of Ernie Banks and Billy Williams, Ron Santo, and a young center fielder named Lou Brock, who in a few days hence would be traded to the Cardinals and immortality.

But we were unprepared. We had no paper, and only a small dull pencil. My father had a plain white matchbook cover with room for only four names. I got Joe Christopher, a hard-hitting outfielder and fan favorite; Tracy Stallard, a journeyman pitcher who had given up Roger Maris's sixty-first homer; and a young Ed Kranepool, who though only ten years older than me at the time already seemed like he had been around forever. I had room for only one more, and I knew who I wanted.

That era's Mets were a collection of has-beens and never-weres. But there was one star, and his name was

Ron Hunt. Hunt was a tough throwback to another era, the kind of player who would do anything to win, and do it well. He would bunt with two strikes and beat it out; he would knock down anyone who tried to prevent him from scoring; he would hit the other way; he would hit for average; and he played impeccable defense. That summer he would start at second base for the National League, beating out players named Mazeroski and Rose, in a vote of his peers. Every white T-shirt I owned was emblazoned with Hunt's name and number in magic marker, to my mother's chagrin.

But everyone knew that Hunt never signed autographs, too focused on preparing for the game. But I was determined to try. We kept calling out his name, to no avail. "Can't now, later," he seemed to say with a nod of his head.

But right over here, signing for everyone, was the great Ron Santo, arguably the best third baseman of his era. "Why not get Santo's?" my father asked. "Aw, Dad, he's a Cub, he stinks," was my nine-year-old's chauvinistic reply, which my father thought was hysterical.

But now, game time was approaching and security was chasing everyone back to their seats—time was running out. Hunt came out of the dugout and was having a pregame catch with another infielder. My father called out one last time, "C'mon, Ron, it's for the kid," and suddenly, remembering us from earlier, here came No. 33 himself, trotting over to me! He signed in the remaining spot, smiled and trotted away, ignoring the pleas of everyone else who came running over.

My mouth stayed open, frozen, my eyes gaping with wonderment. I looked up at my father, and we both just beamed. All the other kids stared with envy. I practically floated to my seat.

Two heroes came through, that long-ago late spring evening. Hunt signed for me and me alone, but far more importantly, it was my father who had gotten it for me. That bond, between my father, myself and baseball, could never be broken.

Now, Dad is long gone and Hunt long retired, his once-promising career curtailed by a series of debilitating injuries, and now remembered mostly for getting hit by more pitches than anybody. Somewhere along the line, through countless moves, those prized signatures faded and disappeared. But from my perspective nearly forty years later, the sunlight still shines on that magical instant.

I've often thought of this story, of how much it meant to me. But until I became a father myself, I never understood just how important it was to my own father, how great he must have felt, how for him, too, it was magical. Baseball truly crosses and melds the generations.

I lean back. The cold winter air feels windlessly fresh against my face. A squirrel jumps across barren branches. In the distance, my eight-year-old daughter fashions a snowball to throw. I smile, content.

Stephen Yudelson

A Little Faith Led to Miracle Catch

Don't be afraid of the space between your dreams and reality. If you can dream it, you can make it so.

Belva Davis

On a June evening, my eight-year-old son, Conor, and I take the 5 P.M. train from Oakville, Ontario, to Toronto to see a Blue Jays game. We plan to arrive early for batting practice in the hopes of catching a ball hit into the seats. The night is full of promise because our tickets are for the front row down the third-base line, a great location for foul ball scooping.

Having umpired semipro baseball after high school, I know many of the subtleties of the game and enjoy teaching them to Conor. The best part is when he asks me a question. I sometimes quote a rule, and if we are at home, we go into the backyard to play it out.

Conor remembers these lessons. At the last game we attended, against Oakland, Rickey Henderson swung and missed for strike three. The catcher dropped the ball, and Henderson ran to first, the runner on first going to second.

Although both arrived safely, the first-base umpire called Henderson out and sent him to the dugout. The two men sitting in front of us were asking each other what was going on when Conor leaned forward and recited in his most confident voice, "The batter may not advance on a dropped third strike with first base occupied and less than two outs."

Tonight we're seated in Section 130D near the left-field fence, where we can expect some flys or one-bouncers from right-handed batters pulling the ball in batting practice. We yank our gloves out of our bag and are looking toward the plate when a Yankee batter lifts a long foul ball directly at me. I settle under it. I hear a man behind me say, "Boy, he's right on it" and I say to myself, *Yes, I am.* But suddenly I lose my focus, everything blurs and moves much too fast, the ball hits the end of my glove and bounces away. I chase it, get my foot caught between the seats and watch helplessly as a teenager in a backward baseball cap scoops it up.

I could sit down and cry. "How could I miss it?" I yell at myself. I'll never get another chance like that. I suddenly feel eight years old myself, bobbing a Peewee League pop-up in front of the whole town. *How could I be such a klutz in front of Conor?*

Conor rescues me. He smiles and stares up at me. "Too much pressure, Dad? Don't worry, we'll get another one. We have good seats." No matter what he might be thinking inside, he doesn't criticize or speak in anger as I have done when he missed a ball I thought he should have caught. Despite his belief in me, I can't forgive myself as easily.

Between batting practice and the game, we leave to get something to eat. There's a sign near the food vendor that says: THE ODDS OF A FAN CATCHING A BALL ARE 300,000 TO ONE, YET EVERYONE BRINGS THEIR

GLOVES. My heart aches and my stomach churns, even before my double chili dog with sauerkraut. I know we will never have another opportunity as good as the one I missed, though Conor remains optimistic. The seats we ordered the previous November are in the first row, he reminds me.

The fellow just on the home-plate side of me and his twenty-something son have their gloves hanging over the field, ready for anything. I saw them during batting practice and hoped our seats wouldn't be close to them because they would scoop up everything that came their way. But, sure enough, here they are in better position than us.

In the top of the first inning, Don Mattingly hits a foul fly down the third-base line. Against all odds, it comes at us again! The fellow on my right and I get up at the same time, his glove in front of mine. Everything blurs together once more and *whap!*, the sound of a horsehide ball in a cowhide glove echoes in my ears. I look in the other fellow's glove for the ball, but it isn't there. I look in my glove, and there, cradled snugly, is Mattingly's fly ball.

"Conor, we got one!" I shout, so excited that I don't even think to show the ball off to the crowd like I've seen others do on TV. I give it to Conor and we sit, heads together, inspecting every square inch of that ball—a black smudge where Mattingly's bat hit it and a brown, rough spot where it had been scuffed in the dirt on the previous pitch. Conor congratulates me. "You see, Dad? I knew we could do it."

The rest of the game has a unique magic: pure and clear. I discover that my neighbor isn't disappointed about missing Mattingly's foul: He scooped a ball during batting practice about the same time I was fumbling my first chance. Our successes had flip-flopped with each other's failures.

At least once an inning, Conor and I get the ball back out of our bag and look at it again. Conor wears No. 10 and plays catcher on our T-ball team because of Pat Borders, his hero. Sure enough, the Blue Jays rally in the bottom of the eighth on Borders' two-run double and win the game 5–4.

My thoughts keep returning to the moment of catching that ball. I never really saw it, didn't follow it at all the last several feet. The oddest part was, I couldn't believe it had gone into my glove. I was sure our neighbor had caught it—his glove was in front of mine. It was a miracle in the middle of a baseball game.

After the game Conor and I stay a few moments to savor our good fortune. Our neighbor gives me a small wave from the river of spectators when he leaves, as if to acknowledge our sharing of games with sons.

Then on the train home, with Conor sleeping against me, I consider the lessons taught tonight. If we tally the results of our little competitions with others, we might find that things usually even out. But most of all, I can now appreciate that miracles do happen, especially when helped along by the faith of an eight-year-old boy in his dad.

Steven Moore

A Father and Son's Fall Classic

There will be many memorable moments from this year's World Series—moments that baseball fans will talk about for years.

For a father and son who live in Lima, Ohio, though, it will be hard for anything that happened on the playing field to match the World Series moment that unexpectedly came to them.

Don Bruns is forty-three; his son Aaron is ten. Aaron loves baseball, and the Cincinnati Reds in particular. He broke his arm in a bicycle accident last summer, and missed the last part of his Little League season. For a birthday present, his dad decided to take Aaron down to Cincinnati for the first game of the World Series. They had no tickets.

"I was hoping that we could find some scalpers who would sell us tickets," the father said. "I explained to Aaron that there was no guarantee we would get into the game. But just being around a World Series, even if we didn't get in, would be exciting."

So they drove the more than two hours from Lima to Cincinnati—Lima is in the northern part of Ohio, Cincinnati is all the way south. For two more hours they walked the streets—Aaron wearing a Reds cap.

"There were a lot of scalpers, all right," the father said. "I didn't realize how much tickets cost. The cheapest ones we were offered were $175 apiece. The most expensive were $300 apiece. I couldn't do that, and I explained it to Aaron. He understood."

Then, the father said, they were approached by a man who asked if they were going to the game.

"He told me his name, and he told me that he was staying at the Omni Hotel," the father said. "I explained about our trip to Cincinnati, and I said that I couldn't pay what the scalpers were asking.

"He pulled out two tickets. He said that my son reminded him of himself fifteen years ago. He handed me the tickets.

"I asked him how much he wanted. He said there was no charge. He said the tickets were free.

"I thought that maybe this was part of a scam or something. I kept waiting for something tricky to happen. We were waiting for the guy to play us for fools.

"But he just said that he hoped we would enjoy the game, and he left. We went to the stadium. The tickets were wonderful. I had never been to a World Series game, and of course my son hadn't. The World Series! It feels different than any other baseball game. The intensity, the emotional high, the excitement level . . . and this guy had just handed us the tickets and walked away.

"During the game my son and I must have turned to each other thirty times and said to each other: 'I can't believe this.'"

Here is the story of the man on the street:

His name is Michael Teicher; he works as an account executive for a company called Phoenix Communications Group in South Hackensack, New Jersey. The company markets TV shows about baseball—the syndicated "This Week in Baseball" and ESPN's "Major League Baseball Magazine," among others.

Teicher seemed surprised when I tracked him down in Oakland, where he had traveled for the second leg of the World Series. I explained what Don Bruns had told me.

"Here's what happened," Teicher said. "I work for a man named Joe Podesta. He hadn't missed a World Series in sixteen years. A month ago, though, he had a mild heart attack, and he's not at the Series this year.

"I guess like a lot of people who have heart attacks, he felt some kind of new appreciation for the preciousness of life. He told me that he wanted to make some people happy. So he told me that when I was at the World Series I should take two tickets and give them to people I thought would be thrilled by going to the game. That's the only ground rule he gave me—give the tickets to people I thought would be thrilled."

Teicher walked around town for some time before seeing Don and Aaron Bruns.

"I had seen a lot of people on the street who I thought might just take the tickets and sell them," Teicher said. "This guy and his son, though—the father was carrying a sign that said 'I Need Two Tickets.' His son was this nice-looking, skinny kid with glasses, and he looked very disappointed.

"I followed them and I heard the father telling the son about how much the scalpers wanted for tickets. I heard the father say they wouldn't be going to the game.

"I looked at them and they reminded me of my dad and me when I was a kid. I would have died to go to a World Series game with my father. But I never did.

"So I went up and I gave them the tickets and I told them to enjoy themselves."

Because of his work, Teicher has begun to regard going to World Series games as almost routine. "I go to all of them," he said. "That makes you forget how important going to the World Series can be."

How important was it to Don Bruns and his son? Here is what Bruns said: "This is the most memorable thing that has ever happened to us. My boy and I will never forget that night."

After Michael Teicher had handed the tickets to the father and son, he watched them walking together toward the stadium.

"The little boy," he said, "it was like all of a sudden he had a bounce in his step."

Bob Greene

"I dunno, Louie. What do you think?
He says they're really good seats. . . ."

The Best Game I Never Saw

Youth comes but once in a lifetime.

Henry Wadsworth Longfellow

It was supposed to be a perfect day. I had tickets to a Cincinnati Reds game in one hand and the hand of my five-year-old daughter, Molly, in the other. She had an excited little skip in her step as we walked up to the escalator that would take us to the stadium gates. What a treat this was going be!

As we walked, I envisioned all the neat father-daughter things we could share. Why, I could teach her the finer points of baseball. We could do the "wave" together. There would be fireworks because the Reds were bound to hit a few home runs and, of course, win the game.

I could tell her all about the famed "Big Red Machine" and how I had rooted for them when I was growing up. We would eat hot dogs and popcorn and sing "Take Me Out to the Ball Game" as we did the seventh-inning stretch. We would give each other high fives until our hands hurt as the Reds made big play after big play.

There was just one problem hovering over our heads. Rain clouds.

Oh, man, I thought. *Not today. Please don't let it rain today, God. This is such a special occasion. All my life I've loved Cincinnati baseball. Never in my life did I imagine I'd have the opportunity to be a father and bring my little girl to a baseball game. It can't rain today. It just can't.*

But it did. In fact, it poured. By the time we found our seats, the game had already started—and been stopped because of rain. The first thing my daughter saw in grand old Riverfront Stadium—the place where I had rooted for World Series champions and seen many dramatic victories—was the ground crew rolling a big tarp out on the field.

I was extremely disappointed. We had driven two hours to see this? It wasn't fair. Maybe, if we were lucky, the rain would stop at least long enough to see a couple of innings. Then I thought of Molly and how disappointed she must be.

But when I looked at her I was surprised to see her smiling. Those trademark dimples of hers were in full bloom when she nudged me and pointed to the ground crew.

"Look at that, Daddy!" she said to the men working side-by-side pushing what looked like a big roll of carpet on the field. "Cool!"

I knew Pete Rose was "Charlie Hustle." I knew Joe Morgan could steal bases like no other and that Johnny Bench was the greatest catcher who had ever lived. But until Molly pointed it out to me, I honestly didn't know just how "cool" the ground crew was.

We watched together in amazement and amusement as they worked to roll that big tarp out on the field. I'd really never paid much attention to what an operation that was before Molly had pointed it out to me.

As the rain continued to fall, the jumbo TV screen in center field began to show highlights of all the great Reds teams in past years. *Good,* I thought. I could at least point out to her who some of my favorite players were. But just as I started to focus on the highlights, Molly nudged me again and said, "I'm hungry, Dad." I reluctantly got up and led her to the concession stand, frustrated all over again. I guess I wasn't supposed to see any baseball—live or taped—on this day.

The rain may have stopped the game, but it didn't stop the exuberance of little Molly. She had that explorer's look in her eye. As most of the fans headed for home, Molly and I headed for a most memorable adventure—the ramps surrounding the stadium.

After devouring a hot dog and some popcorn, Molly and I decided to walk around the stadium. We came to the first of many ramps that wind their way up, down and around that big sardine can of a ballpark. Then Molly's dimples popped out once again.

"Let's run, Daddy," she said.

My first instinct of caution gave way to the "oh, what the heck" spirit. So we ran down one ramp, Molly screaming in glee all the way.

Her spirit was contagious. As we reached the top of another one, no one else around, I decided to scream with her.

Inside the ballpark, those highlights I'd wanted to see were still rolling on the big screen. I could hear the voice of former play-by-play man Al Michaels screaming, "The Reds win the pennant! The Reds win the pennant!"

As Molly and I headed down another ramp, she screamed and I started yelling, "The Reds win the pennant! The Reds win the pennant!"

Up and down we went, ramp after ramp after ramp. Hand-in-hand we went. The rain fell. The crowd had left. The umpires and players were waiting for the official word that the game had been called. And underneath the stadium, Molly and I were having such fun.

It was a lousy day—weather-wise. There were no fireworks. The clouds covered the sky just like the tarp covered the field. But there was a great lesson in the silver linings of those clouds.

Fatherhood is grand, no matter what the weather. If you pay attention and are receptive to your children, it's an event that never gets postponed. Just when things are bad, there is a ramp right around the corner leading to a shining moment. World Series heroes are nothing compared to the magic found within your own children. All you have to do is just look.

I'll never forget that day with Molly. The day we went to my favorite ballpark and never sat in our seats. The day we went to see the Reds and watched the ground crew instead. The day when I didn't see a single inning of baseball but came away from the stadium more exhilarated than ever. Not because the Reds won, but because I was a dad.

It was the best game I never saw.

Darrel Radford

3

DEFINING MOMENTS

*These moments are the soul of baseball:
The ball perfectly hit, perfectly caught,
or perfectly thrown . . . we can unwrap
the moments later, when it's quiet, and
enjoy them all over again.*

Alison Gordon

The Legend

Ability will enable a man to go to the top, but it takes character to keep him there.

John Wooden

My left foot is aching again. It always does when the barometer is falling. For twenty-six years I've been able to predict the weather with my left foot, a very palpable memento of my brush with the legend.

It wasn't a mere brush; actually, it was a collision.

Even as a fourteen-year-old I knew about legends. They were the guys who hung around the playgrounds in the summer and the gyms and bowling alleys in the winter, high-school dropouts mostly, who had once been blessed, or cursed, with bodies that matured too early. They had been bigger and stronger and better coordinated than others their age, young men in a world of adolescents. They had once hit a baseball farther, scored more touchdowns and shot more baskets than their peers in high school. Later, though, they became big-gutted from too much beer and not enough exercise, full of stories of what had been and what, if it hadn't been for a bad break, might have been. Most of them could still dominate us kids. But we knew why they tried: They couldn't compete in the world of men.

My friends and I tolerated them, but we were wise enough not to be flattered when they boasted to us or frightened when they bullied us. We didn't admire them, we pitied them.

I assumed that Joe Bellino was another such legend. Oh, he had done it all for our next-town rival, Winchester High. In the state championship basketball game he stole the ball and drove the length of the court for the game-winning lay-up—in sudden-death overtime. All the big-time football powers were recruiting him. And as a catcher, he was compared by major-league scouts to Roy Campanella.

I wasn't impressed. Another precocious jock—I knew about them.

Still, as I sat on the bench that sunny May afternoon in 1955, waiting to play third base in my first varsity baseball game for Lexington High, my nervousness was compounded by the prospect of playing against Joe Bellino, who was then a junior and already an established legend. I watched him as Winchester went through its infield drills. He had a stocky, Yogi Berra body. His throws to second, flicked so casually, seemed to be still rising when they arrived. He didn't chatter or yell and carried himself with such grace, such sublime self-confidence, that he commanded attention. I was still skeptical; he was no hero, no legend to me. But the more I watched him, the more I began to feel that I, a skinny freshman, didn't belong on the same field with Joe Bellino.

I certainly played as if I didn't belong. The first ball hit to me was the easiest kind of lazy three-hopper. I grabbed at it too eagerly. It hit the heel of my glove, bounced off my knee and came to rest in the third-base coach's box.

An inning later I threw a bunt into right field. I struck out. Twice. My first varsity baseball game (my coach called it my "first debut") was becoming a nightmare. My teammates ignored me, for which I was grateful. The Winchester players didn't say much either. They knew a good thing when they saw it.

In the sixth inning we were losing by five runs, most of them directly attributable to my errors and my failure to hit. I slumped miserably by myself on the end of the bench. When my coach came to sit beside me, I figured he was going to take me out. He didn't look at me, and at first I didn't realize he was talking to me. He seemed to be studying the game from beneath the visor of his cap.

"Errors are part of the game, Son," he mumbled, never taking his eyes off the Winchester pitcher. "Never blame anyone for an error. There! See how he twists the ball in his glove? Curveball coming."

He went on and I listened to him. I began to think of the game and not just my own part in it. My next time at bat, when I saw the pitcher twist the ball in his glove, I managed to bloop a hit into short right field. As I stood on first base I thought, *Two strike outs and a single. I'm a .333 hitter!*

I scored a run and we got a couple more. When we took the field in the seventh, the score was tied.

Bellino, meanwhile, was playing the way legends are supposed to play, hitting line drives and throwing out base runners with impressive nonchalance. Then he was on second base, the potential winning run.

"Watch the steal!" yelled our shortstop. I glanced toward second, where Bellino stood, hands on hips, staring at me and, it seemed, sizing me up. I looked quickly back to the plate, praying for a passed ball, a wild pitch, a base hit— anything so I wouldn't screw up.

When the pitch was released someone shouted, "There he goes!" I moved to straddle the bag. Our catcher's throw was perfect, and as I caught it I turned to face the sliding Bellino. I had him dead to rights.

They told me afterward that he didn't slide, that he caught me with a perfect cross-body block as I was pivoting to make the tag. I don't know. I never saw him hit me. The next thing I knew, I was lying on my back in foul territory, some distance from third base, with an enormous weight on my chest. When I opened my eyes I was staring into Joe Bellino's face.

"You okay?" he asked softly.

I started to answer, but he was gone. I realized I was holding the ball in my glove against my chest. I tried to stand up. That's when I felt the screaming pain in my left foot. I sat looking at Bellino as he perched on third base, arms folded across his chest. He and the umpire seemed to be studying me as they chatted. I saw Joe nod once and look down, tapping the bag lightly with his toe.

"Hey, you're out!" I said from where I sat.

The umpire smiled at Bellino, then shrugged at me. He spread his hands, palms down.

"Wait a minute," I yelled. "I got the ball. See?" I held up my glove for him.

"The runner," pronounced the umpire, grinning, "is safe."

My coach didn't argue with umpires. He felt it set a poor example for us. This time, as he knelt beside me and touched my foot gently, he muttered only, "Bad call." Then he spoke to Bellino, who had come over to look. "I've always admired you, Joe. Not anymore."

The pain took over and I lost interest in the conversation. I lay back on the ground, surrounded by coaches and umpires and players and Joe Bellino, and I couldn't help it, I cried.

After the game, which Winchester won 9–8, Bellino came to the bench where I sat with my throbbing foot. He half carried me to the bus, never saying a word. In spite of my pain, it embarrassed me that my chest was bony where he held me under my arm, and that he was able to bear my weight so effortlessly. He helped me to a seat, then touched my leg and said, "Take it easy." As he walked off the bus some of my teammates called to him, "Hey, take care, Joe" and "Nice game, Joe."

I thought to myself that legends aren't easily tarnished.

The x-rays showed that the first three metatarsals in my left foot had been broken clean through. I wore a cast and hobbled around school on crutches for the rest of the baseball season. For the first few days I was treated like a celebrity: I was the kid whose foot had been broken by Joe Bellino. Senior girls actually volunteered to carry my books. The boys on the varsity team gave me rides in their cars. The local barber even gave me a free haircut.

I should have gloried in all the attention I received. I was almost a legend myself. But not quite. Too often, people I didn't know would stop me in the school corridor or in a store. I had many conversations that went like this:

Stranger: "Hey, I hear you got that," pointing to my cast, "from Joe Bellino, huh?"

Me: "Yeah."

Stranger: "I've seen him play football. He can hit. People, I mean."

Me: "He can hit all right—people and baseballs."

Stranger: "So what was it like?"

Me: "I don't know. Never knew what hit me. Knocked me cold. First thing I remember was lying on my back in the coach's box with Joe on top of me. Ten feet beyond the bag at least."

Stranger: "Wow! I guess he can hit. So, anyway, was he out? Did you hang on to the ball?"

Me (lamely): "Well, I held the ball. I did. But the umpire, he called him safe."

Stranger (terminating the conversation): "Oh, sure. That's too bad. Oh, well."

My story was flawed, my small claim to distinction diminished. I quickly learned to divert those conversations. My cast and my crutches, which by all rights should have been emblems of my courage, became instead my curse. I refused to talk about it. I knew he was out. He was lying on my chest, right on top of the glove that held the ball, and we were yards away from the base. But none of that really mattered. I had to be honest and say he was called safe, and that ruined it all.

I grew to hate Joe Bellino, not for breaking my foot and making me cry, but for being called safe, for having that kind of power over an umpire, for being a legend. I found that there was some stature in being the victim of a legend, but not much.

My foot and my ego healed thoroughly over the course of the summer, with the exception of the ache that I soon recognized could forecast stormy weather. My attitude toward legends remained as skeptical as ever.

The next winter the Winchester basketball team—led, naturally, by all-everything Joe Bellino—was undefeated and on its way to another state championship when we played them. I was a sophomore second-stringer. By halftime Bellino had sixteen points, and we were losing 38–17. I played most of the second half; Bellino didn't play at all.

I was peeling the tape off my ankles in the locker room afterward when someone touched my shoulder and then sat beside me.

"Billy, how you doing?" said Joe Bellino in that soft voice of his.

He knew my name! I glanced up, then returned my attention to my ankles. "Oh, hi Joe. Nice game."

"Good game yourself. You've got a nice jump shot there."

"Sure, thanks."

"Look, I never heard. Your leg, was it hurt bad?"

"Couple broken bones in my foot. It's fine now. No problem."

"Well, listen. I shouldn't have done that. I should have slid. But you had the ball waiting for me, and . . ."

I shrugged. "It's okay. You gotta try to win."

He stood beside me. I picked at the tape. He spoke loudly enough for my teammates in the locker room to hear. "I couldn't believe you held on to the ball. I gave you my best shot. You had me cold. I was out. No question. The ump blew the call." He paused for a moment. "You're a tough kid."

I looked up at him. He grinned and held out his hand. We shook solemnly.

"Accept my apology?" he asked.

"No sweat," I replied.

My teammates seemed to look at me a little differently after that, though perhaps it was only my way of looking at myself. I do know that my attitude toward legends—or at least to that particular legend—changed. I watched Joe Bellino win the Heisman Trophy, a first for the Naval Academy, and later run back punts for the Patriots. I saw him hit people who were considerably better padded than a bony freshman third baseman whose foot he had broken.

Now, when a low-pressure front moves in and that foot begins to throb, it still pleases me to remember one tough kid who hung on to the ball.

William G. Tapply

Living His Dream

The difference between the impossible and the possible lies in a person's determination.

Tommy Lasorda

He loved baseball. Couldn't get enough.

When it rained in Seattle, as it frequently does, and practice was cancelled, it used to make him so mad. That's when he knew he was hooked.

He pestered his dad to hit him grounders in the backyard. He routinely led three younger brothers and a sister out the front door to play catch.

A Wiffle-ball machine was set up in the garage, allowing him to take batting practice at any time. Siblings were paid a quarter or fifty cents to feed the machine.

Posters of Rod Carew and Pete Rose hung on his bedroom wall. He watched games on TV. He was a big, big fan of his hometown team, the Seattle Mariners.

But like most fourteen-year-old boys, he was merely a good baseball player, not a great one. Some day, he would have to channel his energy into something else.

Find another outlet, another passion. Or so everyone thought.

Through a friend on his suburban Pony League team, he heard that the Mariners were hiring. He got on the phone, got an interview, got a job.

Now this isn't some Disney movie, some outrageous fairy tale come true. No one was occupying someone else's body, acquiring magical powers, walking out of cornfields or answering to Roy Hobbs.

He wouldn't be fielding or hitting. Folding and scrubbing were more like it.

He was a clubhouse boy.

For two seasons, he showed up at the Kingdome and wandered the Mariners' locker room. He picked up soiled uniforms, hung fresh ones. He polished shoes, ran errands. He did everything except get in the way.

He was in awe of the big leaguers. He didn't say much. He tried to stay anonymous. Yet he watched all of the activity that went on before him behind closed doors, the good and the bad, the professionalism and the immaturity, and put everything to memory.

"I learned a lot," he said. "I learned when you think people aren't watching you, they really are. I watched the way people acted. Some were really nice."

A few of the players noticed him and took an interest. Mariners second baseman Harold Reynolds, outfielder Bruce Bochte and relief pitcher Dave Heaverlo sat him down and encouraged him. Heaverlo even gave him added work, enlisting him to baby-sit his kids.

One day, he saw one of his heroes, Carew, sitting alone in a Kingdome dugout. He wanted his autograph. He was too shy to ask for it. He turned and walked away.

The dream job ended when it was time for him to go to high school. He couldn't juggle work and play anymore. More than ever he was determined to become a big-leaguer, but most people figured he had come as close to this fantasy world as he would get. How many people get to do what he did, even if it was picking up sweaty uniforms?

For the next seven years, he played high school, community college and college baseball. By now, he had settled in at catcher after trying several positions. Still, he was not a standout. He didn't even make the all-league team in high school.

His baseball career was about to come to an unceremonious end when he showed up for one last collegiate tournament. Something magical happened.

He hit everything thrown to him, threw out every base runner.

Scouts were in the stands. Scouts were on the phone. He was drafted, signed and in the majors before long.

Fifteen years and six big-league teams later, Tom Lampkin now plays for the Mariners. They pursued him and he happily joined them as a free agent. He's been home for three seasons and is a fan favorite, often providing game-winning hits, a familiar face, hope. It's what he always wanted.

"When I started playing, I didn't know the difference between professional baseball and the major leagues, I just wanted to play for the Mariners," he said. "I always wanted to play for the Mariners because they were my hometown team."

He never let go of his dream, actually living it twice, whether it was offering up towels or using them.

Along the way, Lampkin encountered Carew a second time. Yes, he now has the Hall of Famer's autograph. He signs a few himself these days.

Not only that, Lampkin treats all of the Mariners clubhouse boys with ultimate respect.

Dan Raley

That's Why God Made Tall Infielders

I've always felt that the difference between the impossible and the possible lies in a person's determination. Of course, a well-timed prayer every now and then never hurts either.

I discovered this early in my professional baseball career when I was pitching what turned out to be my last Triple-A game against Buffalo. It was the first inning and I had walked the first three batters I faced, loading up the bases with no outs. Now I was 2-and-0 to the next batter and in danger of walking in a run.

I thought there might be some concern on the bench, so I looked over to the dugout and saw the manager with his foot on the top step. I knew what that meant—he was ready to make the walk out to the mound to pull me out of the game.

I grabbed the rosin bag, stepped off the mound, turned completely away from the plate, and put in a request of my own for "relief" on the mound.

"Dear God," I said, "please get me out of this mess."

Well, after a few minutes of standing there with my back to the plate, the umpire, Billy Williams, came out to the mound to see what was up.

"What are you waiting for?" he asked.

"I'm talking to God," I told him.

"Talking to God?" Billy just shook his head—probably something he did quite often around pitchers. "Let's go," he said. "Play ball."

I took a breath to settle myself and threw the next pitch, and the batter hit a screaming line drive down the third-base line, and I thought, *It's all over now.*

But all of a sudden the third baseman made this incredible leap—it seemed like he jumped five feet off the ground—and he snagged the line drive. Then he fired it to second base and got the runner before he could get back to the bag, forcing him out. Then the second baseman whipped the ball over to first base and caught that runner before he could get back, and boom, it was a triple play—and just like that I was out of the inning.

In all of my professional baseball years, including twenty years managing the Los Angeles Dodgers, I've prayed many times—often with good results—but I've never seen another triple play like that one.

Tommy Lasorda
As told to Ernie Witham

A Glove Story

New off the shelf, the baseball mitt cost all of eight dollars. Ten bucks tops if memory serves—the receipt has been long lost.

A "Glove Night" piece of vinyl stitched in Taiwan? Hardly. We're talking about a first-rate first-baseman's glove. A genuine "Major League Model," no less. The best glove ever made, if you ask me.

It should be pointed out, however, that the mitt in study was originally purchased more than a half century ago—by my father when he was a young boy—when eight dollars was half a summer's worth of mowed lawns.

To give you an idea, the glove—circa 1940—is twenty years older than I am. I hope I hold up so well. Shoot, it is not only older than Astroturf, it predates every National League ballpark sans Chicago's Wrigley Field. To be sure, it's a relic from an era when uniforms were baggy and high-fives were still low handshakes and ballplayers didn't go on strike or charge fifteen dollars for an autograph.

A short while ago, I came upon the abandoned old mitt in the bottom of a dresser drawer in my old room in my parent's house. It was battered and tattered and showing its years. Kind of like the Dodgers' bullpen of late. But memories are worth hanging on to. So I shelled out $34.50 to rehabilitate the eight-dollar mitt.

It was a wonderful bargain.

The old friend came back in the mail from the shop as good as new. Better, really, because it was already broken in. You slide your hand inside and feel leather as soft as the hand of your first girlfriend.

It is beautiful. "You look m-a-a-a-h-v-v-elous," Billy Crystal would say if he laid eyes upon the new old glove.

It smells marvelous, too. The intoxicating fragrance of leather took me back to those hot summer days when I was ten or twelve or eight.

Perhaps most marvelous of all, however, the refurbishing treatment made the once blackened writing stamped into the mitt legible: *Frank McCormick. Major League Model.*

In good light, tilted at just the right angle, you can now even make out the *Preferred Model* and the *Horsehide Lining.* It also has an *Inner Processed Palm,* whatever that is.

I doubt they make gloves with inner processed palms anymore, much less with soft horsehide linings. Today's preferred models are made of cowhide. And made in Japan and Taiwan, not Gold Smith Made In USA.

Indeed, Gold Smith was long ago swallowed up by MacGregor; and fewer and fewer gloves are made in the United States anymore. And none are made from horsehide.

"There aren't enough horses," The Gloveman points out. "But back then, 90 percent of the gloves were made from horsehide. It was less coarse than cowhide and lasted as long. The only thing comparable today is kangaroo leather."

No, they don't make baseball gloves like this Frank McCormick first baseman's mitt anymore. It doesn't have fancy buckles or extra straps or Velcro. It looks like a boxing glove for a hundred-pound lobster. Like a catcher's mitt to be sure. It's got more padding than a queen-size mattress. You figure Yogi Berra learned to play with a mitt like this. In its heyday you could probably catch a cannonball without stinging your hand.

But that was before the pocket deteriorated into a spider web of knotted leather shoelaces (confiscated from my dad's old hunting boots) and you didn't dare catch the ball directly in front of your face for fear the ball would break through—and break your nose. Indeed, every catch looked like what Los Angeles Dodgers announcer Vin Scully refers to as an "ice cream cone catch."

All those years I played catch—and even some Little League ball at first base—with that hand-me-down-down-down (from my dad to my two older brothers to me) monster mitt, I never knew who Frank McCormick was—or much cared, to be frank.

I suppose it's kind of like a kid today not knowing—or much caring—who Jack Kramer is, even though Big Jake's name is on their hand-me-down-from-Dad's first tennis racket.

After spending big bucks to have the glove refurbished, I decided it was time to find out who this McCormick fella was.

All he was, it turns out, was a National League MVP!

As luck would have it, a former major leaguer from the 1930s and '40s lives near me in Ventura, California. And better yet Stanley "Frenchy" Bordagaray even played on the Reds with McCormick.

"Of course I remember Frank," Frenchy—himself one of the all-time great pinch hitters for such teams as the St. Louis Cardinals' famous Gas House Gang, Yankees and Brooklyn Dodgers—told me when I inquired about his former Cincinnati teammate. "He was a great player."

"I played with him in '39," Bordagaray recalled as easily as he might his wedding anniversary. "We won the pennant but lost to the Yankees in the World Series. Frank was our fourth hitter, the clean-up man. He didn't swing hard, but—boy!—the ball sure carried a long way."

McCormick blasts carried the outfield fence 129 times in his fourteen-year career in the bigs. I looked it up.

Interestingly, further inspection of the *Baseball Encyclopedia* shows that McCormick and Bordagaray both broke into the majors in 1934. Frenchy, a 5-foot 7½-inch outfielder, retired in 1945 with a .283 batting average. McCormick, 6-feet 4 inches and 205 pounds of muscle, quit in 1948 with a .299 career clip.

"Oh yes! Frank was a good fielder, too," Frenchy replied when asked about McCormick's glovemanship.

Bordagaray was with the Kansas City Blues in 1940 when "Mack" batted .309 with 127 RBIs, nineteen homers and a league-high forty-four doubles for the Reds to garner the National League MVP award. (McCormick's 1939 numbers were actually even better: .332 average, 128 RBIs and eighteen "circuit clouts" as homers were called in that day.)

Nineteen-forty was indeed a banner year for Frank Andrew McCormick as he led the original Big Red Machine to the world title. Ironically, however, my glovesake made two errors in the field during the 1940 Fall Classic, but atoned for them with a key double in Game 7 against the Detroit Tigers to lead Cinci to its first championship in twenty-one years.

Like his model of mitt, the towering right-handed hitting and throwing first baseman was durable. During one stretch, McCormick played in 652 consecutive games, which ranks sixteenth on the all-time iron man list.

I don't really need my "new" antique mitt to play catch in the backyard with my thirteen-year-old daughter or one-year-old son—but I use it anyway. Like I said, it was the best $34.50 I've spent in a long while.

Tucked away in my old dresser drawer with my Frank McCormick glove I also came across an autographed baseball. It's probably worth a small fortune. A few of the signatures are faded and others are scuffed up a little, but you can clearly make out Ernie Lombardi, Whitey Moore, Bucky Walters, Jim Ripple, Morris Arnovich, Paul Deringer, Jimmie Wilson, Gene Thompson, Jim Turner, Lonnie Frey and Joe Beggs.

And Frank McCormick.

I don't know too much about many of those names off that 1940 World Series championship team, except that McCormick fella who died in 1982 at age seventy-one. I know him like the back of my hand.

Make that like the back of the soft horsehide inner processed palm of my Frank McCormick Model first baseman's mitt.

Woody Woodburn

The Heart of the Game

It took a while before you noticed the skinny, tow-headed boy. He was around eleven, smaller than most of the kids playing softball in the park on a warming summer morning. It didn't take long to realize he wasn't a ball-player, however; everything was a struggle.

He never got a hit, not even a foul off a slow pitch. Popped to right field, the occasional looping fly ball would come his way and you'd watch as he hoisted an oversized catcher's mitt and missed, always missed, the catch. It wasn't just the awkwardness of the glove that contributed to the misses; you could see that he was rarely in position to make the catch—and that's when you noticed the leg braces.

The sight of those braces revealed the source of the sound that had been pecking away in the background of the game—*Clack! Clack! Clack! Clack!* They were cumbersome affairs of steel and leather that reached to his knees and banged together as he ran, or jumped, or walked—the only instance of quiet came when he sat at the picnic table with his mother and little sister.

Animated and happy, the boy seemed oblivious to stares or comments from parents and kids. The game was there to be played and he played it. He didn't ask to play—no one else asked.

In this neighborhood park if you were a kid who wanted to play ball, you walked up and started playing. Adults never involved themselves and informality reigned—captains weren't chosen as much as they evolved. Teams ebbed, flowed and played until the last out.

A group of kids would start out together, split up, add players, shuffle positions—this boy knew his role. He'd wait until the team without a right fielder went to the field and he'd walk out and take up his position. Most of the kids knew him; some liked him. So he'd smile and wave, and they'd start the next inning.

Occasionally the random chatter of the game would drift to his mom and the little sister digging in sand beneath the table. Mom would raise her head from the knitting she was doing to pass the time.

A picnic basket waited for the game to wrap up, usually around noon. The end of the game was always signaled by the arrival of the older kids, players from local high schools come to practice. But until then the mom would occasionally raise her head.

"Catch the ball, Boob!" "Geez, he missed again!" "Aw, man—no fair hittin' to him, he can't even get to it." "Hey, new rules, new rules—one hit to right per game . . ." "Hey, yeah? You already hit to 'im twice."

And the mother's face would turn to the small shadowed frame engulfed in the hot green shimmering waves of right field and she would wave as he raised his hand, smiling—always smiling. He'd smack his small hand into that large mitt, bend at the waist and wait for the next moment, the next play of the game.

Clack, clack, clack. "Did you see me, Mom?"

"I did, Ricky, did you catch that last ball?"

"Almost. I almost got it. I got a hit, too."

"Really, when did you get a hit?"

"It was a foul really but I hit the ball. I think if I hit left-handed, I can get a better angle. I tried it and I hit it foul. I'm gettin' better. We got potato salad?"

"We always do."

"Yeah, hey Sissy, you look like a mud duck. Wanna samwich?"

There was a new game now and the older boys played with practiced athleticism and grace. Their expertise revealed greater concentration and a change in their awareness, a sense of the play as something of importance—local fame in the game next week, a scholarship and a career.

The picnicking families watched grounders being clipped hotly to third, listened to the crack of a bat and watched a white blur disappear over the sagging wood fence. There were sliding dusty scrambles into home plate, beautifully timed loping underhanded catches in far left, and back . . . back—a sudden leap in right field then the mitt held high in triumph.

Ricky watched intently, smiling and bobbing his head—sometimes he'd mutter a small grunt of pleasure at a nice play. Mom was reading now; Sissy was napping on her lap.

Ricky was digging his hand into a bag of potato chips when—*craaaack!* His eyes found the ball immediately, looping hard and foul over the shoulder of the batter—hot toward Mom's downturned head. A single *clack!* accompanied his leap, his bare hand stretched, potato chips flying and *whack!* He tumbled to the ground. Mom grabbed Sissy and jumped out of the way—of nothing. It was over. Ricky stood as the catcher walked up, and it was a long moment before he handed over the ball.

The older boy said, "Nice catch," as he took the ball and moved off.

"Thanks."

Mom was smiling as she started gathering things together.

"Nice catch, huh, Mom?"

"Very nice catch, Ricky, very nice."

"Almost beaned you."

"I know, Sweetie, you were very quick. I'm glad you were here to catch it."

I watched them walk away, the sound of their conversation hammered over by *clack! clack! clack!*

Looking back on the sports I've watched or played, I can recall spectacular games and amazing individual efforts of courage and skill. Like you, I can name the greats of the games, the Olympic moments, the last-second plays that won it all, but when I think of that day many years ago I'm not even sure his name was Ricky.

I have no idea how large that catch may have loomed in his life, whether it stayed with him through the years. I like to think that it did though; because without that catch I may never have remembered that day and how much a child can love a game.

It was a small, simple lesson I learned and never forgot: There is always a heart to any game and until you feel that, until the game, whatever it is, lives in your heart you can only *think* the game—and that's no game at all.

Steve Minnick

My First Home Run

All I want out of life is that when I walk down the street, folks will say, "There goes the greatest hitter that ever lived."

Ted Williams, as a young player

Summoning a long-ago memory is perhaps the only exercise more imperfect than the attempt to squarely hit a round ball with a round bat. Both can be akin to flying to the moon and back in a 1976 Gremlin on a half tank of gas. Yet when memory and keen batsmanship collide, imperfection yields to nostalgia. Maybe that's why I can summon the memory of my first home run as clearly as my mother's face.

Saturday, June 9, 1979. Runners at first and second, no one out.

My Bankers Trust team trailing Gordon Gallup Realty by two runs in the bottom of the fourth inning.

I stand in against league ace Brian Lawler. At age nine, he was a year younger than me but a good head taller, and slinging a fastball that bruised many a catcher's palm. In fact, two years later, eleven-year-old Brian would break a batter's ribs with a pitch, sending him to the ground in a plume of dust to cough up half a bloody lung.

Yeah, Brian was big and bad—and in every way my athletic superior. Except on this day.

Brian's first two pitches were in the dirt. His next two were in the catcher's mitt before I could contemplate a swing. But on the fifth pitch, I unleashed a mighty cut that brought Ruth, Gehrig and Foxx from their heavenly seats in applause. And as is inevitable when blazing fastball meets the irresistible force of my bat, the ball . . . well, the ball just kind of dribbled up through the middle, through Brian's legs. Fortunately, the guys on base ahead of me had the good sense to run. For as anyone who has ever played traffic cop at a Little League game can attest, it's a coin toss as to whether base-runners are paying more attention to the action on the field or the stray dog rummaging through the trash barrel at the park's entrance.

So the base-runners ran.

And so did the shortstop and the second baseman—right into each other.

The ball bounded over the heap of mangled flesh that used to be middle infielders and rolled into the outfield, where the center fielder was as much enthralled by the aforementioned dog as the ball I sent crawling his way.

So the base-runners ran, the infielders moaned and the center fielder just stood there. Meanwhile, I traversed a mud puddle created by a leaky sprinkler head and arrived at first base, where a coach instructed me to go to second. I rounded the base and lit out for the next bag. I would have made it there on my feet, too, were it not for the second baseman's 245-pound mother, who had run out on the field to check on her son, pulling a hospital gurney and smelling salts from her purse as she went. By the time I arrived on the scene, the second baseman had regained consciousness, although he was still not sure what day it was, whose team was leading or why a 245-pound woman cradled him in the dreaded maternal headlock.

With so much girth between me and second base, I had no choice but to carom off the butt end of the 245-pound woman. Turned out okay, though, because I fell right on top of second base, and the impact of smacking her fleshy tooshie sent me tumbling toward third.

Once the rolling ceased, I stood on wobbly legs and considered running back to first until, remembering my training, I looked toward my father in the third-base coach's box for further instruction. Ahh, your dad. Gotta love a man who's a boundless reservoir of encouragement and guidance.

"Get your butt to third or you're grounded," my father wailed.

So I went to third, the second baseman whiffed smelling salts and the dog decided to check out a trash can on the other side of the complex.

The center fielder, still entranced by the mongrel, decided to follow. As he turned to give chase, the ball rolled under his foot and shot back toward the second baseman's mother, who dropped the smelling salts while her son whirled and threw plateward in a motion so fluid it would make Roberto Alomar blush. Pretty as it was, the throw still came in high, and the catcher made a valiant but vain leap before the orb struck the backstop some twenty feet behind the dish.

So the catcher ran for the ball, I ran for the plate and the fans crept to the edge of their seats.

Arms pumping, head down, calculating my climbing slugging percentage as I went, I was quite disheartened when I finally thought to look up—seems my mercurial sprint plateward would not be enough to win the foot race with the catcher. I was going to be tagged out.

So the home fans groaned, my dad closed his eyes and I recalculated my slugging percentage.

With no option but to take defeat like a man, I summoned my last bit of strength and belly-flopped headfirst toward home, churning red clay and lime in my wake. Then fate intervened—the catcher tripped over the umpire, who had turned his back to the play to check out my teammate's hot teenage sister.

The dusty cloud I threw above me snapped the ump from his lust-induced trance, and he turned toward home plate just in time to see me slide under the mitt.

"SAAAAAFE!" he shouted, bringing a mob of jubilant teammates from our dugout.

We went on to win, and with a little help from the official scorekeeper (who just happened to be my mother), I had my first home run. At least, that's the way I remember it.

Jeff Kidd

One Hit Makes All the Difference

P. J. Forbes climbed into his car and drove from Pittsburg, Kansas, to Florida for the start of spring training in 1998 on the same day his father was having surgery to remove cancer near his stomach.

His dad made him go. That's how Patrick Forbes Sr. is. His son, Patrick Jr., was a thirty-year-old second baseman still trying to make the big leagues, and it was time for P. J. to continue his quest.

The doctors had only found the cancer after Patrick Sr. had suffered a stroke. It was one of those crazy things— with the stroke he had caught a break.

P. J. Forbes, entering his ninth year of professional baseball, was still waiting to catch his break. After seven years in the Angels organization, Forbes was heading into his second year with the Baltimore Orioles. He'd spent the 1997 season with their Triple-A team in Rochester, his fifth year in Triple-A.

But he'd never played in the big leagues. It wasn't getting any easier, not at age thirty with his dad in a hospital.

"It was a long spring training in that respect," said P. J., who spent the spring trying to take advantage of the at bats Orioles manager Ray Miller was giving him while at the same time worrying about his dad.

Forbes didn't make the Orioles that spring, just like he hadn't in 1997, just like he hadn't made the Angels in 1996 or 1995 or any time since he was drafted in the twenty-first round in 1990.

He went to back Triple-A Rochester. But his dad was getting better.

In the middle of the year, Forbes's father and sister flew in to watch him play when Rochester was playing in Louisville, Kentucky.

"My dad is the eternal optimist," Forbes said. "Whenever people tell me I can't do things, he told me I could do it.

"When he left, he told me, 'See you in three weeks.' I said, 'What?' And he said that's when the Orioles will be in Kansas City."

It was a joke they had shared hundreds of times before. Whenever P. J.'s big-league team was scheduled to be in Kansas City, his dad told his son that he'd be there.

Days later, Orioles second baseman Roberto Alomar broke his pinkie. Forbes was at the batting cage before one of his Triple-A games when Rochester manager Marv Foley came over and put his arm around him.

Forbes was going up. It really was just like in the movies.

He made his major-league debut July 21, 1998, in Baltimore as a defensive replacement. His first start came five days later, when he was 0-for-3 at home against Seattle. The Orioles left town for Detroit, and Forbes drove in his first run July 29.

But he was 0-for-6 when the Orioles arrived in Kansas City, a ninety-minute drive from his hometown.

With one hundred family and friends, including his dad, in the stands, Forbes entered the first game of the series as a defensive replacement in the eighth inning, with the Royals well ahead.

In the ninth, Baltimore rallied. Forbes came to the plate with a chance to keep the rally alive.

He lined a 1–0 single to left. Four days later, he was sent back to Rochester and hasn't been back to the major leagues since. His lifetime average is .100, one-for-ten.

That one hit makes all the difference. A big-league career without a hit isn't a career at all. It's like you were never there, but worse. You had the chance—one at bat, ten at bats, one hundred at bats—and you failed.

"If I don't get back, I'd really be disappointed if I hadn't ever gotten a hit," Forbes said. "But I'm not a settling type guy.

"I was told I'd never get out of Single-A, I'd never get out of Double-A, I'd never get out of Triple-A, I'd never get to the majors and I'd never get back there. If I didn't think I'd get back, I wouldn't waste my time or the organization's."

He's still trying. The 2001 season is his twelfth season as a pro, his second in the Philadelphia Phillies organization. He has a decade of solid minor-league numbers—and that one big-league hit.

After his big game in Kansas City, Forbes met the whole gang of one hundred. He gave his dad the ball from his hit.

"My dad is not a very emotional guy," Forbes said, "but he had a big grin on his face. My mom said he was pretty proud.

"The way it worked out, I couldn't have asked for anything more. God was looking over me that whole year. Not just me. My whole family."

Doug Lesmerises

Catch of a Lifetime

I grew up a Yankees fan. Every time the Yankees played the Anaheim Angels, my friend John Gray and I were there, up front in the bleachers beside the first-base dugout, with gloves, waiting for a foul ball to come our way. Most lovers of the game know this quest. The desire is pervasive; getting the grab is rare—about the same as winning the lottery as far as I can tell, and, in both, failure doesn't dampen the desire.

I'm a grown man now with about one thousand baseball games under my belt. I've yet to catch a foul ball, and certainly not one smashed by the likes of Ricky Henderson. That's why every day, when I notice the one perched in prize position on my wife's dresser, I smile at the vagaries of life.

It happened this way: My wife, Joanne, my dad, Rudy, and I were at a Saturday doubleheader with the Oakland Athletics in town to play the Anaheim Angels. We were there in my favorite spot behind the first-base dugout at Angels Stadium. First inning, first pitch to leadoff batter Rickey Henderson. He hit a high pop-up that came sailing straight at us. Dad and I leapt to our feet. I knew this was it: I was about to grab a foul ball!

Then I stepped back, realizing I had to let my dad get it. But he did the same, stepping back to let his son's dream come true. To our horror, we watched the ball drop between us—right in Joanne's lap.

Looking up with a wide grin, she said, "Honey, I thought you said catching a foul ball was tough."

R. Gregory Alonzo

The Foul Ball

I'm still not sure what made me swing that day.

I hadn't taken the bat off my shoulder in one and a half seasons of Little League, a span of maybe fifteen games and thirty plate appearances. Everyone knew what would happen when I stepped to the plate: I would take every pitch until I either struck out looking or walked.

Despite the patience and encouragement of my coach, the quiet urging of my parents in the stands and the supportive shouts of "C'mon, you can do it!" from the parents of my teammates—even from the parents of the opposing players—I could not bring myself to swing at the ball.

I so desperately wanted to hang a rope into left field. I so desperately wanted to launch a towering fly, and watch the ball trace a parabola through the sky as I rounded first and headed for second. I so desperately wanted to be like my heroes, Hank Aaron and Mickey Mantle.

Before every game, through one summer and part of another, I would tell myself, *This is the day you will swing the bat. Tonight, you will get your first base hit.*

But invariably, my throat would go dry as I put on the batting helmet. My stomach would knot up as I waited in the on-deck circle. By the time I stepped into the batter's box, I was paralyzed with fear, my fate to be determined solely by the umpire's interpretation of balls and strikes.

Oh, how I hated the embarrassment of heading back to the bench after another third strike, my parents' shouts of "You'll get 'em next time" ringing in my ears. How I looked forward to being pulled from the line-up after one or two at bats, thereby avoiding further humiliation.

Who knows why I couldn't swing the bat? Perhaps it was because I was a scrawny ten-year-old with Coke-bottle glasses and a profound lack of self-confidence. I loved baseball, loved the old Milwaukee Braves, loved the pace and beauty and romance of the game.

But it was a different game entirely when I was standing in the batter's box and the ball was whistling toward home plate.

The night I finally swung began no differently than the others. I took three strikes in my first at bat and headed for the refuge of the bench. Our coach walked over and said, "Son, after the next inning you're going to come out." I nodded and breathed a sigh of relief.

But somehow, our team batted around the line-up, and I felt the usual trepidation as I put on the helmet, took practice swings with two bats, and waited in the on-deck circle.

I was going to bat again! Twice, in the same inning.

I walked slowly toward the plate, and the catcher grinned and yelled to the pitcher, "C'mon, easy out here. Just put it over. He ain't gonna swing."

I watched strike one float past.

"Told ya," the catcher yelled. "He's a looker."

He spat out the last word. A looker. That's all I was. There is no bigger insult in all of Little League baseball.

The pitcher grinned back at the catcher, and I felt my hands tighten involuntarily on the bat. He wound up and sent the ball toward the plate and in that instant, something inside me screamed *"NOW!"*

I swung the bat with every ounce of strength I could muster.

Incredibly, I made contact, and I watched in amazement as the ball took flight, looping toward foul territory behind first base. It was one of life's revelatory moments, a precise intersection of time and space in which I suddenly realized I could do something that previously had been unattainable.

I could hit a pitched ball.

I don't remember the rest of the at bat. I don't know whether I got a hit or struck out. But if I did strike out, I'm sure I went down swinging, a much more noble way to go.

In fact, I really don't remember much of Little League after that, even though I played two more seasons and was a starting outfielder for the town champion Tigers.

That was all more than thirty years ago. There would be other sports, then high school and college and newspaper jobs and mortgages and children who are now themselves in college.

But I will never forget that hot summer night in 1966, when I surprised everyone, most of all myself, by swinging the bat and feeling the sweet vibration in my hands and watching the ball trace a parabola through the sky.

It was just a foul ball.

But it opened up a world of possibility.

Gary D'Amato

Hero for the Day

When I was ten, I wanted to play on my grammar
school baseball team so bad I'd go to bed every night and
dream about it. Those were the days long before Little
League, and there were no tryouts. Team members were
selected mostly on a clique basis by class buddies who
had played together since the first grade, and they naturally assumed there was no one else in the class who could
catch or bat as well as they.

The times when the team was short of players due to
chicken pox or measles, I'd beg to substitute, but the team
captain—his name was Buzzy Bennett—always picked
someone else.

Undaunted, I went home and attacked the problem as if
it were a war. I began by coaxing my dad into being my
trainer. We lived on a hill, and Dad would stand at the top
and hit balls while I waited at the bottom to catch them.
This gave the illusion that the balls were coming from a far
distance at a staggering height.

I couldn't afford a mitt. This was the Depression, and
every cent counted. I learned to catch with my bare hands.
I soon built up calluses, but not before I bent fingers,

sprained a wrist and tore off fingernails. But before long, very few lofted balls got past me.

Then I had a stroke of luck. A college student who lived just up the block from me played baseball at a nearby city college. He caught fly balls with me and showed me how to hit. His name was Ralph Kiner, a guy who later had an outstanding major-league career and became a broadcaster.

The day finally came when our class team was scheduled to play the team from the class above us. When you're ten, a kid who is eleven looks as big as a mountain and twice as athletic. The whole school turned out, and everybody expected our guys to lose in a rout. I begged to play, but was totally ignored. There was a little blond girl I wanted to impress, but since I wasn't on the team she didn't give me the time of day.

Then, in the middle of the third with the score nothing to nothing, our team's first baseman was knocked flat by a runner and cracked a rib. Buzzy brought in his right fielder to play first. He then looked around the crowd. Finding no one who looked like he could throw a ball, he stared a long minute at me.

"Okay, Cussler," he finally said. "Go play right field. You should be all right. Nobody ever hits 'em out there."

I ran to the position, still without a glove.

The fourth inning looked like the start of a massacre. We got two outs, but the big guys loaded the bases. The next batter looked like a cross between Babe Ruth and Roger Maris. The impact with the bat sounded like a cannon shot and the ball lifted high in the air. Like a movie in slow motion, every eye on every face was on the ball. I began running back. I stole a glance at the kid in center field. He was just standing there. Now that I recall, he was eating a candy bar.

I ran. Oh, God, how I ran. Out of the corner of one eye I saw the chain-link fence coming closer. I ran two more steps and then jumped. I felt the fence become one with my right hip and shoulder. The ball smacked into my open hand. I had made a one-handed catch of a ball that should have been a home run. And without the help of a mitt.

There was stunned silence on the school ground. Plays like that just didn't happen in grammar school. The months of perseverance with the able assistance of Dad and Ralph Kiner had paid off. The force was now mine. I walked from right field to the bench, slowly tossing the ball up and down, trying to look cool. Only when I passed near home plate did I nonchalantly flip the ball to the opposing pitcher.

Nor did it stop there. I went on that day to hit a single and a triple. Sure, we lost, 6–3, but I was still the hero of the hour. And the little blonde girl who ignored me before the game? Her name was Joy, and she became the first girl I ever kissed.

Clive Cussler

Winning Isn't Everything

Great competitors are bred, and great sportsmen are born. I came to that conclusion at a Little League T-ball game in Davis, California, for which my son, Matt, was umpiring. This conclusion was cemented solidly just last week when a friend of mine related a horror story from her son's Little League game.

"One of the coaches just ripped off a kid's head for making a mistake," she noted. "What does that teach him?"

In both of our books, nothing.

We have become a nation addicted to winning. "We're number one" puts smiles on sports fans' faces. Running a good race doesn't always.

This premise relates to every facet of life, whether at home, at church, at school, at work or at play. Numbers are crunched, awards are pursued, emotions are stifled in favor of one-upmanship. Even the Joneses have a hard time keeping up.

Life too often becomes a tough game with more losers than winners. When claiming the prize eliminates the good in playing, no one wins. Real rewards come from teamwork and playing the game unselfishly for the good of the whole.

On a hot, sunny afternoon, a small boy stepped up to bat. The crowd watched like hawks for his move, waiting for the sought-after home run that most likely wasn't to be. After all, these kids were five and six years old, much too little to stroke a ball past the pitcher, if at all.

The little guy's determination showed in his stance: gritted teeth, slightly bulging eyes, hat-clad head bobbing slightly, feet apart, hands with a death grip on the bat. In front of him was a small softball, sitting perched like a parrot on a lone tee, awaiting the six swings that the batter was allowed.

Strike one.

"Come on, you can do it!" came a solitary voice out of the bleachers.

Strike two.

"Go for it, Son!" the proud father yelled encouragingly.

Strike three.

"Go, go, go . . ." the crowd joined in.

Strike four.

"You can do it!" just the father and a couple of viewers crooned, others losing interest and turning to bleacher conversations.

"YOU CAN DO IT!" And suddenly bat hit ball, amazing the crowd and the little boy, who stood rock still, watching it travel slowly past the pitcher on its way to second base.

"Run!"

The stands rumbled with stomping feet.

"Run, run!"

The little boy's head jerked ever so slightly and he took off toward third base.

"No," the crowd yelled. "The other way."

With a slight cast of his head toward the bleachers, the boy turned back toward home.

"NO!" My son, the umpire, waved him toward first base.

The kids on both teams pointed the way. The crowd continued to cheer him on. Confused, he ran back to third. Then following the third baseman's frantic directions, he finally ran toward first base but stopped triumphantly on the pitcher's mound. The pitcher moved back, not sure what to do next. The crowd stood, shaking the bleachers with the momentum. All arms waved toward first base. And with no thought for his position, the first baseman dropped his ball and ran toward the pitcher.

"Come on," he yelled, grabbing the hand of the errant batter, and tugged him toward first base while the crowd screamed its approval. The ball lay forgotten as a triumphant twosome hugged each other on the piece of square plastic that marked the spot where lives are forever shaped.

Two little boys, running hand in hand, toward a goal that only one should have reached. Both came out winners. In fact, there wasn't a loser in the stands or on the field that summer day, and that's a lesson none of us should ever forget.

Winning is more than being number one. Winning is helping another when the chips are down. It's remembering to love one another, as biblically directed, despite the flaws that sometimes appear in the fabric of daily life.

No one will ever remember the score of that summer afternoon encounter. Competition, usually fettered by jeering remands, lost to sportsmanship, an innate formula for winning.

When you get to first base with opposing teammates, families, friends and grandstanders behind you, a home run is never that far down the road.

Mary Owen

4

HEROES

The sport to which I owe so much has
undergone profound changes. . . . But it's
still baseball. Kids still imitate their heroes on
playgrounds. Fans still ruin expensive suits
going after foul balls that cost five
dollars. Hitting streaks still make the network
news. And the hot dogs still taste better at
the ballpark than at home.

Duke Snider

Man of His Word

There is little difference in people, but that little difference makes a big difference. The little difference is attitude. The big difference is whether it is positive or negative.

Clement Stone

I first met Hank Greenberg in 1947. I was twenty-four years old and in my second season with the Pittsburgh Pirates. Hank was one of baseball's greatest legends, a superstar who had been my boyhood idol. In those days, established stars rarely spoke to young players. But after practice on the first day of spring training, Hank invited me to stick around for some extra hitting with him.

"You've got a lot of power," he said after watching me take a few swings. "But you'll never be a great home-run hitter the way you're doing it." He changed my stance, moving me up in the batter's box and closer to the plate.

Nevertheless, I got off to a horrible start that season. Hank kept encouraging me: "Keep with it—everything's going to fall into place." But by the end of May, I had hit only three home runs. Then I had the worst day of my life, striking out four times. I was worried that manager Billy Herman would send me down to the minors.

Hank went to one of the Pirates owners and pleaded my case: "Don't farm this kid out. He's going to be a tremendous hitter." Then he added, "I'll bet you a new suit that he'll come around." From June until the end of the season I hit forty-eight home runs.

Hank Greenberg brought as much class to baseball as any individual—ever. He was "Hammerin' Hank," the first great Jewish ballplayer, a man whose religious faith, patriotism and sheer love of the game were accompanied by a humble spirit and extraordinary poise. His friendship and his example had an indelible effect on my life. He taught me how to live "the right way."

Hank's hitting feats with the Detroit Tigers in the 1930s and '40s rivaled those of Babe Ruth, Lou Gehrig and Ted Williams. A 6-foot 3½-inch, 215-pound slugger, he put fear into the heart of every opposing pitcher. Season after season, Hank would rack up league-leading totals in a host of categories—walks, doubles, home runs, runs scored, runs batted in. In 1938 he challenged Ruth's record of sixty home runs in a season by hitting fifty-eight; no right-handed batter had ever hit more.

Hank won four home-run championships and was twice voted the American League's most valuable player. He led the Tigers to four pennants and two World Series championships. He compiled a .313 career batting average—and did all that despite a break for four years' service in the Army during World War II.

With his power-hitting and growing fame, Hank was a source of pride and encouragement to Jews of the late '30s when Hitler was on the march. Actor Walter Matthau, a friend of Hank's in later life, remembers growing up on New York's Lower East Side: "You couldn't help but be exhilarated by the sight of one of our guys looking like a colossus."

Nevertheless, as columnist Shirley Povich later noted, "Baseball was not distinguished by lofty intellectuals in Greenberg's time. He was a target of subtle and flagrant anti-Semitism, an earlier version of the bigotry that hounded Jackie Robinson with the Dodgers."

When Hank played for the Pirates in 1947, he was one of the first opposing players to give encouragement to Robinson, who broke major-league baseball's color barrier that year. Robinson and Hank had accidentally collided on a close play at first base. Hank later apologized for the mishap and, noting the taunts and insults thrown at Robinson, said, "Don't let them get to you. You're doing fine." After the game, Jackie told reporters, "Hank Greenberg has class. It stands out all over him."

Henry Benjamin Greenberg was born in New York City's Greenwich Village on New Year's Day 1911, the third of four children of David and Sarah Greenberg, emigrants from Romania. After high school, he briefly attended New York University. Craving the opportunity to play professional baseball, Hank persuaded his parents to let him try. In 1930 he went to spring training with the Tigers.

After three seasons in the minors, Hank burst into the big leagues, hitting .301 in 1933, his rookie year. But it was in 1934, his second season with Detroit, that Hank secured his place in twentieth-century American culture. It was September, and the Tigers were fighting for their first pennant since 1909. Whether Hank would play on Yom Kippur, the Day of Atonement, became an issue not only in Detroit but across the country. When Hank went to temple instead of to the ballpark, he was immortalized by Edgar A. Guest in a popular poem that concluded:

> *Said Murphy to Mulrooney,*
> *"We shall lose the game today!*
> *We shall miss him on the infield*

and shall miss him at the bat,
But he's true to his religion—
and I honor him for that!"

Without Hank in the line-up, the Tigers did lose that day. But Hank Greenberg, winner of four home-run championships and four World War II battle stars, said the only time he really felt like a hero was that day in temple, when he received a standing ovation from the congregation. And the Tigers went on to win the pennant that year.

On May 6, 1941, Hank blasted two home runs to lead the Tigers to victory over the New York Yankees. The next day he reported to Fort Custer, Michigan. One of baseball's first big stars to be drafted, he had registered even though he was beyond the age when he could have been called up.

Hank was discharged as over-age on December 5, 1941—two days before Pearl Harbor. After the attack, he enlisted again. Hank had his priorities: God, country, team.

Hank went into the Army Air Corps as a private and rose to the rank of captain. He spent almost a year in China and was in the first land-based bombing of the Japanese mainland in June 1944.

What a day Hank had when he returned from the Army—July 1945. Sunday afternoon. Briggs Stadium, Detroit, was jammed. In his very first game Hank homered to help Detroit to victory. That was only a prelude to what was to come.

On the last day of the season, he homered again—a ninth-inning grand slam—to clinch the pennant for the Tigers. With a .311 average, sixty runs batted in and thirteen home runs in just three months, he had defied the odds by coming back so successfully after such a long layoff. In the World Series he hit two more homers and drove in seven runs to lead the Tigers over the Cubs.

The 1947 season, Hank's last, was a struggle for him, but it showed his strength of character. He often played in pain; his elbow bothered him all season. Yet he still managed to drive in seventy-four runs and hit twenty-five homers. I got all the headlines, but he was genuinely happy for me and kept urging me on.

After that season, Hank met Bill Veeck, who owned the Cleveland Indians. The two became friends for life. Hank joined Veeck in Cleveland and eventually became general manager and part-owner of the Indians. They won the World Series together in 1948. In 1959, with some partners, Hank and Bill bought the Chicago White Sox. That year they won a pennant.

When Allie Reynolds of the Yankees and I represented the players in negotiations to upgrade our pension fund, Hank and Pirates owner John W. Galbreath were appointed to meet with us and work out an agreement. Through their efforts we were able to agree on an extraordinary deal: Players would get 60 percent of the revenue from the sale of radio and television rights on World Series and All-Star games, as well as 60 percent of net gate receipts from All-Star games, for the pension fund—the foundation for the most generous pension plan in all of sports. Hank told the owners the players deserved it.

Hank cared deeply for people. He lent money to a ballplayer he wasn't particularly close to whose business went bad. He lent money to a sportswriter who had been critical of him in print. Hank held no grudges. He kept trying to bring out the best in others.

In November 1954 my baseball career was just about over. I had been traded to the Chicago Cubs. My hitting had slipped; my back and legs ached chronically. Hank called from Cleveland. "I've got great news," he said. "We've just traded for you. We need you."

The Indians needed me? They had just won the

pennant with an American League record of 111 victories. It was one of the greatest teams of all time—a team Hank had helped put together.

Hank was criticized in Cleveland for acquiring me. Why did the Indians need an over-the-hill Kiner, making sixty-five thousand dollars a season, more than any other player? Hank called me in and said, "Why don't you volunteer to take a cut in salary? Then they'll leave you alone. I'll make it up to you at the year's end." It was unprecedented—a player asking for a salary cut! Hank was right—the criticism stopped. And, of course, he kept his word.

When I stopped playing, I did radio commentary for the Chicago White Sox, owned by Greenberg and Veeck. In June 1961 they sold the team, but Hank helped me get a job broadcasting for the New York Mets, and I've done Mets games ever since.

In the mid-'60s Hank started MG Securities, a small investment company in New York, with a friend, David Marx. He approached his investments the same way he did baseball—devoting himself 110 percent—and made millions.

In 1974 Hank and his wife, Mary Jo, moved to Beverly Hills. He continued to follow the stock market and play tennis—handicap games with Jimmy Connors and Bobby Riggs.

Hank also found another cause. To those who wrote seeking his autograph, he sent a signed photograph in return for a five-dollar charitable contribution—which he matched—to his favorite charity, the Pet Adoption Fund for homeless animals.

In June 1985 Hank learned that he had a cancerous tumor in one of his kidneys. The kidney was removed that August, but the cancer had spread. Hank died September 4, 1986, at the age of seventy-five. The last months of his life were especially difficult, but he died as he had lived, without complaint. His three children were among the few to know of his ordeal.

Hank's son Steve, a Los Angeles lawyer and former minor-league baseball player, tells of the time he asked his father for a photo. A few days later he received one with the inscription, "Kipling said it all for me. Love, Dad."

Kipling's poem "If" was the creed by which Hank lived:

> *"If you can fill the unforgiving minute,*
> *With sixty seconds' worth of distance run—*
> *Yours is the Earth,*
> *And everything that's in it,*
> *and—which is more—you'll be a Man, my son!"*

Honored by induction into baseball's Hall of Fame in 1956, Hank was hailed one more time in Detroit in 1983 when his number, 5, was retired. "When I think of all the great ballplayers who have graced a Detroit Tigers uniform over the years," he told the crowd, "I'm very proud that my name and number will be remembered as long as baseball is played in Detroit."

Hank Greenberg's name will be remembered as long as baseball is played anywhere.

Ralph Kiner

True Heroes Earn the Title

Star athletes have played an important part in the lives of young children as far back as history remembers sports and its heroes. Every youngster has had at least one hero that he worshiped above all others. Such idolization is not always etched in stone, however, and heroes have been known to change for many reasons. I was involved in such a change in 1960.

My father was an Air Force master sergeant stationed at a radar station in Bellefontaine, Ohio. The Cincinnati Reds offered discount seating to military personnel in uniform, and my father decided to take a group of airmen to a game at old Crosley Field. I was included as an afterthought and was thrilled at finally being able to see a big-league game. The doubleheader between the hometown Reds and the Pittsburgh Pirates was going to be a highlight in my relatively short life.

Although I was an avid New York Yankees fan, one of my favorite baseball players, Roy Face, was a star relief pitcher for the Pirates and I was hoping to get his autograph. My father bought me a brand-new baseball just in case. I could hardly contain myself on the drive to Cincinnati.

We arrived at the stadium a few minutes before the players were due to take the field, and I lined up with several other youngsters at the entrance to the Pirates locker room. As the players filed out to enter the runway to the dugout, I looked anxiously for Roy Face. I finally saw him coming and in my best manners stepped up and asked him for his autograph. He calmly ignored me and proceeded down the runway. I was stunned! One of my favorite heroes had brushed me off without the slightest acknowledgment at all. I stood there pondering what to do next when a large arm appeared around my shoulders and a hand took the ball from my grasp. I looked up to see a beaming smile beneath a Pirate hat and a large 21 on the jersey. The man handed me the ball with a wink and headed onto the field. I looked down at the ball and could not believe that it now proudly bore the name ROBERTO CLEMENTE in bold black ink. Roy Face's spot on my hero list had just been filled by one of the greatest players in the game. Clemente played an important part in the Pirates' sweep of the doubleheader that day and helped lead his team to a World Series victory over my Yankees that October. Despite that, he remained one of my greatest heroes until his death in a 1972 airplane crash while flying relief supplies to earthquake victims in Nicaragua. By this time I had followed my father into the air force and was stationed in Southeast Asia. When I learned of Clemente's death, I could only marvel that the man who had helped find me a hero had been a bona fide hero trying to help an entire nation.

Only die-hard fans will remember who Roy Face was, but children who were not yet born when Roberto Clemente died can tell you all about him. That is heroism at its finest.

Michael J. Feigum

The Big Friendly Cop

"MEET THE HOME RUN TWINS, LOU AND BABE."

Paul Simonitsch saw that headline in the *St. Paul Pioneer Press* one morning in 1927 and took it literally: Meet The Home Run Twins. . . .

Young Paul was ten years old the day he saw that headline with accompanying photos of Lou Gehrig and Babe Ruth, and he did what most any boy would do—he clipped it out.

Then he folded it neatly in half, carefully tucked it inside his shirt next to his chest and told his mom he was off to see the New York Yankees play a barnstorming game against the Yankees' local farm team.

Out the door Paul hurried and started walking to Lexington Park. One and one-half miles later he arrived at the ballpark only to discover a problem in his plan. "I didn't have enough money to buy a ticket," Simonitsch, now seventy-eight, recalls from his California living room. "I only had fifty or sixty cents in my pocket. I think the cheapest ticket was seventy-five cents."

What happened next is enough to make you believe in guardian angels. No, an extra quarter did not fall from the sky and land at Paul's feet.

Paul Simonitsch's guardian angel in the outfield did not wear wings, he wore a badge.

"A big friendly cop was standing by the turnstile and for some reason he spotted me," Simonitsch continues.

"What's the matter, fella?" The big friendly cop asked.

"I don't have enough money for a ticket," the sad little boy mumbled, almost through tears.

A big unfriendly cop would have told the sad little kid to "Scram!" But the big friendly cop replied in a deep whisper: "You get in front of me, Son, and just do what I tell you to do."

You can see a twinkle in Simonitsch's steel-blue eyes, a twinkle magnified by the lenses of his glasses, as he repeats the big friendly cop's orders—"You get in front of me, Son, and just do what I tell you to do"—and then he continues with his very favorite story from childhood, perhaps of his entire life.

"He nudged me forward and forward. I was up to maybe his belly button. He pushed me right through the turnstile without anyone asking me for my ticket."

The big friendly cop then took the little lonely boy by the hand and led him inside the ballpark, led him down a flight of stairs, and then down some more stairs until the two reached the box seats directly behind the Yankee dugout.

Then the big friendly cop sat Paul down on the very front cement step in the aisle, an aisle that was right in front of a miniature gate that opened up to allow access to the playing field.

"Stay right here until the game is over," the big friendly cop said. In the fifth inning, Babe Ruth came out of the dugout to coach first base. First base, remember, was right in front of Paul's seat on the cement steps. And the miniature gate leading to the playing field was also right in front of the boy.

"I said to myself, 'By gosh, I'm going to try it,'" Simonitsch recalls.

"I opened the gate slowly," the seventy-eight-year-old grandfather who was that ten-year-old boy continues, "and snuck right out to the first base coaching box."

"I was scared spitless but I pretended I was king of the walk as I went out on the field," he goes on. "I pulled the newspaper clipping out of my shirt and said, 'Mr. Ruth. Will you autograph this for me?'

"He said, 'Well, Son. I sure will.' And then he said, 'Would you like Lou Gehrig's signature, too?'"

Paul, of course, replied, "No thanks," and went back to his seat. No. I'm kidding. The boy looked up at his great hero and replied with a nod—because when he tried to say "yes," nothing came out.

"You come with me now," Ruth told the young gate crasher and then took him by the hand—Babe's enormous hand gently engulfing Paul's little hand just the way the big friendly cop's had—and led him to the Yankee dugout just as the big friendly cop had earlier escorted the boy to a front-row seat.

You get in front of me, Son, and just do what I tell you to do.

"Lou was right inside the dugout in the very first seat," Simonitsch remembers vividly. "Babe handed him my newspaper clipping and said, 'Lou, sign this for the kid.'

"Lou said, 'I sure will.'"

True to his word, the Iron Horse autographed the clipping and then handed it back to Ruth who gave it to Paul.

"Then Babe said, 'Now go back to your seat, and stay right there until the game is over.'"

"I don't think my feet were touching the ground anymore," Simonitsch says of his walk off the field and back through the miniature gate to his seat on the cement steps. "I had an autographed picture of Babe Ruth and Lou Gehrig."

And what beautiful autographs at that! Unlike today's superstars who scribble autographs—if they sign at all— Ruth and Gehrig signed in the smooth cursive script of an elementary school teacher.

Ruth, who would blast an unworldly sixty home runs that very coming season, didn't hit one out of the ballpark that barnstorming day. But young Paul could not have cared less.

"I met the Home Run Twins, both of them! And got their autographs! What a prize!" Paul Simonitsch recalls, still thrilled by the memory all these decades later.

The prize, the proof of that priceless encounter, the yellowed newspaper clipping with the unfaded and perfectly legible signatures, no longer hangs framed on a bedroom wall—first Paul's and then later his son's—as it did for so many years.

Instead, it is hidden away where no one can enjoy it, locked inside a safety deposit bank box, too valuable— "I've been told it's worth five thousand dollars, but it's priceless to me"—to display.

Too bad.

And what about the big friendly cop?

"I never saw him again," Paul Simonitsch says, a trace of sadness creeping into his voice and eyes for the first time all afternoon. "He disappeared. I wish I would have gotten a chance to thank him."

Maybe Paul did. Maybe the big friendly cop was really the Babe in disguise on his way to the ballpark.

Woody Woodburn

Meeting My Favorite Player

My love of baseball and my devotion to the Chicago White Sox began with my grandpa and play-by-play radio broadcasts. Although I was too young to understand the game, I would sit on the floor in front of the huge radio that provided most of the family's entertainment in the 1940s and listen to the sounds of baseball. Bats cracking against balls, the roar of the crowd and the voice of Bob Elson describing the action became an integral part of my childhood.

Sometime in 1947, my father brought home a miracle. It was called television. Now the sounds of baseball took a back seat to sights like the pitcher winding up for the throw, the base runner stealing third and the ball sailing over the outfield fence for a home run.

As I grew into a teenager, I became more and more entranced with America's favorite pastime. I knew every player on the White Sox team, the positions they played and their batting averages.

Although the White Sox hadn't won a pennant since the infamous scandal of 1919, we knew that someday our faith in our team would be rewarded.

It was in the late 1950s that our hopes of bringing another

league championship to White Sox park were really soaring. It was a scrappy hit-and-run team with future Hall of Fame players like Nellie Fox and Luis Aparicio.

We went to as many home games as possible. Ladies Day at Comiskey Park meant ditching school or work to sit in the grandstands screaming for a hit. When the game was over we hurried around to the players' parking lot to get autographs from our favorite players.

The one I most wanted to meet was an outfielder named Al Smith. He was an excellent outfielder, often making unbelievable catches, and at the plate his batting power drove in run after run for the team.

Our trips to the players' lot became a ritual. We got to talk to a lot of the players. Our autograph books were filled with signatures, but the page I had reserved for Al Smith remained empty.

I would call out to the other players, "Tell Al Smith to come out here. Tell him his biggest fan wants to meet him."

They all promised they would give Al the message, but he never appeared.

In 1959, the White Sox finally did it. They won the American League pennant. The city went crazy. Air raid sirens blared, fireworks filled Chicago skies and victory parties broke out everywhere. We were so happy, we were literally dancing in the streets.

Everyone wanted an official team photograph, but they were not easy to come by, and I was not able to get one.

The Los Angeles Dodgers defeated the Sox in the World Series and, before the next season began, many of the players on the championship team were traded away. I felt like it was the end of an era.

I married and began to raise a family so trips to the ball park became infrequent, but I still watched the games on television. Eventually, my husband and I moved our family to Tucson, Arizona. The Chicago White Sox were still my team, but I was no longer able to see them play and had to content myself with the statistics in news broadcasts.

The years passed quickly. With four kids and a full-time job, the only baseball I seemed to have time for anymore were my son's Little League games.

In 1978, I got a real estate license and since my business background was in public accounting, I began working with real estate investors. A few years later, one of my accounting clients, a major real estate firm, offered me a job. I went to their office to talk to the broker, who began telling me about some of the other agents that worked for him.

"Arthur Ashe's aunt works for us. And she's brought us another new agent, Millie Smith. Millie's husband used to be a ballplayer with the Chicago White Sox."

I literally jumped out of my chair. "Al Smith?" I screamed.

"Yes, I think so," he replied carefully.

I could see that he was rather startled by my reaction, but I was too excited to care. "Where is she?" I demanded. "I have to meet her. Al Smith is my all-time favorite player."

"Does that mean you'll take the job?"

I nodded absently as I continued to babble. "Al Smith, how great. He was a fabulous outfielder and what a hitter, always came through in a clutch. I can't believe this."

I had come a long way since my days at Comiskey Park, yet I was suddenly back to a time when a line drive over the center-field fence brought me to my feet shouting for joy.

Millie Smith turned out to be a charming lady and we worked a few real estate deals together. But meeting Al Smith was the best, a dream come true.

My initial introduction to Al took place in the real estate parking lot. When Millie called him and said one of his biggest fans was in the office and wanted to meet him, he got in his car and drove right over. He was delighted to find someone in Tucson who remembered him, and we became fast friends.

In the months that followed, I was able to spend time with Al, talking about baseball, the White Sox and his career.

When I told him I always wanted his autograph, Al gave it to me on the official photo taken of the championship team. He even provided one for my sister.

Today the team photo with Al Smith's autograph is framed and hanging in a special place in my home. Al and Millie Smith moved back to Chicago to be closer to their children and we lost touch, but every time I pass the photo of the 1959 American League champions, it brings a smile to my face.

It took me more than twenty years to meet my favorite White Sox player, but it was worth the wait. I'll never forget the thrill of meeting him, and I'll always be grateful for the twists of fate that caused our paths to cross.

It's been forty years since they won their last championship, but someday it will happen. When it does, a grandmother in Tucson, Arizona, will be on her feet shouting for joy.

Carol Costa

A True Hero

The life of a major league baseball player involves more than playing baseball. Especially for those that are popular.

Jim Abbott was one of the most popular players from the moment he first donned a major-league uniform for the California Angels in 1989. Abbott, just twenty-one at the time, was one of the rare few who skips the minor leagues completely and begins his professional career in the big leagues.

But that's not what made Abbott so special to so many.

Abbott was born without a right hand. In fact, Abbott's right arm extended from his shoulder to just past the elbow joint.

Abbott, though, didn't make the big leagues because people felt sorry for him. Abbott could pitch.

The Angels took a chance on him by drafting him out of the University of Michigan and he proved in spring training that year that he was ready for the big leagues.

Using a skill he developed as a kid, Abbott could pitch with his left hand, then quickly transfer a right-hander's glove from the stub of his right arm onto his left hand, in case he had to field the ball.

If a ball was hit back to him, Abbott would catch it, stick the glove under his right armpit, then pull the ball out with his left hand so he could throw it again. And he did all of this in a second or two.

Abbott became a media magnet. Wherever he went, reporters wanted to hear his story. Abbott was overwhelmed, but never lost his pleasant disposition.

Abbott had a smile for everyone, writers and fans alike.

Many times the media relations department of a major-league team gets requests for fans to meet their favorite baseball players. Abbott was no different.

What was different about one particular fan was what made him similar to Abbott.

The Angels had set up a meeting between Abbott and a young boy from the Midwest. The boy, about nine or ten years old, had lost an arm in a farming accident.

Before one game during a long and arduous baseball season, the boy was brought onto the field to meet Abbott. The boy was obviously nervous, his body language telling the story. Head down, shoulders slumped forward, he had no idea what he was in for.

Abbott and the boy met on the field during batting practice before a game. But they weren't getting much privacy. The media are allowed to remain on the field up to forty-five minutes before game time, and there were plenty of curious onlookers.

So Abbott had an idea. He took the boy down the left-field line and away from anyone who wanted to get close. The two stood in the outfield, talking, watching batting practice and laughing for about an hour.

When the two returned to the dugout after batting practice, the boy's eyes sparkled. His head was up and his chest was thrust forward. Abbott was asked what he said to the boy, but he wouldn't reveal what was said.

That was about ten years ago, and the boy is now an

adult. I often wonder whatever became of him, but after his meeting with Abbott, I have no doubt he is leading a happy and productive life. Abbott, after all, was living proof for the boy that he could do anything he wanted. Even pitch in the big leagues.

Joe Haakenson

The Day I Met
The Splendid Splinter

My autographed Ted Williams baseball sat in my sock drawer for more than twenty years. It's not that I didn't want to display it. It was more like I was afraid someone might steal it or unwittingly throw it out as insignificant clutter. So I was quite unprepared for the day I opened my drawer and discovered that the prized possession had been defaced! There, in bright, bold indelible ink, my three adorable daughters, ages ten, eight and five respectively, had left their collective mark: "Carl Yastremskee Rules," "Your Pal Looe Tiant," "Babe Ruth Was Here," and other random scribbles.

It felt like someone had just pierced my heart. I was furious. If ever there were justification for punishment, surely defacing an autographed Ted Williams ball would qualify—especially with The Curse of the Bambino! As I tried to control my temper, I called for my daughters, and thought back to the day I met Teddy Ballgame. . . .

I was just twelve years old in 1948, but remember the event like it was yesterday. My mother had just come home from the beauty parlor. She told me that Ted Williams's wife, Doris, had her hair done at the same salon. And miracle of miracles, she told my mother their home address. "He lives at Luceile Place," my mother casually mentioned, as if it was no big deal. *How many kids in the world were lucky enough to have the greatest hitter of all time living less than two miles away!*

Ted Williams was my idol. I followed his appearance in every game and could quote his daily batting averages and RBIs. I got into heated arguments with anyone who tried to tell me there was a better player, and even got into one playground fight with a kid who said that Johnny Mize was better. (In 1941, Ted Williams led the American League with a .400 batting average. He was given the chance to sit out the last two games of the season to preserve a mark that had not been equaled in over a decade. Of course, he refused, and in those games went six for eight at-bats, finishing the season for a .406 average. Even today, if it had not been for his call to duty in both World War II and Korea, I doubt that anyone could have eclipsed his record.)

In order to meet Mr. Williams, my timing had to be perfect. I had to make sure that the Red Sox team was in town and that he was home. So I chose a Saturday morning, grabbed a clean baseball and rode my J.C. Higgens bike uphill almost all the way. I told no other kids what I was doing. I knew that Mr. Williams could be difficult with the press and his critics, but I also knew that he liked kids. I hoped he wouldn't mind the intrusion.

I parked my bike outside of his house, baseball in hand. As I stood at his front door and rang the bell, my knees were knocking. *What would I say?* Looking down, practicing my speech, I saw the door open. I looked up, up, up, and there he was, standing there, a giant of a man, smiling at me, a strange kid with a baseball in hand.

"P-p-pardon me, sir. I was wondering if you could sign my baseball for me?" I stammered.

"Sure," he said. "Come on in!"

"Come on in!" He said, "Come on in!" I was in Ted Williams's hallway!

"Would you like a Coke?" he asked.

"No. No, thank you, sir," I managed to say. I was still in shock.

"How do you like the baby?" he asked, pointing to the adjacent baby carriage.

"Oh, he's alright I guess," I blurted out. (I later learned the "he" was, in fact, a "she.")

Mr. Williams laughed at my lack of gender sensitivity and signed my baseball. Then he walked me to the door and wished me good luck.

"Th-thank you, Mr. Williams," I said, still in shock.

The bike ride home that day was magical. When I reached my house I ran in to tell my parents about my adventure. They were hardly amused. Face red and arms waving, my father warned: "Don't you *ever* tell *any*one what you did today, or they'll never give him any privacy. Do you understand me?"

"Yes sir," I said. And I kept my promise.

My mind returned to the present as I looked down at the now-colorful baseball in my hands, and up at the sheepish faces of my three artisan-daughters who stood before me. I realized that to them, Ted Williams was an unknown. In fact, the whole mystique of baseball was void in their world of Barbie dolls and fingernail polish.

I realized then that my girls needed a lesson about baseball: the joy you feel on opening day; the exhilaration you get when you hit another player home; and the kindness shown by a baseball idol who invited a kid in for an autograph.

"Want to know who the first person was to sign this ball? . . ."

Months later, with my daughters' prodding, we organized a girls' softball team in our neighborhood. And while none of them ever made it to the major leagues, they learned a new respect for the game, and none of them has since defaced another baseball.

Ted Janse

Hero of the Game

You can get everything in life you want, if you will just help enough other people get what they want.

Zig Ziglar

Little League coaches aren't supposed to have favorites. But I did. I couldn't help it.

His name was Clyde.

I called him "Clyde the Glide," one of those silly sports nicknames given to a player by a coach on the first day of practice.

I did it as a way to remember a new kid's name. Little did I know that for the rest of my life I would never forget him.

Clyde wasn't a glider. He was a lumberer.

He was big for ten years old, but extremely uncoordinated. He was a special-needs student and, because of it, was often ridiculed by his peers.

He wasn't a good ballplayer. That was okay, I figured, because I wasn't a very good coach.

I was only twenty-three, a young news reporter working

in Williamsport, Pennsylvania, the Little League Capital of the World.

I had extra time on my hands, and I loved baseball. So I volunteered to help an inner-city league a few blocks from my apartment.

It was a tremendous departure from what I had known as a kid. Baseball had become little more than cheap baby-sitting. With the exception of my comanager, my players' parents weren't involved with the team. Only a few mothers regularly showed at games—no fathers were ever in the stands.

Most of my players didn't know the rules of the game. Only one or two had any skills at all.

Then there was Clyde. He was the worst player on a below-average team in a bad league. Still, he kept smiling through all of the strikeouts and errors in right field and taunts by opposing players. He kept trying. He wouldn't give up. And that kept me smiling. Day after day. Game after game.

His first hit was awesome. A blooper right over the head of a shortstop who moments before had been screaming, "He can't hit, can't hit."

I felt great at that moment. Nothing, though, could prepare me for Clyde's day of redemption near the end of the season. After Clyde's bloop single, he went into a slump, striking out in nearly every at bat.

I had noticed he was stepping away from the pitcher each time a pitch was thrown. I assumed he was scared to be plunked with the ball. So one day at practice I put a line of bats behind his feet. And, sure enough, when I threw the ball to him, he instinctively stepped backward and tripped on the bats.

I kept pitching to him with the bats behind his feet until he finally stopped moving out of the batter's box. I thought I had cured a weakness. I thought I was brilliant.

Instead, I had created a disaster.

In our next game, we were trailing one of the better teams in the league by six runs in the fifth inning. Bases were loaded with two outs and Clyde, our last hitter in the lineup, was up.

He had already been hit by the pitcher once that day. And, again, the ball hit him, this time in the center of the helmet.

I rushed from the third-base coach's box to see if he was okay. But before I got there, Clyde was up and smiling and heading to first base.

That's when the umpire roared, "You're out. Third out."

The ump took me aside and explained that Clyde had leaned over the plate and interfered with the pitch. In fact, he had been doing it all day and the ump finally felt he had to call it.

I was stunned. Clyde had never leaned into a pitch before, at least not until I did that stupid thing with the bats behind his feet. Now he was heading in the opposite direction and being called for interference.

I felt responsible. I felt sick. And it got worse.

As I walked away from the umpire, I realized my own players were hurling insults at Clyde. He was trembling, inconsolable.

I looked to his mom for help. I always could count on her to be at the games. She sat motionless in the bleachers. She then bit her bottom lip. There were tears in her eyes. She didn't say a word.

I finally convinced Clyde to head back to the field, but he never looked up. He just stood in right field, head down, glove dangling at the end of his left hand. His chest continued to heave. He didn't stop crying.

In the bottom half of the last inning, my team rallied again.

This time Clyde came to bat with one out and two men on base.

He didn't lift his bat. He didn't shuffle his feet. He didn't move a single muscle for five straight pitches. And he drew a walk.

He eventually reached third with two outs and our best hitter up in a tied ballgame.

I gave Clyde advice on what to do. Told him in which situation he needed to run. He nodded, but I don't think he heard a word I said.

It's tough to explain what happened next.

There was a ground ball to the shortstop that should have been an easy force at second or throw to first to end the game. But the shortstop saw Clyde breaking for the plate. And he threw home.

I yelled for Clyde to slide, but he didn't. He never got dirty. The ball arrived seconds before Clyde—the final out of the game, for sure. That's when something amazing happened. Clyde stopped dead in his tracks about two feet before home plate. And, with his arms swinging, he jumped high into the air and over the crouched catcher's glove.

The bewildered catcher swiped at Clyde's feet. The ball popped loose and Clyde landed with both feet firmly on home plate.

"Safe," screamed the umpire.

Game over. We were unlikely winners.

Teammates mobbed an unlikely hero.

Instinctively, I hugged Clyde and then ushered him and his screaming teammates into the dugout.

I told them that I couldn't be more proud of Clyde and how he had bounced back from the previous inning.

I then presented him with a pack of Big Red gum, my award for player of the game.

His teammates cheered. And Clyde smiled the largest smile I had ever seen on that always-smiling face.

After my speech, I gave Clyde one more hug and then patted his back as he leaped out of the dugout.

Clutching his gum in one hand, he dashed over to the bleachers. I stood and stared at his mother once again. This time, the tears were streaming down her face.

Dan Connolly

The Last Game

It was to be the last game ever for the New Richmond Generals, a team of seventeen- and eighteen-year-olds that were playing in an AABC league in the Cincinnati, Ohio, area. As the parents and teams huddled under umbrellas and dugouts waiting for the rain to end, we were slowly realizing that our last game might not end up being played at all.

The New Richmond Generals had been playing together as a team in one form or another for twelve years. Their coach, Daryl, had put the team together as kindergartners. Over the years some boys left and others were added, they moved from eight years of Knothole to a more select AABC league, but Daryl was their constant. A core group of players, including my son Casey and Daryl's son Aaron, had been with the team from its inception. Others had played for him for eight to ten of the twelve years. In this age of team jumping, kids quitting, coaches quitting and lack of commitment to any one team or person, such dedication was almost unheard of. Yet these boys and their parents had chosen to stay.

During the players' younger years, Daryl worked hard to teach them not only the fundamentals of baseball, at which he was very good, but also the intangibles. He treated each boy individually, knew their strengths and weaknesses, and knew how to bring out the best in each one. I remember him going to the library to look up a certain learning disability so he would know what would be the best way to reach and teach that boy. When he would see a personal problem, he would often visit that boy at home and talk to him and his parents. He gave countless rides to make sure each boy arrived at the games or practices. When the boys were fourteen, he saw their playing potential and the team moved to a more select league, which demanded more of his time and personal financial commitment. Boys that had trouble with paying fees were given or found jobs to help offset the costs and to make them feel responsible. Volunteering to help different sports organizations was greatly encouraged.

On the field, Daryl was not always an angel. Though he mellowed with time, he was a fierce competitor and had a hard time holding his tongue if he thought an injustice had occurred. He expected all the boys to play up to their potential and give all they had. It would not be fair to say he didn't care if they won or not, because he very much wanted to win. But he never failed to apologize to the players if he felt he was out of line, and he let them know he would always stand up for them if they were wronged. He also taught them to respect the game, other players and coaches, umpires, and themselves. If their on-field behavior was inappropriate, he wouldn't hesitate to pull them. There was and still is a deep feeling of mutual respect between him and the boys. Sometimes Daryl was the only adult these teenage boys felt they could talk to.

So many of these thoughts were going through my head as we sat at this last game. The boys were graduating high school soon and going their separate ways, and after taking the team from kindergarten through high school,

Daryl was disbanding the Generals. The parents had planned a simple ceremony to thank Daryl after the game, but the heavy rain was taking away their last opportunity to play together.

We all stood on the field after the umpires officially called off the game. The dreary skies matched our spirits as many of us tried to hold back tears. Daryl had little success holding back as the boys presented him with an inscribed plaque thanking him for his years and friendship, a small token indeed. He then proceeded to thank and praise each boy individually. As he got to the small group of boys who had been with him for the last eight years or so, he gave them keychains engraved with their jersey number and nicknames that he had for them. His good-bye to his own son Aaron was particularly touching, as neither could hold back the tears. He then came to my son Casey. They have had a long, deep commitment to each other, and I could see my almost-eighteen-year-old boy trying to be stoic. Daryl walked to the dugout and pulled out the second base that had always been used in home games. He presented it to Casey with this inscription handwritten on it: "You've stolen this base often enough that I thought you should have it. Remember, good things come to those who wait but only things left behind by those who hustle like you. Thank you for your years of dedication and leadership."

Through my tears I could see Casey giving Daryl a fierce hug and then turning and leaving the field. I tried to catch up with him, but he waved me off, needing me to back away, and to be alone in that way that teenage boys do. That evening, Casey spent his time alone in his room, not wishing to talk about any of the events that happened. I was beginning to wonder if Daryl's gift and words had actually had any effect on him, but a few weeks later Daryl showed me a letter that my son had sent to him, unbeknownst to me. Casey's letter was simple but touching, letting his coach know how much he owed to him and how much of an effect he had on his life. His last sentence was, "If I were ever to receive an award for baseball, you would be the first person I would thank."

Two years have passed since that last game, and Casey and his coach still keep in touch. As college students, many of the players are still in contact and consider Daryl their friend and mentor. When my son started his first year away at college, Daryl called him and encouraged him to work through the tough times. When Casey needs help or advice, or needs to know someone other than his parents support him, he still knows he can go to Daryl for help. And the last time I saw Daryl, he was still carrying with him, folded in his wallet, Casey's letter.

Linda Poynter

CL*O*SE TO H*O*ME   J*O*HN M*c*PHERS*O*N

Even though they were hard to run in,
Don's new shoes made him
a serious base-stealing threat.

One Man, Alone

Branch Rickey was one of baseball's most innovative executives, a visionary who used farm systems to develop future players and introduced batting helmets to protect hitters from bean balls.

Those were dramatic steps, but nothing compared to the one he took in 1945 when he signed Jackie Robinson for the Brooklyn Dodgers.

What made this such a big deal was that Robinson, a former four-sport star at UCLA and Army lieutenant, happened to be African-American, and Rickey had decided he would be the man to integrate baseball.

For a century, from the time Alexander Cartwright first came up with a plan for a new pastime until the end of World War II, the sport had been an all-white operation. Blacks need not apply.

And then Rickey had this idea.

If blacks could fight a war for their country, then they could be allowed to play organized baseball. He quietly sent scouts to the Negro Leagues looking for prospects. He needed a special player, one who not only had the talent to play major-league baseball, but could endure the most severe treatment imaginable.

This move would be the beginning of a great sociological revolution, one Robinson was not at all sure about. He was not particularly interested in being a trailblazer. What he wanted was a job so that he could earn enough money to get married.

Robinson had been playing shortstop for the Kansas City Monarchs when Rickey summoned him to Brooklyn. They sat in the Dodgers office and talked about details of a contract.

Suddenly, Rickey lashed out at Robinson, using every vile racial epithet he could think of, every word he thought a black player—the first black player—could expect to hear on the field. It was a test to see how much Robinson could take.

Finally, Robinson shot back.

"Mr. Rickey," he said, "do you want someone who's afraid to fight back?"

"No," replied Rickey, "I want someone with the guts not to fight back."

After a year playing minor-league ball in Montreal, Robinson was promoted. On opening day of the 1947 season, he was in the Dodgers line-up, batting second and playing first base. Not all his teammates were thrilled with the situation. Some Southern players, including outfielder Dixie Walker and pitcher Hugh Casey, led an attempted revolt, complete with petitions, in spring training. Dodgers management crushed it.

Eddie Stanky, a native of Mobile, Alabama, would bat ahead of Robinson in the line-up and play alongside him at second base. He made it clear that this was not his choice.

"I want you to know something," he told Robinson on the eve of the opener. "You're on this ball club and as far as I'm concerned that makes you one of twenty-five players on my team. But before I play with you, I want you to

know how I feel about it. I want you to know I don't like
it. I want you to know I don't like you."

As expected, every place the Dodgers played, abuse
rained down on Robinson. It was vile and ugly, the most
horrible treatment imaginable.

It followed Robinson from city to city. In St. Louis, the
Cardinals threatened to strike rather than play against a
team with a black man on it. In Cincinnati, there were
death threats. In Philadelphia, the bench jockeys
unleashed a tirade of curses that went beyond anything
Robinson had ever heard.

He went out on the field and took it all, took it silently,
often standing, hands on hips, hearing it all, trying not to
hear it all.

After about a month, the abuse became just too much.
Finally, one Dodger couldn't take it anymore and shouted
into the Phillies dugout.

"Listen, you yellow-bellied SOBs, why don't you yell at
somebody who can answer back?"

The defender was Stanky, the man who had told
Robinson off before the season started.

Robinson was thrown at routinely, sent sprawling on
a daily basis. In the first two months of the season, he
was hit by pitches six times, as many times as any
National League player had been hit the entire previous
season.

Still, he pressed on, becoming rookie of the year as the
Dodgers won the pennant. In the off-season, Stanky was
traded and Brooklyn moved Robinson to second base, to
play alongside Pee Wee Reese, another Southerner, who
had grown up in Louisville, Kentucky.

Robinson was still under orders from Rickey not to
respond to the curses and insults, and he held up his part
of the bargain. It was no easy task for this proud black
man. The abuse was every bit as constant as it had been in

his rookie season. He remained a target—a lonely, helpless target.

One day in Cincinnati, the abuse became particularly ugly. Robinson stood at his position, trying to look impassive, but his head was down, his shoulder sagging. The Dodgers were changing pitchers when a teammate walked over and put his arm over Robinson's shoulder, a silent but eloquent statement that he was not alone in this fight.

When Robinson looked up, the man standing next to him was Reese. They both broke into wide grins, the shortstop from Kentucky and the black second baseman from California. That simple gesture was a turning point. The message was that they were in this thing together and they would come out of it the same way—together.

Hal Bock

5

FROM THE DUGOUT

*I don't know what it is. The big crowds.
The hundreds of reporters, photographers
and television men. The flags decorating the
stadium. . . . Whatever it is, you suddenly
feel the excitement of it all and nothing
that happened before is important.*

Bob Gibson

A Batboy Looks Back

I was searching for baseball ghosts when I took my family on our first trip to the Mall of America in Bloomington, Minnesota. We weren't there to shop. I simply wanted to find the site of where home plate had been at Metropolitan Stadium, the former home of the Minnesota Twins major-league baseball team.

I spent the best days of my boyhood—along with a couple of the worst days—at Met Stadium as a batboy with the Twins. It was a great place to grow up. It's where I learned about sex, race and ethnic relations, and celebrity, and that baseball players were a lot more human than they appeared on their bubble-gum cards.

I'm old enough to have seen construction begin on the Met in 1955. I watched the ballpark emerge from the surrounding corn and melon fields just off Cedar Avenue, the road that ran past my boyhood home. I never saw brighter lights or prettier emerald green grass than the first time I walked out on the runway and looked around the Met diamond. And what a diamond it was.

But the shrine of my youth was torn down when the Twins moved to the Hubert H. Humphrey Metrodome after the 1981 season. That hurt.

Now the nation's largest shopping mall, 4.2 million square feet, sits where the Met once stood. I don't know which is a greater example of gluttonous excess—the overflowing cornucopia at the Mall of America or the greed of major-league baseball players who take stretch limos to their contract negotiations and expect multi-million-dollar contracts for mediocre performances.

Give me back the days when baseball players wore baggy flannel uniforms and appreciated the lives they led and the people who cheered them.

I know we aren't supposed to live in the past, but when it comes to that 164-acre site in Bloomington, I'd prefer to. It took about fifteen minutes to find, but there was home plate embedded in the mall floor at Knott's Camp Snoopy. It was black, bordered in gold and read: "Metropolitan Stadium. Home Plate. 1956–1981."

We were the only ones looking at it. The other people were too busy racing to the hundreds of stores they had to choose from. I would have settled for seeing a Met Stadium hot dog vendor.

"It's kind of sad. It's kind of like a tombstone to me," my wife said while looking at home plate.

There was a time that I wished I was resting comfortably in a casket beneath that home plate tombstone.

It was a balmy summer day in 1964 and forty thousand fans were in the stands watching the Twins play the perennial American League champion New York Yankees.

My main job that day was to make sure that the home plate umpire was supplied with baseballs. The batter—I've forgotten if it was Mickey Mantle, Roger Maris, Harmon Killebrew, Tony Oliva, or one of the team's mere mortals—fouled off a half-dozen pitches. Home plate umpire Nestor Chylak called time and signaled me to bring him a new batch of baseballs.

Not wanting to delay the game, I sprinted toward home plate. But my spikes got caught in the turf. I tripped and slid in the general direction of the plate. The baseballs flew in all directions. Umpire Chylak got into his crouch, pumped his arms and hollered "Safe!"

About sixty major-league players and coaches, four umpires and forty thousand fans were roaring. At me. If I could have crawled under the plate and hid, I would have. I can honestly tell my kids that unless they break a law they'll never face a more embarrassing moment as a teenager.

After the game I remember Killebrew—my favorite Twin—and a half-dozen other players smiling, patting me on the back and asking if I was all right. Twins trainer Doc Lentz asked if I needed a whirlpool treatment. Even I was able to laugh at that.

I went on to become the Twins' assistant equipment manager in 1967 before entering the military. I returned to the team in the same capacity for the 1972 and '73 seasons. By that time I was the same age as some of the players. The best stories from that era—while colorful—probably don't belong in a wholesome publication.

When it comes to the spicier stuff I witnessed and heard, I'll live by the old clubhouse adage: "What you see here, what you hear here, what you say here, when you leave here, let it stay here."

Those memories will never fade. But I wish Met Stadium was still standing and that those players from my past were still able to play the game we all respected and cherished.

Mark Stodghill

Who's on First?

Every professional umpire starts in the minor leagues. For most, the job consists mainly of long automobile drives between small towns to work games under lighting too dim to brighten a porch, dressing in closets, sleeping in hotel rooms so small that if you eat in the room and gain weight you can't get out, and surviving on cold hot dogs and warm soda.

But life in the minors is not just good times. The ballparks are small and the playing fields are terrible. Worst of all are the hometown fans. Durwood Merrill remembers when somebody snapped a lock on the umpire's room after the game, trapping him and his partner. They hollered for almost three hours before a night watchman freed them. Then they discovered the fans had let the air out of all four tires on their car.

Minor-league umpires have to deal with every conceivable situation—as well as many inconceivable ones. They have seen horses in the outfield, rabbits running the bases, fans breaking down the dressing room door. A game in Wilmington, North Carolina, once had to be called on account of a whale. A fan spotted the whale surfacing offshore, and the rest of the fans, as well as the players, left the field to see it.

Rain is always a problem in the minors because few clubs can afford a tarpaulin that covers more than the pitcher's mound and the home-plate area. In order to get in a game after two days of rain in Spokane, Washington, the management soaked the infield with gasoline, and then set it on fire to burn the field dry. Eric Gregg was calling balls and strikes that night.

"The fumes were unbelievably strong," Gregg recalls. "After the first hitter was out, the catcher stood up and said, 'Eric, this is ridiculous. I can barely breathe.' I wasn't feeling so good either, but I suggested we try to finish the inning.

"So he got back down into position and gave the pitcher a sign. Suddenly, whoosh! My whole world started spinning, and I nearly keeled right over his back." That remains the only baseball game called because of gas fumes.

Rocky Roe was umpiring the bases one night when young Rickey Henderson was on first. Henderson took off for second, the catcher made a tremendous throw to beat him, the shortstop caught the throw and put his glove down to make the tag. Henderson came sliding in and pinned the shortstop's glove to the base with his spikes. The shortstop lifted up his hand, leaving his glove—with the ball still in it—wedged between Henderson's foot and second base. "I could see this was going to be a problem," Rocky says.

"Henderson, seeing the glove on the ground, immediately put his other foot on the base, and I called him safe. That brought Stump Merrill, the manager of the other team, running onto the field. 'How can you make that call?' he screamed at me.

"'Well, Stumpy,' I told him, 'unless they've changed the rules in the last few weeks, when a fielder comes up after making a tag he'd better have a piece of leather on the other end of that appendage,' When I said 'appendage,' that sort of confused him, because he asked me what I was talking about. I said, 'He's gotta have control of the ball.' Stump looked, and the glove was still lying there, the ball nestled in the pocket. He shrugged and walked back to the dugout shaking his head."

Chuck Cottier, now a coach with the Seattle Mariners, was managing at a game in Clinton, Iowa, when he witnessed one of those bizarre plays that give umpires nightmares. Perhaps the most difficult call for a major-league umpire is the trap play in the outfield. In the minor leagues, with inadequate lighting in most outfields, it can be an impossible call.

Cottier's team had the bases loaded with one out. Arturo Bonito, his right fielder, was the runner on second. The batter hit a looping fly ball into the darkness, and all the runners took off. The runner on third scored, Bonito rounded third and headed home, the runner from first base was on his heels, and the batter was racing into second. Then the third baseman screamed, "He caught it!"

Cottier was coaching at third, and he remembers it being like a movie projector running in reverse. "Everybody turned around and started racing back. When everything settled down, three of my players were standing on third base, and the batter was on second. I looked at these three guys and tried to think of something helpful to say. Then Bonito sized up the situation and pow! He took off across the infield toward first base. He ran right over the pitcher's mound and slid into the base, just beating the throw.

"We were a little better off now. We had two men on third, the batter on second, and the runner who started on second on first. I didn't have the slightest idea what was going on, so I figured the umpires didn't either.

"Finally they called it a double play. They called Bonito

and the batter out. I have no doubt that if there hadn't been any outs in the inning they would have called it a triple play. Heck, if they needed four outs they could have found them somewhere on that play."

Ray Miller, now the Baltimore Orioles' pitching coach, was on the mound in Dubuque, Iowa, when he helped test an umpire. Again the bases were loaded. The batter hit a grounder back to Miller, who fired a one-hopper to the catcher to force the runner on third. Just as his throw got there the runner slammed into the catcher. The umpire looked on the ground for the ball and couldn't spot it, so he couldn't call the runner safe. Then he looked in the catcher's glove. The ball wasn't there either, so he couldn't call him out. For a moment, everybody stood absolutely still. Then the whole field erupted.

The catcher knew he didn't have the ball, so he started searching for it. The base runners, seeing the catcher looking around, took off. Miller came running in to try to find the ball. The runner from second slid across the plate. The runner from first slid across the plate.

Then Miller saw the ball. In the collision at the plate, the first runner had slashed a hole in the catcher's pants with his spikes, and the ball had gone into the pants. So as the hitter was rounding third trying for an inside-the-pants home run, Miller was grabbing the catcher.

Eventually the plate umpire allowed all runners to advance only one base. He quoted the rule that "When the ball lodges in the catcher's mask or paraphernalia, all runners shall be permitted to advance one base from their position when the first part of the play was made." That satisfied both managers.

In fact, no such rule existed at the time. But one of the first things an umpire learns in the minor leagues is that managers and players don't know the rule book at all. This makes the Bluff Rule a very useful tool. To invoke it, the confused umpire simply must sound as though he knows what he's talking about and do so loudly and firmly. It can get him out of many a sticky situation and might just be his ticket to the major leagues.

Ron Luciano and David Fisher

"Nothing personal, all the signs are printed with Braille on them."

A Game of Life

Coming together is a beginning, staying together is progress, and working together is a success.

Henry Ford

To everything, there is a season. That is baseball. That is life.

Which brings us to the tale of the 1999 New York Yankees—a team drawn together by a round baseball, but a team truly connected by the circle of life.

On October 27, 1999, they won their second straight World Series. They won it at Yankee Stadium, a place of legends, a place of triumph, a place where so many Yankees teams before them had rejoiced in victories much like this one.

Yet on this night, these Yankees did more than just celebrate together. They mourned together.

In front of their eyes, inside their souls, were the highest highs that life can bring and the lowest lows that life delivers.

They had just won a World Series, swept the great

Atlanta Braves, listened as their hallowed stadium shook in the Bronx night. And life was beautiful.

But there, in the middle of this euphoric moment, tears flowed. And life was painful. Two men met on the infield grass—two men whose stories embodied these Yankees' story.

One man was Joe Torre, the manager whose prostate cancer diagnosis in spring training had so powerfully delivered the message that victory is fleeting and baseball is trivial.

Joe Torre spent Opening Day worrying if he would live to see his four-year-old daughter grow up, worrying if those cancer treatments—treatments that had drawn his face and sapped his strength—would get him back to the game and the team that had fulfilled his life's mission.

The other man was Paul O'Neill, right fielder, number-three hitter and grieving son.

Nine hours earlier, he had answered the telephone and learned that his father, Charles, had died of heart trouble at age seventy-nine.

I lost my own father earlier in that same year. So I have no idea how Paul O'Neill managed to play a baseball game that night—even Game 4 of a World Series. But he did.

"My dad taught me how to play the game," he said later that evening, his eyes moist. "I wanted to play."

The essence of these Yankees is that they were a team in which every piece fit together. As baseball players, as human beings, as friends, they fit.

There may be more famous Yankees. But there is no piece more important than O'Neill, the epitome of the selfless mind-set that made the Yankees what they were.

So Paul O'Neill played. He played, Torre said, because "he knows the other guys count on him a lot."

The game, O'Neill would say afterward, was "a blur." He was there. But he wasn't there. His body stood in right field. His brain was often somewhere else.

"It was pretty bittersweet," he said. "My mind wandered off a few times."

He was asked, at one point, how he had gotten through the night. "I don't know," he said with a slight chuckle. "Is it over yet?"

He has had more eventful nights on a baseball field. Yet he has had few more memorable nights. In four trips to the plate, he went 0 for 3 with a walk. He never scored a run, drove in a run or caught a fly ball. But this was the end of an important journey, an eight-month odyssey that had pointed forever toward this night.

So Paul O'Neill played. He played to find three hours of peace. He played because the Yankees' puzzle needed his piece, just as he needed the rest of the puzzle.

"I just kept thinking what it meant to be part of this, with these twenty-four guys," he said. "I didn't want to take anything away from what happened on the field. But it just so happened that my dad had come to New York for a procedure, so my brothers were here—and my mom and some friends. They all knew what I was going through. And they knew why it was so important for me to be out there."

At 11:22 P.M. on this emotional October night, the final out of the World Series settled into Chad Curtis's glove. A 6.0 earthquake erupted on Yankee Stadium's Richter scale. Two dozen players in those legendary pinstripes swarmed Mariano Rivera, the man who had thrown the final pitch. It looked like so many other celebrations that had busted out at Yankee Stadium in so many Octobers—until two men met on the infield grass: Joe Torre and Paul O'Neill.

Then the tears began, for both of them, until they had to escape to the safety of their clubhouse to gather their emotions.

"I just told Paulie, 'Your dad was here to watch this one,'" Torre said. And with those words "all the stuff that had been bottled up inside me just came out," O'Neill said.

"It's all his fault. I was doing fine until I got to Joe. I tried to avoid him, but he found me."

That, however, is how it had to be, because the Yankees spent that '99 season finding each other—on the field and off.

Joe DiMaggio, the greatest living Yankee, had died that summer. So had Catfish Hunter, the first big-name Yankees free agent.

The fathers of third baseman Scott Brosius and of utility infielder Luis Sojo passed away. And the man who holds it all together—Torre—left the club in March to battle cancer, then returned in May to battle the American League. How ironic—so many lows, all leading them up baseball's highest mountain.

"Tragedy's a part of life," Torre said that night. "Just because you're an athlete doesn't mean you're exempt."

Funny, wasn't it? For so many years in the twentieth century, the Yankees were so easy to hate. And then, in the final year of the 1900s, they were so hard to hate. For years and years, they seemed unfairly superhuman. And in the end, they seemed all too human.

Their season of baseball was over. Their season of life went on. And in the end, they taught us all that ultimately, as Joe Torre said, "baseball's a game of life."

Jayson Stark

A Magical Baseball Player

The purpose of human life is to serve, to show compassion, and the will to help others.
Albert Schweitzer

Ken Griffey Jr. is a magical baseball player. When you turn on the sports news at 11 o'clock, you're likely to see him on the highlight shows, knocking another one out of the park or leaping over the fence to turn someone else's home run into nothing more than a long out.

But the greatest feat I ever saw Ken Griffey Jr. perform on a baseball field happened long before the game started. I was in Baltimore hanging around on the field at Oriole Park at Camden Yards, wasting time until I went back upstairs to the press box where I would cover the game that night.

Griffey bounded happily from the Seattle Mariners dugout on the third-base side of the field, making his way toward home plate for batting practice. An Orioles team official leaned to whisper something to him as he headed toward the batting cage, and Griffey looked over toward the Oriole dugout.

There, seated near the end of the dugout, was a pale, sickly looking boy of about ten or twelve in a wheelchair. He wore thick eyeglasses and looked far too thin to be healthy. Griffey walked over to the boy—with his cap on backwards in that little-kid way of his, toting his bat— and stopped to chat with the excited youngster for a few minutes.

I couldn't tell whether the boy had trouble looking straight at Griffey because he was shy or because of whatever illness he had. But Griffey just leaned over a little lower so the two could talk face-to-face.

Griffey stayed and chatted with the youngster for about ten minutes as I watched—transfixed—from about thirty feet away. The whole time while he was engrossed in conversation with the boy, teammates were yelling for him to come over and take his batting practice swings. A shoe company representative kept bugging him to come over to shake hands with a big client who had purchased a lot of shoes from the company.

But Griffey would have none of it. He took his time with the young man, refusing to be rushed by anyone. After about ten minutes, he said his good-byes to the boy and his family, and trotted back to the other side of the field, disappearing into the Seattle dugout.

What a nice moment, I thought to myself. And then I promptly forgot about it, turning my attention to other things.

But Griffey wasn't finished. He reappeared out of the Mariners dugout with a brand new Orioles cap and a T-shirt for the boy. I assume he had sent one of the clubhouse attendants out to the concession stands with some money to buy them for the youngster. Again, he trotted happily over to the young man, said a few words and dropped the new hat and the shirt into the surprised young man's lap. I never forgot the entire tableau.

Ultimately, a few years later, Griffey left Seattle and the Mariners, choosing to sign as a free agent with Cincinnati, where he'd grown up when his father played for the Reds. Much was written and said about Griffey's departure, and the big-money contract he had signed with Cincinnati. Some dismissed him as just another greedy ballplayer.

But none of that meant very much to me. I'd seen on that warm summer evening that Griffey had room in his busy day—and in his heart—for someone nowhere near as lucky as he was. And after seeing what he did that afternoon in Baltimore, I couldn't put much stock in anyone speaking badly about him. I knew better.

John McNamara

Dad's Field of Dreams

Last year's baseball season was miserable. In addition to the bitter aftertaste of the disastrous 1994 strike, the usual drug problems and the players whining, there were other embarrassments. It was bad enough that wealthy stars from the present and past sold their autographs. But several recently pleaded guilty to not paying taxes on this easy pocket money.

Not everybody in baseball is a self-obsessed, immature stiff, of course. There are exceptions, and here's one of them.

"I left Chicago in 1980," said business executive Richard Sturm, "and moved to Eugene, Oregon, to get away from the big city. I wanted to find a smaller town where people still cared about people."

When Sturm's eighty-year-old father died last July 4, he returned to the Midwest for the funeral. Harry Sturm had been a cellist for the Chicago Symphony Orchestra. "He loved music and he loved baseball," Sturm said. "A quiet, nice guy.

"Two days later my brother and I had to go into Chicago to tie up some loose ends. Passing Addison Street, we looked at each other and said, 'We're not that far, are we?'

"So we doubled back and headed for one of Dad's favorite places. Ours too. We got out of the car and just stared. We were kids again, full of excitement. We were standing in front of Wrigley Field.

"Since there was no game that day, we decided to take a walk around the park and reminisce. As we were walking, I pushed on an iron gate and it opened. I said to my brother, 'Let's go.'

"We walked up the stairs, and the field came into view. All the stories Dad had told us came rushing back. How, when he was a boy, he would show up at Wrigley to clean up the stands, put up seats and get into the game free. It was the only way he could afford to see a game.

"I noticed a groundskeeper on the field. Thinking I had nothing to lose, I went over and asked if we could walk on the outfield. He opened the gate and said, 'Sorry about your dad. Make yourselves at home.' We couldn't believe it. We were actually walking on the outfield grass of Wrigley Field, touching the ivy. We were kids again.

"About fifteen minutes later, Mike—that was this groundskeeper's name—walked toward us. I assumed we had overstayed our welcome.

"But he said, 'Here's a couple of game balls. I thought you might want to take them with you.' Then he said again, 'I'm sorry about your dad.'

"It didn't end there. When Mike's boss found out why we were there, he suggested that we might like to sit in the dugout for a while.

"Gosh, you sit in the dugout and see the field like you've never seen it before. My brother said, 'Look, the wind is blowing out. It's a home-run day.' We were sitting where Ernie Banks used to sit. We could look up at the right-field bleachers, where my father caught a home run once.

"We stayed for more than an hour. When we left, I tried to give Mike a couple of twenty-dollar bills. He said, 'No way.' He and his boss wouldn't even let us buy them lunch. They just said it was nice to have friendly people come to the park. They were sorry it was under these circumstances.

"I was wrong back in 1980. You don't have to move to the country to find decent people. We'll probably never see Mike again, but I'll always consider him a friend."

Maybe the team should take away Mike's rake and make him a coach. There's a lot he could teach the players.

Mike Royko

Who's Number One?

*Team spirit is what gives so many companies
an edge over their competitors.*

George L. Clements

I was the new coach of a Little League baseball team and had not yet learned the names of my players. At our first game, I called each boy by the number on his uniform. When I yelled, "Number 5, your time to bat," Jeff Smith came to the plate to hit. When I called for "Number 7," Steve Heinz jumped up. Then I asked for "Number 1," and no one emerged from the dugout. Again I called for Number 1. Still no one.

As the umpire looked on, annoyed at this delay of the game, I shouted, "Who's Number 1?"

That's when the whole team yelled, "We are, Coach! We are!"

Kenneth L. Montgomery

Adam@home

by Brian Basset

Big Leaguers' Little League Memories

When a band of tykes from Toms River, New Jersey, won the Little League World Series during the summer of 1998, the kids got the second thrill of their lives a few days later—the chance to stand proudly next to their New York Yankee positionsakes during the National Anthem at Yankee Stadium. Anyone watching the scene couldn't help but be borne back into the past, when the millionaire Yankees must have been Little Leaguers themselves, sporting the baggy uniforms and big-league dreams.

"I still remember it like it was yesterday," said right fielder Paul O'Neill, who played Little League in Columbus, Ohio. "The games then meant as much to you as these games do now. And you got to go to Dairy Queen afterward!" Added shortstop Derek Jeter, "You didn't worry about making an error or striking out. You just had fun."

Roughly 80 percent of today's major leaguers played Little League baseball, and 100 percent of them recall the experience with immensely fond nostalgia. While baseball remains a child's game, even grown men for whom it's a job remember the child within, and nurture it by remembering the old days.

Baltimore Orioles Iron Man Cal Ripken was honing his workmanlike persona before his age hit double digits. "I shined my shoes after every game," Ripken recalled, "and sometimes wore my uniform to bed because I couldn't wait for the next game." In his first at bat as a Little Leaguer, St. Louis Cardinals slugger Mark McGwire hit— what else?—a home run.

Most of us, of course, never hit a home run or anything approaching it. But even those who enjoyed the most success on Little League fields remember the simple act of trying, of participating. Said the Philadelphia Phillies' Scott Rolen, "It was all so easy then. I think we'd all go back and play Little League again, whether you're an accountant or a baseball player. All you care about is playing baseball and doing the best you can. Unfortunately, you only play six innings. You'd play sixty if you could." Then again—thankfully—even some major-league all-stars struggled. Pitcher David Cone was cut while trying out for his first Little League team in Kansas City when he was seven years old. "I'm still in touch with the person who cut me," Cone said with a laugh. "Whenever I see him I still get on him—'You cut me when I was seven!'"

Cone vividly recalls crying and throwing temper tantrums when he lost games. Sure enough, the intensity that propelled the best to the top percolated inside them as youngsters. Boston Red Sox all-star Nomar Garciaparra was nicknamed "No Nonsense Nomar" when he first started playing in Southern California. He scowled at his less-talented teammates and got so upset with his own mistake once that his own father removed him from a game.

His dad softened up after a while, though, and gave Nomar a brand-new glove that cost $125, way out of the family budget. (Though a shrewd investment on the order of Microsoft's IPO.) The little boy treasured it, carried it with him wherever he went, even slept with it. He never threw it, though, always placing it down calmly on the bench or dugout steps, a tradition he continues to this day in the majors. "The reason my father gave it to me was he knew I loved the game and he probably thought I could take care of it," Garciaparra said. "It was such an honor that my dad would do something like that for me. I didn't want to disappoint him."

No one knew the ten-year-old Nomar Garciaparra, very short and skinny for his age, would later become one of the best shortstops in the history of baseball. The kids generally have more pressing concerns. "The best part was the ice cream afterwards," major-league superstar Barry Bonds recalled. Added Atlanta Braves third baseman Chipper Jones, "We had two teams in our area, the Lions and the Expos. Everybody wanted to play for the Lions because they had better looking uniforms."

"When people ask me what my fondest memories of baseball are," said Nolan Ryan, who struck out more batters and threw more no-hitters than any major-leaguer, "I think back to playing Little League—because we played for the love of the game and the camaraderie. Little League was the first opportunity for children in Alvin, Texas, to get involved in any organized activity. It was one of the biggest events in our lives."

Alan Schwarz

Lessons in Living a Humble Life

Around 1980, when I was a reporter for a weekly news-paper in Albany, New York, I obtained permission from the editor to do a feature story on the New York Yankees. While I would eventually produce a story that ran on the front page, my hidden agenda was no secret to anyone who knew me well: As a die-hard Yankees fan, I wanted to get near the players. With press credentials, I could do more than that; I would be allowed into the team's club-house and dugout, and I could plant my sneakers on the field indented by the cleats of Babe Ruth, Joe DiMaggio and Mickey Mantle.

I knew this opportunity would give me bragging rights for the rest of my life. After all, how many people get behind the scenes of the most famous sports franchise in history?

I received two press passes from the team's public rela-tions office. Puffed up with anticipatory pride, I invited a coworker and friend named Jon Harrington to come along. He worked in advertising, but I decided I could sneak him in with me if I draped a camera around his neck and declared that he was my photographer.

About twenty years older than I, Jon had grown up in New York City and, like me, was a lifelong Yankees fan. I was sure this trip would knock his socks off. He had to be wowed by my "connections," even though they consisted entirely of making a phone call or two to the Yankees press office.

When we got to the Bronx and I flashed the press credentials, we were waved past security guards and into places only imagined by ordinary fans. Once inside the bowels of the stadium, I held tightly to the secret hope that Jon was impressed with me. But I soon noticed that he was a very reluctant participant. He seemed nonchalant as I fulfilled my boyhood dreams and collected autographs (violating a basic journalistic code). In the fabled clubhouse, as the players dressed for batting practice, I chatted with sports stars while he stood quietly in a corner. When I headed toward the dugout, he trailed behind me. As I was about to trot up the steps to the field that some of the most famous ballplayers in history had run on, Jon called to me.

"I'm going to go to our seats," he said. "You go ahead."

I was stunned and a little miffed. *He had to be jealous of me,* I concluded. What else explained his hesitant behavior? What avid Yankees fan would be so shy about talking to players? What keen student of the game wouldn't want to plant his shoes on the grass of Yankee Stadium?

The questions lingered in my mind as I finished my assignment, and they remained throughout the game. On the drive home, after I poured out stories about the players I had talked to, from famous outfielders to journeymen infielders, I asked Jon, "How come you didn't seem impressed? Was something wrong?"

"Not at all," Jon replied. "Thanks for bringing me. It's just that I've been there before."

I nearly drove off the Thruway. "What are you talking about?" I asked. He had never told me any such story, and we had worked together for nearly ten years.

"My father was a cop who walked a beat in Times Square, back when Times Square was the center of New York life," he said. "He got to know a lot of celebrities, including sports stars like Jack Dempsey. He introduced me to them. When something big was happening at Yankee Stadium, he would be assigned there. Sometimes, he took me with him and introduced me to the players he got to know. So it didn't mean as much to me as it did to you. But I'm glad you had the chance."

His voice trailed off. Sometimes, getting Jon to talk about himself requires a chisel and crowbar.

"Like who?" I asked. "Who did you meet?"

Jon shrugged, "Oh, Lou Gehrig, for example. Babe Ruth. All of the Yanks from that era."

Now I fought to keep the car's wheels on the highway. "Gehrig!" I shouted. "Ruth!"

Jon continued, "My dad would let them take me into the stadium with them. I would do errands for them. Lots of times, I ran to a bakery about two blocks away and got them cakes. We hung around a lot."

He said "we." Meaning "me and Lou Gehrig." I was amazed. "Who else?" I said.

"Several times," Jon continued, "my dad brought Grover Cleveland Alexander home, and he stayed overnight."

The Great Alexander! The Hall of Fame pitcher who spent twenty years in the bigs! The hurler portrayed by Ronald Reagan in a movie with Doris Day as his wife! The notorious tippler who sometimes needed a friendly place to dry out! A friendly, cozy, baseball place like Jon's house when he was a boy.

No wonder he wasn't impressed by my half-hour in the clubhouse. He had spent his entire youth hobnobbing with some of the game's greats. I had sought to impress Jon by giving him the chance to shake hands with the Yanks' second-string catcher. But he had palled around with the Iron Horse and the Sultan of Swat, and served breakfast to Alexander—and never felt the need to say a word about it.

Jon is like that about other aspects of his life—his Army service in Italy during World War II, for example, or the hundreds of good things he has done for charities when no one is looking.

Two decades after our trip to the Bronx, Jon and I remain good friends and avid Yankees fans. We talk about all sorts of things, but I am smart enough never to bring up my feeble attempt at impressing someone who lives with such memories—and such humility.

James Breig

Play Ball!

Sports have always played an important role in my family's life. My father has been involved in every type of sports activity known in the free world. He especially enjoys the game of baseball. As a youngster, he played constantly, and when he was unable to play, he found alternatives. My dad loved the game of baseball so much that he actually moonlighted from his job at U.S. Steel's Carrie Furnace to sell peanuts at Forbes Field while watching his beloved Pittsburgh Pirates play ball. No problem, until he was so enamored with the game that he failed to see his boss sitting in row five waiting for a snack. Thankfully, his boss loved the game as much as he did. My mother even tells stories of being seven months pregnant and walking all over the eastern suburbs of Pittsburgh looking for kids for my dad to play ball with. He loved every aspect of the game and he attempted to bring this same fierce love to his hometown by being involved with Little League baseball.

When I was young, our family did not know what a family vacation at the beach was all about. We shared the lives of seventy-five or so young boys each summer. My dad coached, umpired and even took a swing at running the local league. Anything that needed to be done, he was there ready to help. We have countless stories to share about the numerous things that took place over my dad's twenty-five years in this game. Perhaps our favorite story involves his brief stint as an umpire attempting to brave a real fan—namely, one little lady that went by the name "Mom."

As I stated, my dad would do anything to help. One night in late June 1972, the local coaches could not find anyone to umpire an important game between the crosstown rivals of Tri-Town and the Eagles. This was an important event for our small town located in southwestern Pennsylvania. Being that it was an important game, Dad decided he would umpire and take home plate. He swaggered up to the plate and in his deep, infectious voice filled with excitement, he bellowed, "Play ball." My dad is a fair man and he takes this game seriously. He began calling "strike, ball, strike" and so forth. Each time that he offered his decisive shriek of "strike" during Tri-Town's turn at the plate, he was greeted with this voice from center field offering numerous insults in a tone that equaled his. He heard everything from, "Can't you see?" to "Go home, ump." This badgering continued throughout the first three innings.

As the game wore on, Dad began to become frustrated. This was evident in his voice. Finally, after calling a strike for a young lad about eleven years old, he was thrown a good jab at his need for glasses. My dad stood straight and slowly removed his mask. He called time and began to leave the playing field. He opened the gate and walked down the right side of the fence. He continued and began to round the center-field fence. He took his time and slowly approached the center-field bleachers. He then chose a seat beside his debating partner and introduced himself.

He proudly said, "Hi, I'm Bill Shearer. I'm glad to meet you." He then looked at the playing field and pointed his finger and hooted loudly, "Play ball!"

Everyone looked stunned, especially the small lad that now occupied the most conspicuous spot at Connellsville's major-league field. One of the coaches looked puzzled; finally, Dad politely offered, "If she can call them from here, so can I! Play ball!"

The crowd erupted with a thunderous round of applause and laughter. This was the last time that my dad umpired anything, including family squabbles.

As I stated, this is one of my favorite stories related to my dad. I think it brings a famous quotation by John Wooden to light, "Sports do not build character, they reveal it."

Sharon Shearer Harsh

Roger Maris and Me

I grew up in the shadow of Yankee Stadium and just fell in love with baseball.

When Roger Maris came to the New York Yankees from the Kansas City Athletics in 1960, I was eleven. I had been burned in a fire in August, so I was laid up for a while and followed baseball even more closely. I remember a headline that said Roger Maris "rejuvenates" the Yankees. I had never heard the word before, but it made me think this Roger Maris was someone special.

For me, there was something about the way he swung the bat, the way he played right field and the way he looked. I had an idol. In 1961 the entire country was wrapped up in the home-run race between Maris and Mickey Mantle and Babe Ruth's ghost. I cut out every single article on Roger and told myself that when I got older and could afford it, I would have my scrapbooks professionally bound. (Eight years ago I had all of them bound into eleven volumes.)

I usually sat in Section 31, Row 162-A, Seat 1 in Yankee Stadium. Right field. I would buy a general admission ticket, but I knew the policeman, so I would switch over to the reserved seats, and that one was frequently empty.

I'd get to the stadium about two hours before it opened. I would see Roger park his car, and I would say hello and tell him what a big fan I was. After a while, he started to notice me. One day he threw me a baseball during batting practice, and I was so stunned I couldn't lift my arms. Somebody else got the ball. So Roger spoke to Phil Linz, a utility infielder, and Linz came over, took a ball out of his pocket and said, "Put out your hand. This is from Roger Maris."

After that, my friends kept pushing me: "Why don't you ask him for one of his home-run bats?" Finally, when Roger was standing by the fence, I made the request. He said, "Sure. Next time I break one."

This was in 1965. The Yankees had a West Coast trip, and I was listening to their game against the Los Angeles Angels on the radio late one night, in bed, with the lights out. And Roger cracked a bat. Next morning my high school friend called me, "Did you hear Roger cracked his bat? That's your bat."

I said, "We'll see."

When the club came back to town, my friend and I went to the stadium, and during batting practice Rog walked straight over to me and said, "I've got that bat for you."

I said, "Oh, my God, I can't thank you enough."

Before the game, I went to the dugout. I stepped up to the great big policeman stationed there and poured my heart out: "You have to understand, please understand, Roger Maris told me to come here, I was supposed to pick up a bat, it's the most important thing, I wouldn't fool you, I'm not trying to pull the wool over your eyes, you gotta let me. . . ."

"No problem. Stand over here." He knew I was telling the truth.

I waited in the box-seat area to the left of the dugout, pacing and fidgeting. Then, just before game time, I couldn't stand it anymore. I hung over the rail and looked down the dimly lit ramp to the locker room, waiting for Rog to appear. When I saw him walking up the runway with a bat in his hand, I was so excited I almost fell. I don't know what he thought, seeing a kid hanging upside down, but when he handed me the bat, it was one of the most incredible moments in my young life.

I brought the bat home, and my friends said, "Now why don't you ask him for one of his home-run baseballs?"

So I asked Roger, and he said, "You're gonna have to catch one, 'cause I don't have any."

Maris was traded to the St. Louis Cardinals on December 8, 1966—a dark day for me. That year, I went off to college at the University of Akron, in Ohio. My roommate had a picture of Raquel Welch on his wall, and I had a picture of Roger Maris.

Everyone knew I was a big Maris fan. My friends said, "You say you know Roger Maris. Let's just go see." So six of us drove two and one-half hours to Pittsburgh to see the Cardinals play the Pirates. It was May 9, 1967. We got to Forbes Field two hours before the game, and there was No. 9. It was the first time I had ever seen Roger Maris outside of Yankee Stadium, and I figured he wouldn't know me in this setting. I was very nervous. Extremely nervous, because I had five guys with me. I went down to the fence, and my voice quavered: "Ah, . . . Roger."

He turned and said, "Andy Strasberg, what the hell are you doing in Pittsburgh?"

That was the first time I knew he knew my name. "Well, Rog, these guys from my college wanted to meet you, and I just wanted to say hello." The five of them paraded by and shook hands, and they couldn't believe it. I wished Rog good luck and he said, "Wait a minute. I want to give you an autograph on a National League ball." And he went into the dugout and got a ball and signed it. I put it in my pocket and felt like a million dollars.

In 1968, I flew to St. Louis to see Roger's last regular-season game. I got very emotional watching the proceedings at the end of the game. I was sitting behind the dugout, and Rog must have seen me because he later popped his head out and winked. It touched my heart. I was interviewed by the *Sporting News*, who found out I had made that trip from New York City expressly to see Roger retire. The reporter later asked Maris about me, and Roger said, "Andy Strasberg was probably my most faithful fan."

We started exchanging Christmas cards, and the relationship grew. I graduated from college and traveled the country looking for a job in baseball. When the San Diego Padres hired me, Roger wrote me a nice note of congratulations.

I got married in 1976 at home plate at Jack Murphy Stadium in San Diego. Rog and his wife, Pat, sent us a wedding gift, and we talked on the phone once or twice a year. In 1980, Roger and Pat were in Los Angeles for the All-Star Game, and that night we went out for dinner—my wife Patti, me, my dad, Roger and Pat.

When Roger died of lymphatic cancer in December 1985, I attended the funeral in Fargo, North Dakota. After the ceremony, I went to Pat and told her how sorry I felt. She hugged me, and then turned to her six children. "I want to introduce someone really special. Kids, this is Andy Strasberg." And Roger Maris Jr. said, "You're Dad's number-one fan."

There is a special relationship between fans—especially kids—and their heroes that can be almost mystical. Like that time my five college buddies and I traveled to Pittsburgh to see Roger. It's so real to me even today, yet back then it seemed like a dream.

I'm superstitious when it comes to baseball. That day I sat in Row 9, Seat 9, out in right field. In the sixth inning

Roger came up to the plate and, moments later, connected solidly.

We all—my friends and I—reacted instantly to the crack of the bat. You could tell it was a homer from the solid, clean sound, and then we saw the ball flying in a rising arc like a shot fired from a cannon. Suddenly everyone realized it was heading in our direction. We all leaped to our feet, screaming, jostling for position. But I saw everything as if in slow motion; the ball came towards me like a bird about to light on a branch. I reached for it and it landed right in my hands.

It's the most amazing thing that will ever happen in my life. This was Roger's first National League home run, and I caught the ball. Tears rolled down my face. Roger came running out at the end of the inning and said, "I can't believe it." I said, "You can't? I can't!"

The chances of No. 9 hitting a home-run ball to Row 9, Seat 9 in right field on May 9, the only day I ever visited the ballpark, are almost infinitely remote. I can only explain it by saying it's magic—something that happens every so often between a fan and his hero. Something wonderful.

Andy Strasberg

[AUTHOR'S NOTE: *On August 3, 1990, I received a phone call from Roger's son Randy and his wife Fran. They were calling from a hospital in Gainesville, Florida. Fran had just given birth to their first son. Fran and Randy wanted me to know that they named their son Andrew and asked if I would be his godfather. To this day I still can't believe that the grandson of my childhood hero Roger Maris is my namesake and my godson.*]

$\overline{6}$
HEADING FOR HOME

*B*aseball *is continuous like nothing else among American things, an endless game of repeated summers, joining the long generations of all the fathers and all the sons.*

Donald Hall

My Father's Voice

Words have an awesome impact. The impression made by a father's voice can set in motion an entire trend of life.

Gordon MacDonald

What I remember from that day is the rhythmic scuffing of metal cleats across asphalt, followed by the sudden quiet in the hot Nebraska sun. I was only one of a small band of boys that stopped in awe of the colorful archway of clapping flags lining the entrance to the ball fields. It was the moment every kid dreams about. The banner read: Welcome to the Continental American World Series.

I had arrived from New Jersey having had the flu all week. I couldn't stop vomiting on the plane, and then I had exited the airport into the worst August heat you could ever imagine. Still, nothing could stop me from being with my team. I swung my bag of gear from one shoulder to another, shading my eyes with my hand, trying to take it all in.

I looked behind to see my mom pick up her pass at the gate and shook off the last argument with my dad. "You're cavin' your left leg on the inside pitches, and you're not comin' up fast enough from the crouch. You gotta' teach 'em respect." In a way, I was almost relieved that he couldn't come. Still, the image of him as I waved from the plane haunted me.

This is it, I tried to convince myself back to reality, *This is the World Series. . . . Dad would love this.* It felt like I had stepped into the *Field of Dreams,* right down to the rolling cornfields that went as far as the eye could see.

My thoughts were broken by the sound of Mom's voice, soft and encouraging. "If you feel weak or tired in this heat, just tell the coach . . . let him rest you. You have a lot of games to play."

I frowned up at her, but on the inside I was screaming, *The biggest game of my life and you're telling me to take it easy?* Now Dad would have said something like, *If you feel like you're gonna pass out—just call time and splash some water on your face.*

I put on my chest protector and pulled the mask over my helmet, searching the faces of my opponents. *Move with the pitch,* I could hear my father say. *Stay on your toes and move behind the plate. Soft hands, Jake . . . soft, quick hands.*

Mom strolled by the dugout, "Good luck, boys!"

Good luck, I thought. Dad would have said, *Get out there and kick some ass!*

"Batter up!" the ump's voice bellowed, and I snapped back to the present. Their lead-off batter got a single and was now getting ready to test me. He started to run on the wind-up. I caught the pitch, came up and threw with all my might, but the boy was already on second. *Damn, these guys are fast.*

"Good try, Jake," Mom yelled from the bleachers.

I didn't turn around, but heard my father say, *Should've gotten him! Come up faster and fire!*

When the same boy tried to steal third, I was way ahead of him. I pivoted and nailed him cleanly, even with the slide.

Teach 'em respect, Dad's voice echoed in my ears. I picked up my helmet and adjusted my catcher's mask.

"Way to go! Good throw!" Mom yelled.

I chuckled as the words of my father echoed, *Good throw, but you should've gotten him at second!*

I watched a new pitcher from the batter's box, confident that I could hit him. I stood outside the limed rectangle swinging my bat to the rhythm of the warm-up pitch. There was that voice again, *Square up your shoulders, step in toward the plate. Keep your eyes on the ball and don't forget to widen your stance. Teach 'em respect.*

As I waited to deliver my lesson, I heard my Mom's advice, *Above all, Jake—have fun.*

Boy! I never heard Dad say that!

I walked up to the plate repeating his words, *Gotta stay level on the swing, widen my stance and commit hard.*

What I got was a satisfying double and an RBI.

The seventh inning went down like quicksand. There were errors in the field and the other team rallied in hitting. One error led to another, and soon we were sinking fast. The more we fought, the deeper we got. We walked away that day with an 8–5 loss.

Mom and I rode back to the hotel. I was thankful for the silence. Dad would've wanted to discuss every mistake. I would always answer him by rolling my eyes and hearing him say, *You've got a lousy attitude! If you can't take criticism, you'll never get better.*

Mom finally broke the baseball silence when we got to the hotel, "Tough game, but you played well. You and your team put up a fight today. You should be proud of your effort."

Now Dad would've said, *You played tough, but not tough*

enough. Now, can I give you just a little bit of advice? I rolled my eyes just thinking about it.

"I'm gonna call your father and tell him how you made out. He felt so bad that he couldn't take time off from work. I know he's home goin' crazy waiting for our call." She dialed and turned to me. "Do you want to tell him?"

"You tell him." I didn't want to explain

She didn't argue, "Hi, Hon. We just got back. It's hotter than the hammers of hell out here—and not a tree in sight. A hundred and ten on the field, do ya believe that? These poor boys . . . and Jake being sick all week and wearing all that heavy gear in this heat . . ." I couldn't stand it. She made me sound like a wimp. I yanked the phone from her hand in midconversation.

"Hello? Dad? Well . . . we lost our first game. My throws were late to second—these guys play far off-base and run on everything. I know, Dad, but I'm only as fast as the pitcher gets the ball to me. Dad! . . . Dad! . . . will you listen to me? I got two men at third, one at home—boy, was that a great play. Yeah, two outs, first and third, and I called the trick play. . . . You know when I look like I'm throwin' down to second, but I go to short and he fires back to home . . . and the guy hammered me and I still held on. I got on base every time, three singles and a double with two RBIs . . . And Dad?" All of a sudden there was a kind of choking silence between us and some kind of liquid began to fill my eyes. The words just spilled from my throat, "I really need you, Dad—I mean, I wish you were here. . . . I love you, too, Dad."

I handed the phone back to Mom and she was silent as she listened. "Well, you have to do what you have to do." She tossed a pillow playfully in my direction as she hung up the phone. "Your dad's getting a flight out tonight. Work is gonna have to do without him. Somethin' about his boy needing him."

And I realized at that moment I knew the true meaning of respect.

Jake Mannon
As told to Lois J. Mannon

[AUTHOR'S NOTE: *Jake is now a Division 3 college catcher, varsity starter and team captain. When asked about his ability, he always credits his dad—and yes, they still argue after every game.*]

Spring Sounds, Spring Dreams

Fatherhood is responsibility, it's definitely humility, a lot of love and the friendship of a parent and a child.

Denzel Washington

Reluctant spring finally shows up in our town Wednesday. The balls, bats and gloves are on the sofa when I returned home from work.

"Thayer, Dad?"

"Definitely."

Thayer Field, named for the philanthropists who once owned half our community, stretches off a back road behind the elementary school. Twin diamonds, soon to bustle with ballplayers, beckon like long-neglected lovers. Pines, seventy- or eighty-foot-tall green monsters, line the ball fields' eastern edge. An occasional passing car, a train moaning through the distance, and a dog's bark or bird's whistle are the only sounds that carry through the still, clean air.

It is a good place to be on the first real day of spring, a good place to be with a boy who loves baseball.

"You want to hit?"

"Nah. Hit me some first."

The boy pulls his hay-colored fielder's glove onto his left hand and trots toward second. Crabgrass that took root last summer lies brown and dead in the spots where pivoting shortstops and sliding baserunners had sprayed away the infield's stone dust.

Thwack. I stand under a great gray backstop that hovers like a giant's catcher's mitt above home plate. I swing the wooden bat and hit a soft grounder to the boy. He scoops it up, tosses it back on a bounce.

Thwack, thwack. I hit grounders, soft, then harder—at him, then to his left, to his right. "Stay down," I say, but the boy knows. He fields with ease, a pretty fair ballplayer.

Thwack, thwack. I hit pop-ups and liners.

The boy comes in and I go out to the mound. I pitch. Soft straight throws at first, harder now and harder still.

Thwack, thwack. The boy rips his blond thirty-inch Louisville Slugger around, sending line drives into the wet yellow-brown grass of the outfield.

"Try to pull it," I yell. He drills a shot that kisses the line in left. "Hey, hey," I yell to the season. I feel mechanical-legged, like a Babe Ruth running from death, as I chase the ball down. I feel like a lucky man.

I know a man in my town, a quiet, friendly man. He comes alive when he coaches soccer, pounding up and down on September fields with his sons and the other players, shouting instructions to the kids in the crisp evening air of autumn. I stand at the pitcher's mound. I know how he feels. Here I am, a man who flopped at Little League, pitching to a son who loves the game, a son who can flat-out hit, a son who dreams the truest American dream.

Will the dream come true? Will it take him all the way, forty miles beyond the tall pines to Fenway Park? Probably not. But who cares? Hearing that *thwack, thwack, thwack,* that sweet song from the sweet spot, is enough.

The minutes pass quickly. The sun drops behind the western horizon, painting the sky around the clock tower of the 175-year-old Bulfinch Church in pinks and blues and purples. A man who had been pitching to his son and another boy on the other field calls it a day. I almost shout "Isn't this great?" as he drives past. But I don't. The other boy rides his bike over, puts on his glove and joins us in the field.

"John," a woman's voice calls from an unseen house five minutes later. "John."

"See ya," the boy says to us. "Thanks." He slides his glove onto his handlebars and pedals off.

Dusk comes a'creeping. The sparrows sitting in the maple saplings along the chain-link fence sing louder, railing at the end of such a day.

Dong, dong, dong, dong, dong, dong sounds the bell in the Bulfinch tower.

"That's it," I say. "I can't even see the ball."

"One more," he says. Always the boy says, "One more." "One more."

I wind and deliver. I listen for the thwack, fearing the ball my eyes can no longer pick up, delighting that the boy can hit it hard enough to frighten his old man.

He's eleven now. Some year soon he will not want to play with Dad. But Jewel and Lisa, my little girls, ah— Jewel is four and already she talks about playing soccer. I think about pounding down a September field with her. *Oh, lucky man,* I say to myself.

Paul Della Valle

A Little League Mom

While raising our first three sons, my wife had put aside her dislike of sports and served as a Little League mother. Now, eight years after the birth of our last son, she was about to have a fourth child.

After the baby arrived, the nurse came out to the hospital waiting room to get me. My wife was on a stretcher being wheeled back to her room when I caught up with her. "Your husband doesn't know what you had," the nurse said, prompting her.

My wife looked up with a drowsy smile and answered, "Another four years of Little League—that's what I had."

Harry Del Grande

A Guide to Little League Parenting

Kids should practice autographing baseballs. This is a skill that's often overlooked in Little League.

Tug McGraw

Congratulations. You've just reached another Kodak moment in the great photo album of life. You've become a "Little League parent."

What's that? Hanging back a little because you're new? Not quite sure what's expected of a Little League parent? Well, fear not. I was a rookie not too long ago just like you. If you want to look seasoned here are some hints.

First, as a Little League parent, you'll want to have been "quite a good little ballplayer yourself, back in your day." This allows you to join the other parents in the pregame, advice-to-the-coaches and warm-up sessions. Your extraordinary experiences—before the trick knee developed, cutting your promising young career short—will be cherished by all.

Then there's the jargon. You'll use expressions that are not that common in everyday life. Like "good eye." Good eye, of course, means letting a ball go by that was too fast to see anyway, but it turned out not to be a strike.

I suggest practicing these expressions during everyday life. Like when your accountant finds a little something in your favor. "Good eye, Bob," you might say. "Way ta look 'em over."

Another common expression is "Atta boy, got a piece of it." This means your kid hit a foul ball. For some parents this is the most exciting it ever gets. At this point you are allowed to jump up and down and say clever things like "Okay now . . . hit 'em where they ain't." Some of you may even be tempted to leap over the fence to hug the little darling. Of course that's strictly against the rules.

Oh? You didn't know there were rules? Oh sure. They hand them out at the same time they hand out the concession-stand duty sign-up sheet.

Rule one: Parents are not allowed in the dugout or on the field—team cap or no team cap.

Rule two: Parents are not allowed to feed kids while they are playing ball. This includes trying to slip them something just before they bat, like a double-fudge sugar cookie and a caffeine-laden Jolt cola.

Rule three: Parents are not allowed to boo the other team's parents.

Rule four: Parents are not allowed to curse the umpire. I did that in one game early on and guess what? Next week I was the umpire.

Rule five: Parents may not offer the coach free Amway products to just let their kid stay in until Grampa Earl figures out how to get the stupid batteries in the video camera.

Rule six: Parents must allow younger siblings to eat stuff like snow cones that will easily spill onto their clothing and Gummi Bears that stick to their teeth. This makes getting Little League sponsors like Community Cleaners and Valley Dental much easier.

Speaking of clothing, there are some dos and don'ts here also. For instance, ladies should refrain from wearing miniskirts in the stands. It distracts the other spectators, the coaches and some of the older Little Leaguers. Fat men with white legs should not wear shorts. The glare can blind the infielders and it causes hot dog sales to plummet. All parents should avoid wearing anything that does not look good with gum stuck on it.

Finally, we have the after-game etiquette. This means hand slapping for the kids. The two teams must line up in rows and march toward each other saying things like "good game" and "nice try." Parents should approach the opposing bleachers in much the same manner, but are allowed to make excusatory comments about the wind, sun, playing conditions, poor coaching, bad calls, day of the week, recent illnesses and heavy scholastic load.

They are also allowed to make excuses for their kids' performances.

Now that you know the rules, glad to see you out there. Little League needs all the athletic supporters it can get.

Ernie Witham

THE FAMILY CIRCUS By Bil Keane

"Can we delay the start of the game, Coach?
My dad's recharging his camcorder battery."

Reprinted with permission from Bil Keane.

Yerr Out!

Setting a good example for your children takes all the fun out of middle age.

William Feather

My father gave me a great example of self-control when I was a boy watching a church-league softball game.

Dad was forty-three at the time and very active. Though he wasn't known for hitting grand slams, he was good at placing the ball and beating the throw. Singles and doubles were his specialty, and he did the best he could with what he had.

This particular dusty, hot Phoenix evening, Dad poked a good one right over the second baseman's head, and the center fielder flubbed the snag and let the ball bloop between his legs.

My dad saw this as he rounded first base, so he poured on the steam. He was 5 feet 10 inches, 160 pounds, and very fast. He figured that if he sprinted for third and slid, he could beat the throw.

Everyone was cheering as he sent two of his teammates over home plate. The center fielder finally got his feet under him and his fingers around the ball as Dad headed toward third. The throw came as hard and fast as the outfielder could fire it, and Dad started a long slide on that sun-baked infield. Dust flew everywhere.

The ball slammed into the third baseman's glove but on the other side of Dad—the outfield side—away from a clear view from the ump, who was still at home plate. Our team's dugout was on the third base side of the diamond, and every one of the players had a clear view of the play.

Dad's foot slammed into third base a solid second before the ball arrived and before the third baseman tagged his leg. But much to the amazement—and then dismay—and then anger—of the team, the umpire, who hesitated slightly before making his call, yelled, "Yerr out!"

Instantly, every member of Dad's team poured on to the field and started shouting at once—Dad's teammates were intent on only one purpose: They wanted to win, and by golly they knew they were right!

The two runners who had crossed home plate before Dad was called out had brought the score to within one. If Dad was out—and we all knew he wasn't—his team was robbed of a single run.

With only one inning left, this one bad call could cost them the game.

But just as the fracas threatened to boil over into a mini-riot, Dad silenced the crowd. As the dust settled around him, he held up a hand. "Guys, stop!" he yelled. And then more gently, "There's more at stake here than being right. There's something more important here than winning a game. If the ump says I'm out, I'm out."

And with that, he dusted himself off, limped to the bench to get his glove (his leg was bruised from the slide), and walked back into left field all by himself, ready to begin the last inning. One by one, the guys on his team gave up the argument, picked up their own gloves, and walked out to their positions on the field.

I've got to tell you, I was both bewildered and proud that night. My dad's character was showing, and it sparkled. He may have been dusty, but I saw a diamond standing out there under the lights, a diamond more valuable than all the runs his team might have scored.

For a few minutes that evening I was a rich kid, basking in my father's decision to be a man, to hold his tongue instead of wagging it, to settle the dust instead of settling a score. I knew his character at that selfless moment was worth more than all the gold-toned plastic trophies you could buy.

Dad held court that night and the verdict came down hard and he was convicted of being a man . . . and the evidence that proved it was his powerful use of that awe-inspiring weapon. Self-control.

Clark Cothern

The Cold Breeze of Baseball

Believe in something larger than yourself.

Barbara Bush

It was the high school county tournament, the one that would determine who was the best, and it lasted only one day. As we all stepped off of that big yellow bus you could see in our eyes that this day was unlike any other. The bleachers already had a crowd. The parents were already trying to get the best seat so they could see their son become the next Joltin' Joe. And as I entered the dark and damp dugout, a strange, cool breeze ran down my spine.

As I started to loosen up my arm, every single throw I made seemed like it had to be perfect. Every single shag I took in left field felt like I was running down a game-winning hit. But at the same time everything about me was nervous!

Earlier in the morning over a plate of hotcakes and sausage, my father told me he would try to make the game as soon as he got off work. But I knew from his hectic work schedule that it was doubtful. He isn't the kind of guy who cheered when I had a good time. A retired Navy veteran, he kept his emotions to himself, and I had always wished I could change that with hard work and dedication through baseball. Maybe my wish would come true.

Our first seed pinned us up against the toughest team in the tournament. Fortunately, due to a strong coaching decision, our number-one ace was ready to go. He had the width of Fernando Valenzuela and the height of Randy Johnson and, with that combination, he was deadly. One, two, three innings went by and not a single hit. With the score 3–2 in the ninth, we felt bold, confident of a win. Our clutch relief man came in and struck the first two guys out—both looking. The next man up was definitely going to strike out! Right? Wrong! A hit to left center looked like it came out of one of those old pirate cannons. I reacted and took an angle at this ball where I would have to be moving fast. I sprawled out like a cheetah across the thick grass. With my eyes still scared shut to see the outcome, I opened them and to my amazement there was the ball on the top of my glove like a snowcone on a summer day. The game was saved. But still as I trotted proudly back to the dugout, I gazed to the stands and didn't see my father. *He isn't going to show,* I thought to myself.

At a single elimination tournament we had just knocked off the toughest team and were halfway to a championship. The next team we had to face was one we had dealt with before and one that had beaten us in extra innings on a humiliating home run.

One hour later, after enjoying the glory of victory, we were back on the field. Our third-string catcher was in, so we knew that our offense was going to have to step up to make this a ball game.

Again, we had a tight game all the way through with the score of 5–3, not in our favor. The game seemed to move very slowly for us on the offensive side. A couple of singles brought us the three runs, but it didn't seem like this game was going in the right direction.

Being the lead-off hitter for the season, I felt it was my job to get something started or maybe even something to end! All of a sudden it was the top of the ninth. On our squad we all gathered in the dugout and said that this was it. This was the last chance we have to prove that we are the champions. With a little advice from our coach and our rally caps on, we were going to turn this game around. First guy up walks—next batter hits into a double play! Already two outs and no one on! Our hopes started to dwindle as a cold breeze came through again. Perhaps this was the sign of a change? The seventh and eighth hitters both walk. The next batter hits a screamer at the second baseman. As the runners are advancing the second baseman bobbles the ball and all of a sudden it is bases loaded with two outs.

Here I come to the plate, palms drenched and wide-eyed, realizing that it has all fallen on me—5-3 in the top of the ninth inning. The coach from the other squad comes in and brings in his relief pitcher, Butch. I remember to this day the diabolical look in this guy's eyes and the sound of his name over the loudspeaker. I step up to the plate and wipe my brow, dig my cleats into the dirt, and sit and wait on the pitch. One ball, two balls, three balls. Am I going to walk? One strike, two strikes. Am I going to strike out? As a full count quickly sneaks up on me, I take a good step out of the box and look to the crowd. Maybe I will see some kind of answer? Maybe someone can help me? At that very moment, still in his suit from work, I see my father. He doesn't know that I see him and I quickly turn back to the hitter's box and dig in again. I choke up on the bat about two inches and take a half step up in the plate.

The next pitch looked like a melon to me. It came at me with such a perfect spin and speed that when I made contact it felt like I actually didn't hit anything at all. As I swing through I look, and this white object that was coming at me around eighty miles an hour is quickly going the other way at the same speed. The crowds' cheers are a low hum to me as I concentrate on the flight of the ball. It travels deep into left field and slams against the fence. I round second base and make a diving, head-first, Pete Rose–style slide, into third. "Safe!" As I lay in the dirt with my mouth full of some of the best dirt I have ever tasted, I gaze up and see my father throwing high fives with the other fans and turn to me and wink. Game won, 6–5.

That wink from my father showed acceptance and emotion I have never seen. To this day, we speak and joke about that game, the snowcone catch, the famous triple and the Pete Rose slide. And it is because of the game of baseball that this can happen.

Dale Wannen

Bringing Up Son . . .
and Father, Too

*Until you have a son of your own . . . you will
never know the joy, the love beyond feeling that
resonates in the heart of a father as he looks
upon his son.*

Kent Nerburn

His children are growing up. This is not exactly a news
bulletin, he tells the woman on the bench next to him. It's
what children do. It's their thing.

Still, he says, facing the baseball diamond, he thought
all this growing up would be gradual. Instead, his kids
seem to lurch from one age to the next, the way his oldest
takes the corners in his driving lessons, shifting from one
gear into the next with the most unnerving sounds.

He remembers when his oldest was only three. The
nursery-school boy holding his hand said hello to someone on the street. How could the son know someone his
father didn't know? Even then, he felt a tiny electric shock
of independence.

Now they were going through rites of passage again. The oldest is getting his license. The youngest is heading for junior high school.

On cue, the thirteen-year-old came up to bat. In a matter of weeks, months, the boy has gotten it together . . . the wrists, the stance, the eye. It was as if his body had been preparing for today's final exam. He passed it with a solid double.

The father watched him as only parents watch their own. Too proud one minute and too critical the next. To be a parent is to know excess. But today he felt something else, between wonder and wistfulness, between love and loss.

Maybe, he says to the woman, he is going through a kind of adolescence himself. Maybe parents go through a second one with their kids: caught here between the pleasure of seeing them grow and the pain of letting them go.

He chronicles the little things. The projects they bring home from school have changed. A butcher-block table replaces the first raw wooden-block candlestick. A sixteen-page civics paper replaces the crayons. The boy heading off for camp once had anxiety; now he has a list and extra socks.

While they talk and watch, the teams change sides. The thirteen-year-old swoops by to pick up a glove and heads for third base. Someone hits a line drive right at him, and the boy drops it.

The father is on his feet in a second and then back down again. He tells the woman: Two years ago the boy would have been in tears; now he recovers quickly. The woman tells him: Two years ago you would have been compulsively coaching; now you are a spectator.

Yes, he says, we are both growing up. But, he adds grumpily, the difference between my son and me is that I have been his age and he has never been mine. The two laugh. This is a difference that makes no difference.

Yes, once upon a time, this man thought he knew a great deal about fathering. He had, after all, been a child, had a father. He pictured himself guiding his children around the potholes of his own youth. He would pour everything he had learned about life into their heads so that they would be protected from the worst.

He thought his life would be a foundation they would build on from where he left off, like skyscrapers.

But his children are more like what he HAD been than like he wished he had been. Now, gradually, he was beginning to accept what Doris Lessing once wrote, that "his son, all of them would have to make the identical journey he and his contemporaries had made, to learn lessons, exactly as if they had never been learned before."

In turn, he was learning what his father had learned before him: about the intensity of feeling and wanting for his children, about the need for letting go. The game ended. The lanky younger son loped over. He handed the forty-two-year-old man a glove and a ball. He took three dollars to buy pizza with the team and took off. Halfway across the field, the boy yelled, "Hey, Dad, thanks for coming."

The man waved after him. It is okay. It is what happens. They grow up.

Ellen Goodman

Something Wonderful

One home run for my entire career.

The shot came on a Saturday in June when I was ten years old. I still smell buttered toast whenever I think about the ironed blue-and-white uniform that my mother left on the bed that morning. She folded the pants and shirt, leaving them close to my pillow.

I remember pulling on the white pants with blue stripes and looking at myself in the mirror. Back then, the hair was brown and cut in the style of the day, which is to say a flattop. Looking in that mirror, I didn't realize another eighteen inches and about one hundred pounds would come to me.

A two-inch black leather belt went around my waist before putting on a white T-shirt and then the short-sleeved baseball shirt.

Mom kept my cleats in the hall closet near the front door. That day, I remember sitting on the staircase steps, lacing up the cleats and telling her that I felt something wonderful was going to happen.

Just have a good time, she said.

Our last game of the season was played on a field we called Fleet Street in Forest Hills, Queens. We already made the play-offs and were eager to finish the regular season. Our record was 8–1 and we faced a team hoping to win the last play-off spot.

Six months short of my eleventh birthday, my dream was to play first base for the New York Yankees when older. I wore No. 7, played first base and learned to switch-hit. Like Mickey Mantle, I took the first pitch and batted fourth in our line-up.

My father came to every game. Usually he stood against the brown iron fence on the third-base line. Back then, his hair was jet black and he was never without a smile.

The opposing pitcher that Saturday was short even for a ten-year-old. His team was sponsored by a pizza parlor that gave us the second soda free. His father coached and older brother played shortstop.

The first three times at bat, Brian Kugleman got me to fly out to left field. That season, I tagged the outfield fence twice, only to kick the dust while running toward first base.

Kugleman was one of the better pitchers in the league. Good control and knew how to move the ball around the plate. His first pitch to me in the last half of the seventh nicked the outside corner and the umpire called strike one.

There were two outs and nobody on base. I knew this was my last at bat of the day.

His next pitch was inside and forced me out of the batter's box. I looked down the third-base line and saw my father leaning over the fence. He yelled words of encouragement but I heard none of his advice. Then, when our eyes locked, he clenched both his fists as though he held a bat. He motioned for me to swing faster just like when we practiced in the backyard.

Thirty-five years later, I still see the ball coming toward the plate and Kugleman's black cap falling on the mound. My left foot moved forward in the brown dirt before the bat and ball connected. The crack of the wooden bat hitting that ball remains louder in my memory than when one of the children cries.

The ball went in a slow arch over the fence in the gap between left and center fields. I remember hearing my father call out my name. Never again would he cheer as loudly for me as he did that day.

When rounding first, my heart beat through that short-sleeved shirt just as it would many times years later. The second baseman, a third-grade classmate, hit me with his glove as I passed him. Going from second to third, there was a wide smile on my face. I still see my father slapping the iron fence with his right hand and can hear the sound of the fence rattling.

Rounding third toward home, I saw teammates crowded around the plate. Somebody yelled out, "Don't forget to touch the plate." I remember that, because one foot away from home, I stopped and then jumped on the plate with both feet.

We went on to win the game 7–3. While walking back to our car, I passed Kugleman. He was crying because his team didn't get into the play-offs. "Nice shot," he said.

Back home, I told Mom what had happened even before the screen door closed behind me. In my hand was the ball, signed by our manager and my teammates. She looked at the ball and then at me.

"Told you something wonderful would happen," I said.

Robert Remler

The Bravest Man

When I was in high school we had to read a play once about a man who was sentenced to death. I don't remember too much about the play except that the man who was about to die was terribly scared and the chaplain of the prison—or somebody who had come to visit him in his cell—tried to comfort him by telling him a line of poetry from Shakespeare. I'm not much on poetry and I don't know very much about Shakespeare, but I have never forgotten the line because the prisoner on his way to his execution kept repeating it. It went, "Cowards die many times before their deaths; the valiant never taste of death but once."

The bravest man I ever knew was my father. He died the winter after my first year in the major leagues, when I was twenty and he was only forty-one. He died of Hodgkin's disease, a form of cancer like leukemia. He knew he had it. He knew it for a long time. He was a tremendously strong man but the disease weakened him so much that he was like a shell of what he used to be. He never told me he was sick, and I believe he never told anybody, until we found out about it by accident.

Here's how I learned about it. In the second game of the 1951 World Series, which was my first World Series, I fell while chasing a fly ball in the outfield in Yankee Stadium, and I hurt my knee badly. I was taken home to the hotel where I was living in New York City, and then I had to go to the hospital. My father had come up from home to see the World Series and he had left the game with me and come to the hotel. Now he went with me in a taxi to the hospital. He got out of the cab first, outside the hospital, and then I got out. I was on crutches and I couldn't put any weight on the leg that was hurt, so as I got out of the cab I grabbed my father's shoulder to steady myself. He crumpled to the sidewalk. I couldn't understand it. He was a very strong man and I didn't think anything at all about putting my weight on him that way. He was always so strong. Well, the doctors took him into the hospital, too, and they examined him and then they told me how sick he was. It was incurable, they said, and he had only a few months to live.

After the Series was over and we had gone home to Commerce, Oklahoma, my wife Merlyn and I took my father up to the Mayo Clinic in Rochester, Minnesota, to see if they could do anything. They gave him treatments that eased his pain, but there was nothing anybody could do to cure him. He went home again to Commerce, but then during the winter he decided to go out to Denver. He said there was some hospital or other out there that said it could cure him, and he said he thought he'd go out there and see.

He knew they couldn't cure him. But he went out to Denver so that the little kids in our family—I'm the oldest and my sister and three brothers were all just little kids at that time—wouldn't see him wasting away, getting thinner and thinner and sicker and sicker. So he went out to Denver, and he died there. He never complained, he never acted scared, and he died like a man. That line from that play fitted him for sure: "Cowards die many times before their deaths; the valiant never taste of death but once."

My father was brave in lots of ways. I was the oldest child and I was born in October of 1931, right in the middle of the Depression, in Spavinaw, Oklahoma. Kids nowadays don't have any idea of what the Depression was like—it's just a word in the history books—and that's great. But it was a hard time to bring up a family, especially where we lived, which was one of the poorest parts of the country. Even in wealthy parts of the country, people were standing in line for food. Finding work and earning money were the hardest things in the world to do, and keeping a family alive and fed and happy at the same time was even harder. But he did both, he and my mother (she was pretty brave, too; she had to make do without very much—she did all our cooking on a wood stove, for one thing—but we never felt we were without anything). My father never quit, never admitted defeat.

One year he traded our house in Commerce, where he was working as a miner in the lead and zinc mines we have there, for a farm out in the country. It wasn't much of a farm—we lived in Dust Bowl country and a lot of people had quit and gone to California (you've heard of the Okies, haven't you?). But he thought maybe a farm might mean a better life for us kids. The very first year he had it, there was a flood and the river came up over the farm and ruined it. My father just picked up, went back into town, and down into the mines again.

My father loved baseball and he always wanted me to be a ballplayer. He named me for Mickey Cochrane, the great catcher who was at his peak about the time I was born. Actually, Cochrane had a bad World Series the month I was born, when Pepper Martin and the St. Louis Cardinals were stealing bases on him and running wild. Cochrane was criticized, but baseball men said it wasn't his fault so much as it was his pitchers', who didn't hold the runners tight to their bases. Anyway, one bad Series couldn't affect my father's admiration for Cochrane, and maybe he named me Mickey just to show people that he was still loyal to the man he admired.

When I was growing up my father used to take me with him all the way to St. Louis to see major-league games. That was the nearest big-league town in those days, and he and friends of his would drive six hundred miles up and back on a weekend to take in a couple of games. My father always took me with him.

I guess my making the major leagues was one of the happiest things that ever happened to my father, and I often think how glad I am that I made it before he died. Though I almost didn't.

That first year I was with the Yankees, when I was nineteen, I struck out an awful lot. Casey Stengel was the manager and he played me a good part of the time, but even though I got some hits now and then, I kept striking out. It was terrible. Finally, in July, the Yankees decided to send me down to the minors to get rid of the strikeout habit. It is a depressing thing being sent down to the minors, and I felt low. I thought I had missed my big chance. I figured they had looked at me and didn't want me.

The Yanks sent me to Kansas City, which at that time was a Yankee farm club in the American Association. There I got even worse. I believe I got one hit in my first twenty-two at bats, and that was a bunt. My father came up from home to Kansas City to see me play. I was living in a hotel there and, boy, was I glad to see him. I wanted him to pat me on the back and cheer me up and tell me how badly the Yankees had treated me and all that sort of stuff. I guess I was like a little boy, and I wanted him to comfort me.

He said, "How are things going?"

I said, "Awful. The Yankees sent me down to learn not to strike out, but now I can't even hit."

He said, "That so?"

I said, "I'm not good enough to play in the major leagues, and I'm not good enough to play here. I'll never make it. I think I'll quit and go home with you."

I guess I wanted him to say, Oh, don't be silly, you're just in a little slump, you'll be all right, you're great. But he just looked at me for a second and then in a quiet voice that cut me in two he said, "Well, if that's all the guts you have I think you better quit. You might as well come home right now."

I never felt as ashamed as I did then, to hear my father sound disappointed in me, ashamed of me. I shut my mouth. I didn't say anything more about quitting and going home. I kept playing. Things got better and a month later the Yankees called me back up to the majors.

I have wondered sometimes exactly what it was. I know that I wanted my father to comfort me. He didn't. He didn't give me any advice. He didn't show me how to swing the bat any different. He didn't give me any inspiring speeches. I think that what happened was that he had so much plain ordinary courage that it spilled over, and I could feel it. All he did was show me that I was acting scared, and that you can't live scared.

A year later he was dead. I realized then that he was dying when he came to see me in Kansas City, though he never gave any sign to me. He didn't die scared, and he didn't live scared.

Mickey Mantle
and Robert W. Creamer

A Game of Catch

I waited in the backyard with my thirty-year-old Rawlings PM5 fielder's glove while my nine-year-old son, Jonah, at my suggestion, bolted upstairs in search of the mitt I'd recently bought him.

In 1955 in Lubbock, Texas, it had been a crisp, sunny day much like this one when my team, the Scrappers, had beaten the Rockets 3–2 in an extra-inning Little League game. We had a new field (built by the Lion's Club), new bleachers (Ace Hardware), and an official, built-to-perfection, Little League specification pitcher's mound. On that special day, I'd been atop it.

I threw the ball hard that day. I pitched good. My teammates chattered, "You got him, Babe," "You're in charge, Richard," "Hey batter, hey batter," and—best of all— "You're the one, Big Rick." In one game I'd gone from plain Richard to "Big Rick." "Elated" fails to adequately capture how I felt that day.

The memory intensified my desire to "play ball!" I wished Jonah would hurry.

Hurry up, I thought, stepping off the official Little League distance between an imaginary pitching rubber and home plate. Jonah and I could build a mound on that spot where grass hardly grew anyway. Home plate could go over there, and the fence would be a backstop. Today, though, we'd just play catch. Or maybe I'd toss the ball lightly to him, and he'd tap it back to me with the bat. *It'll help Jonah learn to keep his eye on the ball,* I thought. He probably won't be a home-run hitter. I wasn't. But he'll be a solid, reliable hitter. And a great pitcher. Good arms run in the family. I'll help him take care of his arm. No curves for years. I threw too many. Probably why my pitching career peaked at sixteen. I don't like to think about it.

Where was Jonah, for goodness' sake?

I tossed myself several pop-ups, catching them Willie Mays–style. Willie was the best. I'd seen him play an exhibition game in 1956. I was eleven. Willie, the incomparable and world-renowned center fielder for the Giants, had looked at me and nodded. He looked right into my eyes. I'd been too starstruck to nod back, and it's a moment I'd like to live over. This time I'd say, "Say hey, Willie. Say hey." Willie used to say "Say hey" a lot, or so I'd heard. Too bad Jonah never saw Willie play. I'd tell him about Willie Mays, but I'd emphasize the importance of learning the fundamentals of fielding before trying to catch Willie-style.

Where was Jonah?

I threw a few onto the roof and, as they rolled off, I scooped them out of the air, faking a perfect peg to home. I reminded myself to tell Jonah to keep the ball low on his pegs when playing the outfield and to remember to check where his runners were before every pitch. He'd have to watch runners as a pitcher, too, and learn to throw from a stretch.

So much to learn. We'd have to start now. I went inside and yelled. "Jonah, hurry up. Jonah, what's up, pal? Jonah?"

I ran upstairs. No Jonah. I sprinted downstairs and into the front yard, still sporting ball and glove. My wife, Leti, was repotting a plant.

"You seen Jonah?"

With a side glance, she said, "He's at Brennen's playing Nintendo."

My denial systems flew up like an armored shield. "No," I said, as if she were sorely mistaken. "He and I are going to play catch."

"All I know is, Brennen came by, Jonah asked if he could go play Nintendo, and they left."

No catch. No high flies. Nintendo? Freckle-faced Brennen chosen over the pitching ace of the Scrappers? My heart fell into my stomach.

I skuffed back through the house to the backyard. Disappointment is a feeling like no other. It wracked my guts and made my bones ache. Seconds later, a funny loneliness set in—a longing—for Jonah, for somebody to play catch with, for times past. To be "Big Rick," maybe. I thought, *This is how little boys feel when their dads are too busy for them, not how dads feel when their little boys are too busy for them.* I fielded a few more off the roof, but there was no zip in it.

Later, after supper, I told Jonah that he'd left me stranded and I was miffed. He looked at me with the wisdom of a sage, put his hand on my shoulder, and said—I swear—precisely these words: "Dad, I love you and I like you and we have the rest of our lives together. Don't worry about it."

It was exactly what I needed to hear. I felt soothed, yet off balance. Who was the older, wiser one here, anyway? There must have been a typo and Opie had gotten Andy's lines.

It's been that way with Jonah and me a few times since because, drat it, there is no script. He's never been my son before, nor I his dad. This puts us in the position of figuring things out as we go along. It's not a bad deal. In fact, all in all, I like it. While life experience is valuable, there's something to be said for a fresh point of view. There's an essence to who we really are. It's had many labels: "soul" for one.

There are many wise souls on our planet. And it's possible that some of them are housed in small bodies, love Nintendo and have never heard of Willie Mays.

Rick Carson

THE FAMILY CIRCUS   **By Bil Keane**

"Anytime you're ready, Daddy,
I'll be sitting outside growing older."

Reprinted with permission from Bil Keane.

A Father's Glove

A wise father teaches skills. Courage. Concentration on the job at hand. Self-discipline. Enthusiasm. A spirit of enquiry. Gentleness. Kindliness. Patience. Courtesy. And love.

Pam Brown

The story about my new baseball glove, bought shortly after my forty-second birthday, starts with a line drive hit straight at me from thirty feet away by my son, Ben, who was then seven years old. I wasn't wearing a glove, and the ball nearly tore my hand off. I immediately rolled around on the ground, yowling and cussing.

Ben dropped his bat and came running over. His lower lip was trembling and his eyes were filled with tears. "I'm sorry," he said. "Are you hurt bad?" "Not that bad," I said, though in truth my hand felt as though it had been run over by a truck. "The yowling and cussing help considerably. No need to be sorry. That was one wicked hit, partner." His lip stopped trembling then, and he grinned. "Yeah, it was," he said. We looked at each other for a minute, neither of us saying a thing. A change had taken place, and we both knew it. Ben folded his arms, narrowed his eyes and kicked the dirt a couple of times. "Maybe you ought to get a glove," he said. "I guess I better had," I told him. The two of us had been working out behind the house for more than a year, since the night Ben announced he wanted to learn to hit a baseball. He wasn't quite six and could barely swing the lightest bat I could find, but he was determined to become a hitter. Night after steaming-hot Florida night, Ben stood beside the plate we had made out of plywood; I faced him on the mound—on more of a swelling, actually, that had formerly been inhabited by fire ants.

"Hold the bat up," I would say. "Keep your eye on the ball." We had picked a spot just in front of our neighbor's chain-link fence, which served as a backstop. When the ball struck the fence it made a clanging sound, and for the longest time the backyard litany was, "Hold the bat up. Keep your eye on the ball." *Clang.* When Ben did make contact, the results were ten-foot dribblers, foul tips and the occasional five-foot pop-up; but he refused to quit. Neither rain nor attacks of no-see-ums could move him inside. Some nights we played until it was so dark I could barely see him, and he could hardly see the ball. I could hear him inhale as the pitch neared him and exhale when he swung, often sending drops of perspiration farther than the ball. "One more pitch," he'd say. "I can't go in until I hit a good one."

Time passed. The dribblers became slow rollers, the dinky pop-ups became short fly balls, and the prospect of eventually smacking one over the six-foot wooden fence at the far end of the yard—of hitting a "real home run," as Ben put it—loomed as a distinct possibility. Still, there was nothing to suggest I needed a glove, although Ben brought the subject up a number of times, particularly when we weren't pitching and hitting but simply having a good old catch. He had a glove. It seemed only right that I have one, too. He even organized a futile search through a garage full of old cartons and trunks for the glove that got me through Babe Ruth League and high school before disappearing during one of a multitude of house moves.

"Listen," I told him. "I'll be fine without a glove. Just worry about your hitting and catching." The fact that I might be insulting my son, or at least violating his sense of correctness, was somehow overshadowed by the notion that buying a baseball glove in middle age was more frivolous than necessary. The line drive, however, clearly set me straight.

My hand had swollen up to the size of a cow's udder, so it was several days before I made the trip to the baseball section of a sporting goods supermarket. There I was surrounded by a profusion of gloves and enveloped in a rich, intoxicating smell of new leather that instantly took me back to the hot summer afternoon in 1957 when I walked into Wood's Sporting Goods in Burlington, Vermont, and plunked down every penny of the thirty-five dollars I'd made in a week of caddying to buy a Warren Spahn personal model, the last glove I had owned.

Now, in addition to various shades of brown, you can buy black, blue or even red gloves. You can get them with all sorts of interesting buckles and straps and intricately designed webbing. These gloves were a good deal larger than I remembered them, too. They cost a whole lot more, as well, with the best of them up around $150, but they still creaked when you first tried them on, and the familiar feeling of confidence, agility and grace produced by merely smacking a fist into the pocket made time stand still and the price irrelevant.

I was about to forgo dining out for two months and buy a $140 beauty, when the store manager came over with a glove almost as nice. "Gonna surprise your kid with a new glove, huh?" he said. "Well, you're lucky he's left-handed. We got four of these from a place in Tampa that went out of business, and this is the only one left. Cost over a hundred dollars originally. You can have it for thirty-five bucks."

"My kid isn't left-handed," I told him. "I am, and I'll take it."

It was a Wilson, George Brett MVP model, with snap action. Buying it brought back memories I'd kept locked away for nearly thirty years, not because it cost the same as my old Warren Spahn, but because of a question from my son. The two of us were sitting on the floor in my study that night rubbing neat's-foot oil into our gloves, folding and bending them every which way, spitting now and then into the pockets and generally getting ready to resume playing serious backyard ball, when suddenly Ben looked up at me. "Did your father have a glove?" he asked. Ben never knew my father, but he'd been named after him, and from an early age he'd wanted to know every-thing he could about the man. "As a matter of fact, he did have a glove," I answered, and I told him a story I'd for-gotten until just then.

My father was a country doctor, the kind who made house calls late on cold winter nights and sometimes came home with a basket of vegetables from a farmer who had no money to pay him. He had little free time, but one day, when he was leaving the house after dinner to make his rounds at the hospital and he saw me chucking a baseball up against the side of the garage, he stopped, came over and put his arm around me. "You want to throw a few?" he asked me. "Yeah," I answered.

I was eleven, an outfielder on a Little League team, and had a burning desire to be a pitcher. We went around behind the house, paced off the appropriate distance, cut a plate and a rubber from an old hunk of linoleum and began. He had been a pitcher once, in high school and on a semipro team, but he quit to work his way through college and medical school. He still had his old glove, torn, floppy-fingered, without an ounce of padding in it. He might as well have been catching me with a wet napkin stuck to his palm. "You ought to get a catcher's mitt," I told him. "Don't worry about me," he said. "Just get the ball over the plate."

We played almost every night after that. He'd come home with his stethoscope sticking out of his pocket. He would take off his suit jacket and lay it over the back-porch railing. I'd already have the ball and gloves ready. He'd loosen his tie, roll up the sleeves of his starched white shirt and squat down behind the square of linoleum. I was wild at first, as left-handers are supposed to be. "Throw smooth and easy," he'd tell me. "And get the ball over the plate." That was his litany.

My control improved. My speed increased, too. I was sure I was hurting his hand, but he never said a word. Complaining wasn't something he ever did. Then one day he came home with his medical bag in one hand and a paper sack in the other. He lay his jacket over the railing and pulled a brand-new catcher's mitt out of the sack. It was a very cold spring evening, but I remember we were both in our shirtsleeves. As I sat there on the floor with my son, I could hear the sharp pop my pitches made in the clear, still night air when they hit that mitt's pocket. I remember I was grinning so much I could hardly throw, but when I did, the ball seemed to move faster and with more authority. I remember how close I felt to my dad.

A week later, I pitched my first game for my team, the Tigers. We won 4–3, but my father had to deliver a baby at the time, and he missed all but the last inning. I didn't know he was there at all until I heard him honking his car horn from way back behind the right field fence. As I was walking off the field from the pitcher's mound, I turned around and saw him waving with his new glove.

My father taught me to throw a curve, a screwball and a change-up, and though I never amounted to very much as a pitcher, the two of us kept on playing out back of the house from mud season in spring until it began to snow. Then one day, with no warning, my father died. I stopped playing baseball and instead spent my free time backpacking.

My son didn't say a thing to me after my story. He just gave me a big hug and went off to bed. The next night he hit another line drive that caromed off the wooden fence. A week later he drove one over the fence and then began doing that so regularly we decided we had to move to a large field down by the lake near our home.

We were playing there one night when, just as I was about to throw a pitch, he stepped away from the plate and leaned on his bat. "What happened to your father's glove?" he asked. "It got lost along with my Warren Spahn," I told him. "It's too bad he died," he said. "It would've been fun to have him in our game. But I guess in a way we do. I'm real glad you finally bought a glove. Even if I lose it, I've got the story. I'll never forget that."

Philip Singerman

7

FIELD OF
DREAMS

*The romance of baseball . . . is in its capacity
for stirring fantasy. We are never too old or
too bothered to see ourselves wrapping up a
World Series victory with a homer in the
final inning of the seventh game.*

Ron Fimrite

The Chase

Ability is what you're capable of doing. Motivation determines what you do. Attitude determines how well you do it.

Lou Holtz

When I arrived at the *Kansas City Star* in 1989 and began covering baseball, the only George Brett who I knew was from a distance. I'd heard the legendary stories. There was, of course, the Pine Tar Incident. The chase for .400. And the famous three-run homer off Goose Gossage in the 1980 play-offs that helped propel the Royals to their first World Series (that homer is still chilling on replays more than two decades later).

But by 1989, Brett was not the same player that he was in his prime. His knees ached, his right shoulder often throbbed, and the subtle rust on his game saddened me because I never had the privilege of witnessing his greatness firsthand, and knew I probably never would. I had to rely on the accounts of others to relive all of his great moments.

Yet there was one part of Brett that had not fallen prey to the relentless pursuit of time: He was still a warrior, driven by a passion for winning and for being the best. I could see that in his eyes and through his demeanor as he often sat slumped on a chair after one of the frequent losses the Royals experienced in the early 1990s. It still hurt Brett to lose. And I could sense that it hurt his pride that he couldn't lift this team and this organization back to the top as he once did.

But for one glorious moment in 1992, Brett did rise up again, right before my eyes, and defied all probability. I did get my chance to witness his greatness.

As the Royals prepared to wrap up yet another disappointing season in 1992, their fans at least were treated something akin to a pennant race: Brett's race toward three thousand hits. It was, by most definitions, a race. Brett was thirty-nine years old. Rumors persisted that he was about to retire. I even reported a story the previous off-season that then-Royals owner Ewing Kauffman had asked Brett to retire because he felt Brett's skills had diminished too much and because the team needed to make way for its younger players. Brett was crushed. Two days after the story appeared, Kauffman called a press conference to publically apologize to Brett. But the damage had been done, and Brett himself admitted during the 1992 season that his playing days were near an end.

That, of course, made the timing of Brett's pursuit of three thousand hits critical. He obviously wasn't going to retire without getting his three thousandth hit, but with two weeks to go in the '92 season, he was still about twenty hits short. Our newspaper had started the countdown with about two months to go but when he got to 2,975, we began putting the magic number to three thousand in a big box on the front of the sports section every day. Seeing that huge number every day in the newspaper was just another reminder for Brett, I'm sure, of the pressure he was under to get that hit before the season ended.

I knew he didn't want to force himself to come back in 1993 just so he could get to three thousand hits. That would be cheating, in his mind, just milking the game for some self-serving statistic. Not exactly George Brett's style.

With less than two weeks to go in the '92 season, Brett was still ten hits away from three thousand and the hits were becoming harder and harder to come by. Brett's aching shoulder was killing him, and he had immense pain every time he pulled the bat down toward the incoming baseball with that shoulder. But as the team embarked on its final road trip in 1992—a seven-game trip that would start in Minnesota with three games and end in Anaheim with four—Brett started to finally get a bit of luck. He dropped in a few hits during the three-game set in Minnesota and raised his total to 2,995. Brett now had seven games left to get five more hits—four games in Anaheim, and the three-game final home series back in Kansas City. Better yet, Brett now had a realistic chance of getting those five hits in Anaheim, less than half an hour away from where he grew up in El Segundo, California. How perfect. Sportswriters covering the team saw the story lines dropping into our laps.

But unbeknown to us covering the team, Brett had seriously reinjured his shoulder during his last at bat in Minnesota. On the plane ride to California, Brett was in tremendous pain. He never said a word to us about it. Neither did the team's trainers. Monday night, during the first game against the Angels, Brett managed one single but it became apparent that something was wrong with his swing. He was grimacing with each yank of the bat. After the game, he fessed up. He might not be able to finish the season. The pain was intolerable. I could only imagine all that was going through Brett's mind. He had hundreds of friends and relatives at Anaheim Stadium,

was ready
s and bad

to get his
ingful for
s. But we
do it in
Anaheim
a night
al night, a
sically get
uotes, get
hen send
done on a
ree thou-
cause that
icted. Yes,
in Kansas

flared No.
er hit, No.

g a rat'
n to

and they were all there to see
h hit. Now he might not even
season. I know he felt he was

oyals scheduled an appoint-
orthopedist just outside San
covering the team (normally
rs but now there were more
reporters on the three thou-
the way to the appointment.
appointment, he managed a
iscuss the results of his exam-
ore he spoke with us. So back

re the game, Brett and the
he media and announced that
playing again that season, that
the swelling in his shoulder
ing game.
sn't in the starting line-up. He
ow, there were five games to go,
ay night came and went the same.
o go, four hits to go. Brett was dis-
reasons. So was his entourage at
hich included his brother, Ken, who
io analyst. "Man, I know he'd like to
d right here," Ken told me that night.
much."

night, though, it seemed a foregone con-
here was any chance of Brett getting three
in 1992, it would have to come in Kansas
the final three-game homestand. But before
rett began swinging off the batting tee in the
ading to the Royals dugout. The pain was begin-
ubside. A cortisone shot taken a day earlier was

starting to work. He told manager Hal McRae he
to give it a shot. Of course, this was good new
news for us reporters.

Naturally, we were privately rooting for Brett
three thousandth hit in Anaheim—it was mear
him and a great "homecoming" storyline for u
also were crossing our fingers that he would
Kansas City—the two-hour time difference from
to Kansas City made newspaper deadlines o
game almost unimaginable. As it was on a norm
beat writer might have twenty minutes to phy
down to the locker room, grab a few players for c
back up to the press box, compose a story and
it by modem to the paper. The same magic act
night a future Hall of Famer was getting his th
sandth hit would require ten times the effort be
story needed to be as special as the event it dep
we were privately pulling for Brett to pull it off
City.

But Brett had other ideas. In his first at bat, he
2,997 to left. In the fourth inning, he lined anoth
2,998 to left-center.

Uh-oh. We in the press box began experiencir
strange mix of emotions from awe and admiratio
panic. By the time Brett came up to the plate fo
at bat in the sixth inning, Anaheim Stadium wa
Fans were standing, teammates were standin
eyes were fixed on Brett. Well, some of our eyes
on our computer screens, too, and we scrambled
some verbs and nouns together that would mak
sense to be reprinted. Bang. Another hit for
2,999. By then we knew. Everyone in the stadi
ably knew. Brett, ravaged shoulder and all, wa
do it in front of his friends, his family, his mothe
brothers, thirty miles from where he grew up.

that Brett was going to get another at bat and we knew he was going to somehow get his fourth hit of the night.

Then, at about 9:30 Anaheim time, Brett came up for that at bat in the ninth inning. First pitch, *whack.* Brett drilled a one-hopper that nearly beheaded second baseman Ken Oberkfell and sizzled into right field. Number three thousand. The ovation Brett received lasted longer than ten minutes. Tears streamed down his cheeks and he raised his batting helmet and saluted the crowd. He had done the improbable one more time.

I finally got to see that Brett greatness in person. (And I made the deadline, too.)

Jeffrey Flanagan

[EDITORS' NOTE: *Brett, by the way, did come back and play in 1993, and made that his final season.*]

Hot Dog Heaven

It was 1959, and I was an insecure junior-high-school kid in Duluth, Minnesota. The local paper, the *News-Tribune,* ran a contest to choose the batboys for the city's minor-league baseball team, the Dukes. Kids throughout the city sent in essays. Mine was pretty straightforward, noting that I got up at a quarter to five every morning to proudly deliver their wonderful paper. The flattery worked, and I was chosen as one of six finalists.

The contest was put to a citywide vote, with ballots printed in the paper every day to elect two winners. The one with the most votes would be the home-team batboy, and the one with the second most would be visiting-team batboy. I hoped to come in second, because that would mean working with a lot more players, including the Fargo-Moorehead Braves. Like everybody else in that part of the Midwest, I was a big fan of Fargo-Moorehead's parent, the Milwaukee Braves.

The paper ran head-shots of all six of us every day for several weeks. I had the poorest excuse for a duck-butt haircut that any kid of the '50s ever wore, so I wasn't going to win on the basis of looks. But I ran what was, in retrospect, an effective campaign.

I bought a classified ad in the paper, saying "Vote for Steve Carlson for Batboy." The six words cost me less than a dollar, easily affordable with my pay from delivering papers. A popular columnist for the newspaper noticed the ad, and he wrote a piece about the fine, enterprising young man who not only delivered newspapers every morning but knew the power of advertising in the classifieds.

The other key to my success was a random bit of luck. At the time, I was being picked on at school by a popular jock. To make a long story short, the jock also insulted a very popular girl, who retaliated against him by volunteering to manage my campaign for batboy. She gathered hundreds of votes on my behalf.

When the votes were finally counted, I came in number two, and the next summer I was visiting-team batboy.

It's worth pausing for a moment to exclaim the importance of baseball in general, and the Milwaukee Braves in particular, at that time and place. To Minnesota teenagers, the Braves were kings of the world. Their names evoked a sense of magic and glory. Hank Aaron, Eddie Matthews, Warren Spahn, Johnny Hodges, Billy Bruton, Wes Covington, Lew Burdett, Del Crandall, Del Rice. . . . Heck, it just seemed natural that the greatest team on earth would have not just one but two catchers named Del. Everybody in school was chronically bleary-eyed from staying up late, listening to Earl Gillespie's play-by-play and Blaine Walsh's color commentary, brought to you by "those famous names, Miller High Life, Clarke Super 100 Gasoline, and Kent with the Micronite Filter." In our school, if Frank Torre and Elvis Presley had walked into the cafeteria at the same time, Elvis would have been ignored.

Equally, we all hated the New York Yankees. Oh, there were great individual players such as Mickey Mantle and Roger Maris, but the team itself, which seemed to always win the American League pennant, was despised. If, in any given year, the Braves lost the National League pennant to their arch rivals, the Brooklyn Dodgers, we'd all change allegiances and become Dodgers fans during the World Series.

In those heady years of baseball, it was a thrill to deliver bats and chase balls for minor-league players, knowing that some of them would ascend to the majors. When the Fargo-Moorehead Braves were in town, they brought intense excitement, and not just because they were Braves. One of their players—Frank Torre's younger brother, Joe—was burning up the Northern League. It was obvious to everybody that Joe Torre would not only make the big leagues, but would become one of the all-time greats. The fact that I was right down there on the field, able to hear his every comment, even every swear word that Duluth kids had never heard before, made me feel like I was experiencing history.

In late summer, my parents decided, rather abruptly, to move to Vermont. That meant giving up my privileged position. I'd heard some good things about Vermonters, but was apprehensive. These people didn't even have a minor-league team at the time. And the major-league teams they rooted for were, well, could you believe it? The Red Sox and, more unbelievable still, the Yankees? This was going to involve some culture shock.

My last night as batboy was with the Fargo-Moorehead Braves. To me, this was the end of an era, and it needed to go well. The game was unexceptional, other than Joe Torre's performance, which was always exceptional.

But then, something terrible happened. A player tossed me a nickel and asked me to get him a "soda." He was from the South, and as a life-long Minnesotan, I had no idea what he meant by "soda." Baking soda? Soda crackers? Where I lived, the fizzy stuff was always called "pop." So I just sat there, not knowing what to say, and the player got angry at me, berating me for being lazy. It was a total communication breakdown. He thought I was being lazy and insubordinate, when in fact I just didn't understand what he was asking for.

When the game ended, I was in a deep depression. The team members went back to the showers, and I just sat in the dugout. In my last game as batboy, a stupid misunderstanding had destroyed everything. What a way to end what was supposed to be a glorious time of my life.

After what seemed like a long time, sitting with tears in my eyes, I felt a presence next to me. I turned, and it was Joe Torre. He looked me in the eye and said, "The concession stand isn't closed yet. Would you like a hot dog?"

The rest of the conversation is a bit of a blur in my mind. I just remember that the worst evening in my life was suddenly transformed into the best. And even after all these years, I'm amazed that this man, who was already a popular sports idol, was sensitive enough to notice what a depressed kid I was and take the time to cheer me up.

Joe Torre's career, of course, has turned out to be pretty much what we expected: one of the all-time greats. And it's certainly no surprise to me that he has become widely recognized as one of the nicest people in the game.

There's been just one major surprise. Who could have ever guessed back then that Joe Torre would become the manager of the dreaded Yankees?

Steve Carlson

Home Free!

*You are never too old to set another goal or
dream a new dream.*

Les Brown

I hadn't played softball in five years. My career had
ended abruptly back in 1990 when I collided with Paul
McLaughlin, a 6-foot 2-inch, two hundred-sixty-pound
heating and air-conditioning contractor. That was at
Westways on the shores of Lake Kezar, where some local
guys meet every Thursday night during the summer for a
pickup game. I was playing left. Paul was at short. We both
were going for a little Texas leaguer. Paul caught the ball
and me all in one motion. I was knocked cold. When I
came to, I picked up my glove, straightened my glasses
and saw that it was time for me to hang up my cleats. At
forty-five, I was through.

Then this past summer my wife, Ruth, planted a bug in
my ear. "It's Thursday," she said. "Why don't you go up
and play softball?"

"I beg your pardon," I said, putting down my book and
looking out at the lake. It had been raining all week, but
the late afternoon sun had finally broken through.

Sunbeams were dancing on the water. It was going to be a nice evening.

"I said, 'Why don't you go play softball,'" Ruth said much louder.

"Are you kidding? I'm too old to play softball. I've got bursitis and I can't see anything with these new bifocals."

"Plus you don't hear half the time," she added gratuitously.

That wasn't true. After twenty-five years of marriage, I've just become more selective in my hearing, but I wasn't going to tell that to Ruth.

"My hearing has nothing to do with my softball," I said, "but I don't know. I haven't played in five years. Most of the old guys are probably gone and I don't know any of these new kids."

"With all this rain, they might need an extra man and if you don't like it, you can always come home."

Ruth knew how much I loved Thursday night softball. All through the eighties, it was one of my greatest joys. I played every week. I was one of the guys. Outsiders are always welcome at Westways, but Stephen King and I were the only summer folk ever asked on a regular basis.

I could feel the old juices starting to stir. It would be good for me to get out. With all the rain, I was suffering from a slight case of cabin fever and Ruth was right, if I didn't like it, I didn't have to stay. I rocked out of my chair, pulled my Playmate cooler from under the porch, tossed in a six-pack of Moosehead, dug out my glove, boxed my hat and strapped on my bifocals. I was ready. "I'll drop by and see what's happening," I said to Ruth. "If some of the old guys are still there, I might stick around for a couple of innings."

I'd forgotten just how special the little diamond at Westways is, how it glows in the evening sunlight, how it's nestled among the towering pines, how it looks out over Kezar Lake into the White Mountains.

I pulled in next to a row of battered pickups and marveled at the green of the grass, the blue of the lake and the
purple of the mountains. The sound of balls slapping
against leather and the ping of a metal bat said that it was
Thursday night. I grabbed my Playmate, straightened my
hat, spit in my glove and headed for the field. I was back.

Ruth was right. Normally, there'd be fifteen to twenty
guys warming up. Tonight, there were barely a dozen,
most of them familiar faces. John Bliss, the local surveyor,
was busy laying out the bases. Tom McLaughlin, the former first selectman, was playing catch with Eddy Nista,
the current chairman of the board of appeals. Angelo
Campo, a dead ringer for a short, husky Fidel Castro, was
hitting fungoes to Bob Drew, the plumber who first introduced me to Thursday night softball.

Bob Aiken, the manager of the K-Mart over in North
Conway, was raking away the puddles around home plate
with Mark Tripp, the caretaker at Westways. A ball went
streaking over their heads and banged off the top of the
backstop. Sure enough, there was Steven Bennett in deep
center field loosening up his powerful but ever erratic
arm. On the bench drinking a beer was Hopie, Lovell's
oldest and best hippie. "Hey, look what the cat dragged
in," Hopie said as I approached the bench.

"Well, with all this the rain, I thought you might need an
extra glove."

"Damn straight," Hopie said. "It takes a few innings for
these new kids to show up. No dedication. Lousy values."

"Stephen King still come?" I said, trying to give myself
some credibility.

"Naw, Steve's too old, but his kid plays every now and
then."

So much for my credibility.

When we got to sixteen players, John Bliss and Eddy
Nista quietly stepped aside to pick the teams. I always

liked the way the teams were chosen. Nobody ever knew when they were selected. I used to fancy myself as a top pick. Now, I was just happy to be drafted.

"Dave, we're in the field," John Bliss said to me when they were done. "Where do you want to play?"

"I'll take right," I said. "That way, maybe I can stay out of trouble."

"Okay, but try not to run into anyone, haw, haw."

My first at bat came at the bottom of the second. There were two outs and men on first and second. Steven Bennett was on the mound. Even with slow pitch, Steven was having trouble finding the strike zone. "Come on, Dave, there's two ducks on the pond," John Bliss said as I picked up one of the new aluminum bats and stepped into the box. "All we need is a little bingo."

A little bingo, my eye. I was going for the woods. I was going to reintroduce myself with a three-run blast. I went right after the first pitch. It was a just above the letters, but any decent ball player should have been able to reach up and get it.

Thanks to my new bifocals, I reached too high and topped the ball. It dribbled toward third. I chugged toward first. Tom McLaughlin, who usually has a vacuum cleaner for a glove, slipped on the wet grass and bobbled the ball. There was no play at third or second, so he rifled a shot to first. Mark Tripp gave it one of his classic stretches and even with Tom's bobble, I was out by a yard.

"Gee, Dave, looks like you've lost a step or two, or three, or four," Hopie said as I hobbled back to the bench.

My next two at bats were equally disappointing. A little pop to short, followed by a soft liner to second, all with 'ducks on the pond,' all snuffing out a potential rally. Thanks in large part to my anemic performance, we were down by eight runs going into the bottom of the seventh. I was tempted to call it quits, especially when a couple of pickups pulled in and a bunch of young bucks piled out. True to Thursday night softball, they immediately worked their way into the line-up. The best ended up on our side and their powerful bats quickly whittled away at the eight-run lead. Steven Bennett shook his head in disgust as shot after shot sailed into the woods. Going into the bottom of the ninth, we were down by just one.

Like all good athletes, Steven and his side began to bear down. Our first batter sent a scorcher down the third-base line, but Tom McLaughlin looked like a young Brooks Robinson as he neatly backhanded the ball and fired to first. Our kid was fast, but not fast enough. Mark Tripp gave it his best stretch and Hopie, the catcher, called him out.

The next kid launched a rocket to center. It had extra bases written all over it, but the young buck playing center sprinted back and made a Willie Mays over-the-shoulder catch. It was unbelievable. As I popped my last Moosehead, I was glad the game was almost over. These new kids were way out of my league.

Angelo waddled to the plate. He was our last chance. He gave his Fidel Castro beard a tug and cracked the first pitch deep, deep to left. The ball bounced off a big pine and rolled into the woods. It would have been a homer for almost anyone, but Angelo was lucky to make third. He fell on the bag huffing and puffing. Now the tying run was just sixty feet from the plate.

"Atta boy, Angie!" John Bliss said. "Who's up?"

One of our kids hopped to his feet, his muscles swelling under a "Maine Coon" T-shirt. "Must be me," he said.

"Whoa, wait a minute," Hopie said from behind the plate. "Dave's up."

A dejected look swept down our bench. Hopie was right. I was up. What a terrible way to end a great game. We almost had come back. Fortunately, even the young guys were too polite to say anything. I chugged what was left of my beer and trudged over to the bat box. The heck with these new light metal sticks, I needed some real timber. I rummaged around until I found my old bat, the Ball Buster. It was my favorite when I was a legitimate threat. Now I hardly recognized it. The Ball Buster's bright red gloss had been bleached white, its lettering barely discernible. We were a good match. A couple of relics trying to recapture the past. I took a couple of practice swings and stepped into the box.

"Hey, Dave," Hopie said from under his mask, "here's your big chance. Hit one into the woods and you'll be a hero." Hopie's voice dripped with sarcasm. Gone was the sincerity of the sixties.

I didn't say a thing. I was too busy looking for some hole in the defense. Tom McLaughlin, knowing my power was gone, had everyone playing in tight. Bob, the manager at K-Mart, was the only one out of position. Bob was playing right and seeing that I was a righty, he'd shaded me too far to the left. My only hope was to try to punch one down the right-field line. To do that, I'd need an outside pitch. No more swinging at anything close. I was going to have to wait Steven out.

Steven's powerful arm still couldn't find the plate. His first three offerings were high, low and inside. With a 3-0 count, a new strategy emerged. I could go for a walk. No decent ball player ever walked at Thursday night softball. Anyone with three balls and anything less than two strikes automatically took a mock swing at ball four. Not me. Not anymore. I wasn't going to lose this game. I was too old to be humiliated. I'd take a free pass if Steven offered it.

"Come on, Steve," Hopie yelled from behind me. "Pitch to this guy. Make him hit."

Steve's next pitch came floating over the outside corner of the plate. It would have been a ball, but instinct took over. The Ball Buster reached out and smacked it. It was a beautiful shot, perfect in every way. Mark Tripp leaped into the air, but he didn't have enough spring. The ball zoomed six inches over his outstretched glove.

I raced to first, my old legs churning like a teenager's. I watched the ball bounce just inside of the big birch that marks the right-field line and dug deeper as it skipped into the woods. Bob was running after it. One of the young guys was moving over to take the cutoff, but it was going to take them awhile to catch up with that shot. Angelo was home.

This game was tied and I was going for two, maybe more.

As I motored toward second, I could hear a chorus of rich Maine accents yelling from our bench, "Home free! Home free!" As I rounded second, the cry got louder. "Home free! Home free!" I couldn't believe it. They were telling me to go for home. I was going to score. I was going to win this freakin' game.

I could see the amazed look on Tom McLaughlin's face as I streaked around third. Base coaches are far too formal for Thursday night softball, but who needed a third-base coach? The cries I heard coming from the bench were now almost hysterical. "Home free! Home free!"

Hopie was standing at the plate. He discarded his mask and pounded his glove obviously trying to deke me out. What did he think I was, some rookie? Couldn't he hear the screams. I was going "Home free!"

I was about twenty feet from the plate when Hopie casually caught the ball. There was no chance of me stopping and trying to scramble back to third. I had too much momentum. I was like a supertanker heading for an iceberg. "Too bad," Hopie said as he tagged me out.

John Bliss caught me just before I collapsed. "Jeez, Dave," he said, "why'd you keep running?" It was the question everybody was asking.

"I heard you all yelling, 'Home free! Home free!' I thought I had it," I gasped.

"Home free?" John said. "We were yelling 'Hold three, Hold three.' A triple would have been plenty from you."

That was it. The game was over. The sun had long set behind the Presidential Range. Evening's shadows crept over the field. Nobody cared about the tie. A tie was fine for Thursday night softball.

"Not too bad for an old man," Hopie said as I was getting into my car. "Only next week, take the potatoes out of your ears."

I wasn't sure there'd be a next week. Already I could feel my body stiffening. I'd be sore all over in the morning. Still, it was worth it. Seeing that ball bounce into the woods, running the bases, hearing the cheers. I couldn't wait to get back and tell Ruth. I just wouldn't mention the part about "Home free!"

David E. Morine

Trying to Fulfill a Dream

It was 7:45 on a Saturday morning at the Chicago White Sox's spring-training facility in Sarasota, Florida. The sun was still on the rise.

Birds chirped in the distance. The grass glistened with morning dew. It was so early that only one player was working out. Spring training had just begun; only pitchers and catchers had reported. But the player in the batting cage was neither a pitcher nor a catcher. He was a minor-league outfielder, working on his swing.

He was Michael Jordan, trying to fulfill a dream.

Jordan had turned to baseball the previous year after retiring from the NBA for his first time. He needed a break from basketball. He also wanted to honor the memory of his late father, James, who had urged him to try baseball.

Yet his attempt was not warmly received.

In fact, Jordan was harshly criticized, most notably in a *Sports Illustrated* cover story that suggested he was embarrassing the game. Jordan, the story said, "has no more business patrolling right field in Comiskey Park than Minnie Minoso has bringing the ball upcourt for the Chicago Bulls."

Well, Jordan never made it to Comiskey—he batted .202

with thirty stolen bases and fifty-one RBIs in his only season with the Double-A Birmingham Barons. As he prepared for his second season, the major-leaguers were on strike. By then, he seemed anything but an embarrassment to the game.

Jordan didn't take a cavalier approach to the sport, coming and going as he pleased, demanding to play for the White Sox immediately. He paid his minor-league dues, spending hours on the bus, playing through the hot summer, learning how to fail.

That last concept was new to Jordan. At one point, his spirit was so broken, he considered quitting. In basketball, Jordan exerted his will on opponents, teammates, perhaps even the basket and ball. But baseball, he said, "was beating me mentally.

"It got to one point in the season where I didn't feel like I was of use to anyone and that I was making a very big mistake," he said. "I sat down and talked to the coaches. They gave me positive feedback. It kept me moving forward.

"That's when I started to jell as a baseball player. I was willing to accept failure as something that happens to baseball players. I didn't understand—you fail seven out of ten times and you're a superstar. I had trouble accepting that. In my game, it wasn't that way."

His solution, however, was the same as it was in basketball—work, work and work some more. Never were his hunger, dedication and commitment more evident than in his second spring with the White Sox.

That one Saturday morning, Jordan arrived nearly two hours before the pitchers and catchers were scheduled to work out, and four days before the rest of the White Sox minor leaguers were due to report.

Walt Hriniak, the White Sox hitting coach at the time, stood behind a screen fifteen feet away, pitching balls to Jordan underhanded.

"Like that one?" Hriniak would ask Jordan.

"I was on top of it," Jordan would reply.

This went on for the better part of an hour. When the session was over, Jordan emerged from the cage, his face dripping with sweat.

"Actually, I'm a little late," he said. "Normally, I'm up early. But the family's in town. I figure I'm the only guy here before the pitchers and catchers. I can get here at 8 A.M."

No one knew it at the time, but a month later, Jordan would return to the NBA. The baseball strike had left him with little opportunity to improve, and he had no intention of becoming a replacement player. So he went back to basketball, back to complete his remarkable career with the Bulls.

Try as he might, Jordan never could generate major-league bat speed. He looked gangly in a baseball uniform, out of place. But he gave the sport everything he had, even reconditioning his body before his second season.

"In basketball," he said, "I never had to train this hard."

At one point, he made a Nike commercial with Spike Lee poking fun at his frustration with the game. Stan Musial, Willie Mays, Ken Griffey Jr. and Bill Buckner all offered the same reaction to his futile efforts: "But he's trying."

He tried, all right. Tried to honor his father's memory. Tried to master a sport that leaves even the greatest athletes humbled. Tried nobly to fulfill a dream.

Ken Rosenthal

The Second Time Around

If you can dream it, you can do it.

Walt Disney

Jim Morris is living proof that dreams, even the most improbable ones, do come true. His wife, Lorri Morris, still cries when she recalls the moment she saw her husband standing in his big-league uniform that evening in September 1999. She and the three kids had made the three-and-one-half-hour drive from San Angelo, Texas, to Arlington, arriving at the ballpark just as the Texas Rangers and Tampa Bay Devil Rays were finishing their pregame warm-ups.

Jim Morris, called up from the minors earlier in the day, had already taken his place in the Tampa Bay bullpen when his family showed up. His son Hunter camped by the dugout hoping for a glimpse of his dad, while Lorri and the two girls made their way around the ballpark to see if he was with the other relievers.

As they peeked over into the bullpen, they saw him for the first time in three months. He was twenty-five pounds lighter than he'd been, but he was smiling and he was a few hours from becoming baseball's oldest rookie pitcher in thirty-nine years—a thirty-five-year-old left-handed reliever who returned to baseball last summer after a ten-year retirement.

"It was just hard to believe," Lorri Morris said. "I cried. He cried. It's just unbelievable."

Four months earlier, he'd been a science teacher and high school coach making the 140-mile round-trip drive from San Angelo to Big Lake (population: 3,672), learning the lonesome landscape that inspired the songs of James McMurtry and the politics of Lyndon Johnson.

His dream then was to land a high school coaching job in Fort Worth that would allow him more time with his family. And then one day, he challenged his high school team in Big Lake by saying, "What's it going to take to motivate you guys?"

Actually, Morris doesn't remember exactly what he said. What he remembers now is that as he was challenging his kids, they were challenging him in return.

"They'd been knocked out of the basketball play-offs on a fluke, and they were down in the dumps about the base-ball season," Morris said. "I kept trying to motivate them. Basically, they threw it on me. They said they could tell by the way I coach and look at the game and how I feel that I still want to play. One of them said something like, 'You tell us to do one thing, but you're not willing to do it yourself.'"

At that point, Morris made his players a promise that's now a Disney movie project.

"I just told them that if they made the play-offs, I'd go to a big-league tryout camp," he said.

David Werst, owner of the local newspaper, the *Big Lake Wildcat,* and father of first baseman Joe David Werst, recalled, "He was telling them the usual stuff that coaches tell kids. 'You guys are good, you can be good, keep a positive attitude,' all those things. They said, 'What about you?' It might have been Joe David who said it first, but several others picked up on it. I mean, they knew he was throwing hard, but they didn't know it was that hard. It's just fantastic the way it has turned out."

The Fighting Owls did make the play-offs, and a few weeks later, Jim Morris fulfilled his end of the deal by loading the three kids into a dusty Cutlass and driving to his hometown of Brownwood to participate in a Devil Rays' tryout camp.

Veteran scout Doug Gassaway, who had made the two-and-one-half-hour drive from his home near Lake Whitney that morning, recalls that about seventy kids showed up.

"Typical tryout camp," he said. "None of them could play."

Morris, soft-spoken, polite and wearing a softball uniform, was the last guy to approach him. He walked up with a beer gut and an eight-year-old trailing behind him, a five-year-old hanging on one leg and a one-year-old in a stroller.

Gassaway asked which one wanted the tryout.

"Me," Morris said, smiling.

Gassaway rolled his eyes and said, "C'mon, Jimmy, I'm hot and I'm tired. Let's get this over with so I can go home."

Morris originally had planned to attend a tryout camp in Dallas because several teams would be there. He decided on Brownwood because he had to keep the kids while Lorri worked and because "there were fewer people to embarrass myself in front of. I figured all I was doing was fulfilling my promise to my high school kids. After that, I could go and get another job in teaching and get back on with my life."

Morris took the mound and threw a ninety-four-mile-an-hour fastball.

Gassaway saw the reading on his radar gun and said to his assistant, "Something's wrong. Must be some electrical interference."

The assistant shook his head. He had also clocked the pitch at ninety-four miles an hour.

Then thirty-five-year-old Jim Morris threw twelve consecutive ninety-eight-mile-an-hour fastballs.

Gassaway was speechless.

"This is crazy," the scout said, "but I'm going to call my office and see what they say. I'll let you know one way or the other."

When Morris returned home that evening, Lorri asked: "What are these messages from Doug Gassaway?"

Gassaway had telephoned Devil Rays General Manager Chuck LaMar to tell him he'd found a left-handed pitcher who threw ninety-eight miles an hour.

"Sign him," LaMar said.

"Chuck, he's thirty-five years old," Gassaway said.

Gassaway told LaMar the whole story: As a high school football star for legendary Brownwood High Coach Gordon Wood, Morris had turned down football scholarships to Penn State and Notre Dame because he wouldn't be allowed to play baseball. Instead, he went to Angelo State on an academic scholarship, and the Milwaukee Brewers drafted him in 1981.

In six seasons, he never made it higher than Class A, and he retired after having surgery on his elbow and his shoulder. He had returned to Texas, earned his teaching degree and married, and now was the father of three. Yet even as he looked for a simpler life, he could not shake what Texan Robert Earl Keen described as "this crazy cowboy dream."

Two days later, Gassaway had Morris back on the same mound. In a steady rain, Morris was clocked at around ninety-six miles an hour—at least five miles an hour faster than he'd ever thrown before retirement. Two days later, he said good-bye to his wife and kids and headed for Florida and a job that would pay him twelve hundred dollars a month. In simpler terms, he would be making one thousand dollars a month less than he'd made as a teacher (in the majors, he started at the major-league minimum of two hundred thousand dollars, but Lorri has kept her job at Angelo State).

"I honestly don't know how Lorri made it," Morris recalled, his voice choking. "I'm here now because of her. I know God had a plan for me that was different than my own plan. I was really homesick, and we were struggling financially. When it seemed like we couldn't go on, something would happen. One time, it was a contract with a (baseball) glove company. I had them send the check to her. Little things like that would happen to me."

The Devil Rays pushed him through an abbreviated spring training–type program, and after he appeared in three games for Class A Orlando, he was promoted to AAA Durham.

"One day our scouting director, Dan Jennings, came in my office and said, 'I've got a story you're not going to believe,'" Devil Rays Manager Larry Rothschild said. "We didn't bring him up here because he's a good story. We brought him up because he's a left-hander with a good arm. He's thirty-six years old—you're not going to take your time with him."

In eighteen games at Durham—yes, the team of Crash Davis and Nuke Laloosh—Morris was 3-1 with a 5.48 ERA and sixteen strikeouts in twenty-three innings. Then came the word that the Devil Rays were bringing him up for a September look-see.

He arrived in Arlington on the afternoon of September 18, and a few hours later—and eighteen years after the Milwaukee Brewers had first drafted him—Jim Morris made his big-league debut by striking out Rangers shortstop Royce Clayton on four pitches that were clocked at ninety-five miles an hour or better. After the game, Jim, Lorri and the kids celebrated with pizza in his hotel room.

"We heard about him a month or so before he got called up," Devil Rays catcher John Flaherty said. "I remember the guy *Sports Illustrated* made up—Syd Finch. He was supposed to throw 105 miles an hour, and Jim's story sounded an awful lot like that. I really didn't believe it until that night in Texas when he came out of the bullpen."

Morris appeared in five games during September and was impressive enough to win an invitation to the spring big-league camp. At thirty-six years old, he made the Devil Rays as a left-handed specialist and appeared in sixteen games before being sent back to the minors. He was disappointed about going back to the minors, but still amazed at how far he'd come.

His velocity has declined a bit since last summer, but he has a nice slider and a decent curveball. He struggles with his composure at times, but that's not surprising considering everything that has happened.

"He's the best guy in the world," Flaherty said. "You see kids come up now who think they should have everything handed to him. This is a guy who hasn't had anything handed to him. He appreciates every day he's here. He's trying so hard to learn. He's had some success and he's had some failure, but he's handled it all in a first-class manner."

Richard Justice

Rediscovering My Dream

Isn't it funny how the passage of time can make you forget to tingle? Years and the worries of adulthood can take a dream come true and turn it into some kind of cruel practical joke. Be careful what you wish for, little guy; it may one day be fixed around your neck, squeezing tighter and tighter each day.

These thoughts were not fully formed as I sputtered down the Deegan Expressway on May 17, 1998, a bright, beautiful Sunday morning that was lost on me. But they were there in the back of my mind. I was running late as usual, and, thanks to the obligatory large Dunkin Donuts coffee, the tardiness and the stop-and-go traffic were affecting me, as per usual.

And just where was I going? To another baseball game. Big whoop.

The Yankees were playing the Twins that day, a nothing game. The *Hartford Courant's* main man on the Yankees, Jack O'Connell, took the day off and I was asked to cover. I never knew how to say no to an assignment, even when it was the last thing in the world I wanted to do. My regular assignment at that point was the football Giants and this, May, was supposed to be my time off. My Sunday off.

But faced with the choice of staying home and staring at the walls of my condo until I couldn't take anymore, or going to, sigh, another ball game—well, I took the lesser of two tortures. I did maybe twenty games a year. I could see it now: ball one, ball two, strike one, ball three. By the third inning, I'd be wondering why I didn't have a life like everyone else. Just what had I DONE to myself? Four hours of drudgery, followed by a flood of locker-room clichés and then the one part of this job I still loved, trying to make it interesting in roughly eight hundred words.

I made it to the stadium, convinced the parking lot attendants that, yes, I belonged in Jack's space, and got into the stadium just in time for manager Joe Torre's pregame speech. Nothing new was offered.

Then a horrible breakfast of cold, powdery eggs and up to the press box. For a minute, as always on bright Sundays, I stopped to look out at the stadium. *You know, it's still a beautiful place,* I thought. Still, those 1923-vintage outer walls have the ability to block out all the ugliness just outside and protect the pristine, pastoral setting within. The sun has the place looking wonderful, just as it did the first time I saw it.

That would have been 1972, Old Timer's Day, when the days I went to Yankee Stadium were the biggest days of the year. We didn't have a car and Dad didn't drive, so it meant a long, hot ride in old, fetid passenger cars bequeathed by the late New Haven railroad, and a hot, smelly subway ride. All of which was worth it for the moment the No. 4 train emerged from its tunnel, just on the Bronx side of the river where it becomes an elevated train. The train breaks out into daylight and the first sight is the stadium, bigger than life. God, that was great. Where did that sensation go? In 1976, sitting out in left field for the first game in the refurbished stadium, another Yankees–Twins game, I looked up at the press box and decided those guys have the best job in the world.

So then and there, I chose this life, and now from the press box I was looking out at the left-field grandstand. I was through the looking glass.

First pitch, sentiments disappear. This isn't fun anymore. When you grow up, it's not supposed to be fun. Growing up really sucks, by the way.

I'm already thinking about Yankees-win angles. They're in first place and the economic climate of the game has made it impossible for the Twins to field a major-league line-up. Never heard of half the guys playing. In 1972, I could have told you every team's line-up, bench and Class-A hopefuls. But that was so long ago, so many traffic jams, large coffees (cream, no sugar) and lost loves ago. Now, I just wanted to know the bare minimum. Who's pitching for the Yankees today? Oh, yeah, David Wells.

So, yes, David Wells is going to play the hero in this feel-good story. Can you beat that? May 17, 1998. Is that enough of a hint for you? The first seven Twins batters went down easy. So easy. Sooooo easy. I said, to no one in particular, "This guy's gonna pitch a perfect game."

I said it, but I didn't believe it. Would you? But the innings rolled by, and Wells retired every batter. The Yankees put four runs on the board, and Wells kept mowing them down. In the seventh, when he went 3–1 on Paul Molitor, you got worried. He came back to strike him out.

Meanwhile, something was happening. I was covering a PERFECT GAME. Thousands and thousands of games had been played, and there had only been fifteen perfect games. I was going to cover one, and more important, I WANTED to see it. This was important to me again. Like it was 1978 again and the Yankees had to beat the Red Sox, just HAD to. The fat, bald stooge on the mound had to do this, he was going to do it.

Ninth inning, and it was easy. The last batter flied to

right. This was a day game, no deadline pressure, and I stayed in the locker room to hear everything I could about what happened, stayed until there were only a handful of writers left and Wells was opening the champagne George Steinbrenner had sent. "This is something nobody can ever take away from me," Wells said.

I agreed.

My story did not win a Pulitzer Prize, although, if I do say so myself, it came out pretty good. But that wasn't the point. For the first time in a long time, I thought, as I drove home, *This life I chose isn't all that bad.* My dream had been to cover baseball, live with a team, preferably the Yankees because, well, they were the Yankees. I had given up. *Wouldn't have wanted to live that lifestyle for a million bucks a year,* I always thought. But now, the dream was chasing me and I was asking myself, *Just what I was so afraid of?*

A year later, I was offered the chance to leave football and do the Yankees full time. I said yes.

Nearly three years later, I am making plans for my second spring training and I am looking forward to it. Can't WAIT. The problems still exist. No wife, no girlfriend. Still trying to lose weight. Pushing forty. Everyone has these problems, right?

But not everyone can say they wanted to do something when they were fourteen, something only a handful of people get to do, and end up doing it. A Subway Series HAPPENED, and I was in the park for every pitch. The dreams are coming true so fast, I can't keep up anymore.

I don't know what the lesson is from all this. Positive thinking? Sure. Dwell on the successes of life instead of the failures and the shortcomings, since we all have plenty of both? Maybe. Or maybe it's this:

Baseball, for all its faults, can be counted on to rise and set like the sun. I hate to differ with Bart Giammatti, but it wasn't really designed to break our hearts, or leave us to

face the fall and winter alone. It remains to heal and reju-
venate, whenever one is ready to open up again and let it
back inside.

Dom Amore

Days of Heaven

When John Stancel told the guys at work what he planned to do, they wanted to know why he would spend that much money to be laughed at.

Stancel, a forty-one-year-old engineer from Pottersville, New Jersey, is a large, gentle family man. Not an ounce of the impulsive or flamboyant runs through his conservative veins. Yet at this moment Big John is rummaging through the garage for his high-school bat, asking his kid to throw a few balls in the backyard and going on long walks in the surrounding hills to get into shape. He is preparing to take his arthritic knees and his bum shoulder to Scottsdale, Arizona, where for $2,195, plus meals, he and sixty-two other men over thirty-five will spend a week in "spring training" with members of the 1969 Chicago Cubs. And on the final day they will play a game against the team that lost the division race to the Miracle Mets. In a stadium. Wearing uniforms. Before a crowd.

"I've got to admit," says Stancel, "that there is a dark side to this fantasy, that deep within me there is the fear of looking real bad."

For the first few beats of this men-will-be-boys odyssey, it appears that Stancel's friends were right, that this package put together by Allan Goldin, a Chicago Cub nut who ordinarily runs baseball camps for kids, is going to be one big sitcom with a running laugh track. As lawyers, doctors and commodity brokers whose ages stretch to sixty-three struggle to suit up the first morning, former Cub catcher Randy Hundley makes his first announcement: "The jockstrap goes on under the pants."

Taking an early look at the batting cages, 1980 Cy Young winner Steve Stone expresses mild concern for the team he will manage in the Big Game: "They say Earl Weaver was a good manager, but he had the players. Me? I got Fefutznick and Plotstein."

Wandering over to the infield drills, where a network crew is zooming in on a forty-five-year-old psychiatrist flubbing grounders and offering his profound analysis that "You have to be crazy to do this," Stone asks former Cub coach Bobby Adams if he's seen anyone with talent. Adams says it's too early to tell. "Then have you seen anyone who might die before the end of the week?" Stone asks. "You might keep your eye on the guy at first base," Adams replies.

The laugh track ends when a thirty-eight-year-old real-estate developer pivots to throw, collapses in pain and is carted off for knee surgery. Five minutes later a forty-six-year-old Chicago cop is through for the day with an injured arm, and the question now is whether this gimmick has degenerated from the amusing to the sick joke.

Then, just like that, it all turns around. As opening jitters fade, old skills slowly return. Stancel is scooping them out of the dirt first. Two Long Island, New York, buddies, Bob Margolin, thirty-six, a publisher whose mother made him promise not to slide, and George Altemose, forty, an engineer who designed a circuit that injects jelly into doughnuts, have been playing hard back home, and they're good. The sixty-three-year-old, a corporate pilot who had once been offered a Yankee contract, can still get them over the plate. And, *mirabile dictu*, the psychiatrist of limited talents has heads nodding in disbelief as he leaps beyond his ability and hauls in a wicked line drive.

"You won't believe it," former Cub Gene Oliver tells Hundley, "but I just saw a fifty-five-year-old with a *good* arm. I mean a good arm." The arm in question belongs to Ken Schwab, a Peoria, Illinois, grain farm owner who was offered a minor-league contract by the St. Louis Browns in 1947. Before this week is over he will rendezvous with glory by reaching back for something extra and throwing a swinging third strike past Hall of Famer Ernie Banks.

Oliver is not the only Cub with growing enthusiasm. Ron Santo is soon shouting encouragement to infielders. And Billy Williams is grinning with satisfaction because an Iowa attorney has followed his advice to shift his weight to the back foot and is making good contact with the ball. The former pros are, after all, middle-aged men them-selves, and they seem delighted to be back in uniform, teaching what they know to men who are hanging on every word.

In the whirlpool and the hotel bar later that afternoon, tired, sore, happy men are showing off calluses and brag-ging about how long it's been since they last held a bat. "So far," says Stancel, "the reality is better than the fantasy."

In a distant corner of the practice the next day, Ferguson Jenkins, who won twenty-one games for the '69 Cubs, fourteen for the '82 Cubs and needs twenty-two more to become a member of the prestigious "300 Club," is patiently showing a retail executive how to rotate his hip when releasing the ball. Jenkins lets a few fly—by way of demonstration. Squatting the proper 60 feet, 6 inches away, Dennis Ferrazzano, a stocky, bearded attorney and law instructor, catches them. "I don't believe this,"

Ferrazzano says, his grin breaking through his mask. "Ten years from now I'll take my kids to Cooperstown, where this guy will be in the Hall of Fame, and I'll be able to tell them that I once caught for him."

The rest of the week is devoted to intersquad games, and spirits soar as Bob Margolin hits a ball that goes far enough for him to round the bases without having to slide. Ferrazzano is also getting good wood, and Altemose has just belted one that Santo said would have gone out of any major-league park.

Elsewhere, the stock market may be doing whatever and the kid may have a cold, but here, in this wonderful, fragile bubble that has been created, the only truth is that men are lining up early for Harry the trainer to perform miracles on their hamstrings and staying late for him to ice their arms. Reporters are hovering around as though this were the real thing, and everyone is smiling.

"Last night I laid in bed thinking how much I would take to have not been part of this," Stancel says. "I had just turned down twenty thousand dollars when I fell asleep."

As the Big Game approaches, its outcome no longer seems to matter. The talk now centers on what this week has meant. There is mention of male bonding, of camaraderie that long ago gave way to marriages and work.

What is it about this game of baseball that lingers on in grown men's souls? That caused some players to send their deposits Federal Express?

"I don't know the answer," Ferrazzano says, "but I'll tell you this. I'm making ten times more money than I ever thought I would. I'm a respected teacher. But if I could have just one year in the sun . . ." He stops speaking, because, he remembers, real ballplayers don't cry.

With two days to go, several guys are talking about playing in the Big Game even though they are hurting. It doesn't seem to bother them. "The pros play with injuries

because they know they have the whole winter to recover,"
Stancel says. "Me? I've got my whole life to recover."

History will little note nor long remember that on
January 21, 1983, in a game attended by four thousand
paying fans, the 1969 Chicago Cubs defeated their adoring
opponents 23–6 in a game that Steve Stone would say was
not as close as the score might indicate.

What sixty-three men will never forget about that day
in Scottsdale Stadium is the sound of their cleats running
up the concrete ramp, the roar of the crowd as they lined
up on the first-base line to hear themselves introduced,
the sight of Cub manager Leo Durocher making his first
appearance from the dugout, the American flag waving in
a gentle breeze during the singing of the national anthem
and the call of the umpire: "Play ball!"

What will remain for this sportswriter is the autographed baseball he carried back with him. Between the
seams on one side are the names of four immortals. They
are Fergie Jenkins, Dennis Ferrazzano, Ernie Banks and
John Stancel.

Philip Ross

"I understand that my rookie card is
going for more than my salary."

8

WISDOM OF THE GAME

Every day is a new opportunity. You can build on yesterday's success or put its failures behind and start over again. That's the way life is, with a new game every day, and that's the way baseball is.

Bob Feller

The Unforgettable Charlie Brown

Charlie Brown was standing on the pitcher's mound before yet another pounding as his Beethoven-loving catcher went over the signs.

"One finger will mean a fastball, which isn't very fast anyway," Schroeder said. "Two fingers will be your curve, which doesn't curve at all. Three fingers will mean your change-up, which hasn't fooled anyone yet. Four fingers is a pitchout, but we won't use that one."

"Why not?" Charlie Brown asked.

"Everything you throw looks like a pitchout."

Cartoonist Charles Schulz chose many ways to torture Charlie Brown—having Lucy always pull away the football, entangling him in the kite-eating tree, paralyzing him with fear before the little redheaded girl. Yet his favorite motif was baseball. Over his fifty years of drawing "Peanuts," Schulz made Charlie Brown the game's most lovable loser.

No pitcher yielded more homers or squandered more games as a manager. Line drives disrobed him. Fastballs baffled him. He didn't need a tape measure for his team's home runs because, he muttered, "Our hits can be measured quite adequately with an eighteen-inch ruler."

Charlie Brown got so tired of his team's ineptitude that one day he ran a classified ad, searching for a new managerial job. He received one reply—from his own team.

But the losing finally ended for Charlie Brown on February 12, 2000, when Schulz died from colon cancer at the age of seventy-seven. Baseball gave Schulz his most longstanding device. He gave back by giving us some of its best laughs.

Charlie Brown's team, the losingest, silliest, what-in-the-world-are-they-doingest of all time, lost all but a handful of games over fifty years, sometimes 40–0, 123–0, even 200–0. His classic double-play combo featured Snoopy catching balls in his mouth and spitting them to his second baseman Linus, who toted his ever-present security blanket.

Charlie Brown's favorite player, Joe Shlabotnik, once got demoted to Stumptown of the Green Grass League after hitting .004. (Shlabotnik later was fired as a manager because he called for a suicide squeeze bunt with the bases empty.) Charlie Brown got so consumed with his baseball failures that the sun, then his own head, turned into a baseball. He asked his psychiatrist, "Is this the last of the ninth?"

In one of his more sadistic moments in the '60s, Schulz had Charlie Brown's love for baseball betray him at what could have been his finest moment. In his class spelling bee, he was asked to spell "maze."

"M-A-Y-S."

"AAAAUUUUGGGGHHH!"

Some years later, Charlie Brown had just given up yet another home run when his fussbudget right fielder, Lucy Van Pelt, walked on to the pitcher's mound.

"I wonder why I do this," Charlie Brown grumbled. "I wonder why I stand out here day after day losing all these ball games. Why do I do it?"

"Probably because it makes you happy," Lucy said. To which a perturbed Charlie Brown yelled, "You always have to be right, don't you?"

Schulz was unabashed in his love for the game. "I could draw baseball strips every day," he once said. "It really is funny. Baseball is ideal because little kids do play it at that age, and they aren't very good. But they do suffer at it."

Schulz suffered at it, too, growing up in St. Paul, Minnesota. He enjoyed going to St. Paul Saints minor-league games at old Lexington Park and cherished the Ollie Bejma souvenir bat his father bought him in 1938. But his fondest moments came when he played—even though he once did actually lose a game 40–0.

"We had teams that we would just make up in the neighborhood," Schulz said. "There was no league. We'd find out that some other neighborhood's kids had a team and so we'd play them."

It has been said that we are a nation of failed baseball players, and Schulz was no exception. His own persona as the hapless underdog was cast as a good-field, no-hit catcher and third baseman. Later, as a sergeant stationed in Germany during World War II, Schulz got one of the thrills of his life simply by playing a pickup game.

"I was so flattered that these guys should like some unknown guy from Minnesota to be on their team," Schulz remembered. "Isn't that funny? Something as totally meaningless as that, really, in the history of mankind and baseball, a game played in an unknown area that didn't mean a thing, and yet it meant so much to me. That's what sport does for us."

The first cartoon Schulz sold after the war displayed a little boy and girl with the caption, "Judy, if your batting average was just a little higher I could really fall in love with you." He began "Peanuts" in October 1950 and soon began using real baseball events in his work.

began using real baseball events in his work.

In 1962, when Willie McCovey lined out to the Yankees' Bobby Richardson to lose the World Series for the Giants, Charlie Brown cried to the heavens, "Why couldn't McCovey have hit the ball even two feet higher?" Seven years later, Charlie Brown joined major-league baseball by lowering his pitcher's mound because, he explained to Lucy, "It seems that we pitchers dominated the game too much last year." (Lucy walked away howling.) Charlie Brown later wondered if he could trade her to Oakland A's owner Charlie Finley—noted fussbudget himself.

Schulz did finally get a little sentimental in 1993 by allowing Charlie Brown to hit a game-winning home run. "I think it's a mistake to be unfaithful to your readers," Schulz said, "always letting them down." Soon, however, the losing began anew, to the delight of readers of twenty-six hundred newspapers in seventy-five countries and twenty-one languages.

"Winning is not funny," Schulz explained. "Winning is great, it's wonderful, but it's not funny. Victories are fleeting, but losses we always live with."

Charlie Brown's will live forever.

Alan Schwarz

Three Strikes of Life

The Organic Produce Little League team was taking pregame batting practice. The stars were smacking the ball hard. Everyone else was missing. After a bit, an old man in brown suit pants put his fingers through the chain links of the backstop. He looked eighty, though his shoes looked only half that.

"You kids want to hit the ball better?" he asked. The better players laughed. What did an old man know about hitting? But a handful of the lesser players tentatively put their hands up. They were willing to try anything.

"Listen up," the old man said. His hands trembled until they fastened around an aluminum bat. Then they seemed strong. His eyes were red and his complexion was mottled, with a stubble of white whisker on his cheek.

"You get three strikes," he said. "Each one's different. Each strike, you change who you are."

The kids squinted.

"The first pitch is your rookie pitch. The pitcher doesn't know you. Anything can happen. Maybe you close your eyes, you get lucky and beat one back up the middle.

"But usually you don't. You miss, and all the weaknesses of the rookie come down on you. You're thinking about failing, and getting ready to fail. You're scared of the pitcher, scared of the ball. You get revved up. You forget what your coaches say and swing crazy, hoping to get lucky. Or you stand like a statue while the umpire calls a strike.

"Most young hitters give up now. They swing at the next two just to get it over. They don't grow in the at bat. The bat's a white flag, and they're waving it to surrender.

"To have a good rookie pitch, you have to be good inside. Good rookies go up to the plate respecting the pitcher and humble about their odds. They respect the ball, and they shut out everything else.

"You need courage on the first strike pitch, because you're a stranger in a strange land. You put yourself in harm's way, close to the ball, close to the plate.

"Maybe you'll get drilled. It'll hurt. But only a bit. You stand close anyway, because good things happen when you put yourself in a little danger.

"You need faith that if you do it in the right spirit, things will work out.

"That's the *rookie pitch.*

"By the second pitch, you're in your prime. Now you know what the at bat is about. You've seen the pitch. You know what you have to do to turn on it. The first strike filled you with adrenaline. Now you're strong. You feel electrified. You feel good. You grip the bat tight.

"The prime pitch is when good things usually happen. You're ahead of the pitcher, even with the first strike. Because you know what he's got, and you feel good. If you fail on the prime pitch, it's because maybe you felt too good. People in their prime get overconfident. They swing too hard. They miss.

"That's the *prime pitch.*" The old man spat but the spit dripped out at about five points, and he had to wipe some off his lip.

"Third pitch. Now you're a veteran. You're at the end of your rope. If you fail now, there won't be another pitch. It's life or death. You're like an old prizefighter, and you stand almost perfectly still, waiting for your moment. The bat's loose and tight at the same time.

"You're not relying on luck, like the first pitch. Or talent, like the second pitch. Now you're calling on your guts, and everything you've learned.

"You mess up on the *veteran pitch* when you're angry at the pitcher for making you miss the other two pitches. The bad veteran is always making excuses. He's making up excuses for missing before he misses.

"But the good veteran welcomes the battle. It's serious, but it gives him joy, too. He knows that baseball means pain, and he welcomes the suffering. He may go down, but he's grateful he ever got up. If he goes down, it will be swinging."

"Sir, what if you strike out?" asked one kid, shielding the sun from his eyes with his glove.

"You just hope there's another game, and you're in it." The old man scanned the horizon to the west. "I gotta go, kids. Good luck out there." And he turned and was gone.

The kids mumbled as they got their equipment together. Did anyone know who that guy was? Maybe a retired sportswriter, someone suggested. Or an ex-player. Maybe even a Hall of Famer, one wishful thinker said.

"No, it's just my dad," said a slender infielder. "He was in the sixties."

The players nodded sagely and they took the field. In the game, the Organic Produce team skunked the Subway Sandwich team 14–3. And every one of the kids who listened got a hit.

Michael Finley

fooling around, showing off for the benefit of some twelve-year-old girls who had come to flirt. I put my cap on backward, and my shoes were unlaced in a deliberately sloppy manner to elicit laughter. "Fix your hat and shoes, Jordan!" my uncle barked at me. "Look like a ballplayer!"

I sulked for the entire game. Afterwards, as my uncle drove home, I sat in glum silence. I felt humiliated. He tried to explain why he had snapped at me over such an inconsequential matter.

"It's important how you look, Paddy," he said. "Details, like wearing your uniform just so, add up. They count. If you do all the little things right, then when the big things come it'll be easier to handle them. And sometimes the little things are all you have in life. You can take great satisfaction in those details."

As a child of twelve, I only vaguely understood what my uncle was talking about. I understand now, of course. He was talking about pride in oneself. He was talking about his own life really.

People came from all over the state to see me pitch that year. In the six games I pitched, I threw four no-hitters and two one-hitters. And our team also won when I wasn't pitching.

My uncle's secret to success was to know the limits of his boys, never push them beyond those limits. He kept things simple and orderly. Other managers overextend their players by concocting elaborate plays that always seemed to backfire and humiliate the boys in front of their parents. Those managers wanted to show the fans how much they knew. My uncle always managed in a way that kept the attention on us, not him.

We were a heavy favorite to win the state championship on our way to the Little League World Series at Williamsport, Pennsylvania. But we lost our final game and were eliminated. I pitched a one-hitter that day before

My Uncle and Me

It's not whether you get knocked down; it's whether you get up.

Vince Lombardi

My uncle Ben Diamond was a draftsman, and it was the perfect job for him. He had a clear, logical mind and an esthetic sense to go along with his devotion to detail. He dressed in a preppy way, navy blazer and gray flannel slacks, and his gestures were mesmerizing. A courtly man, he seemed to move a beat or two slower than others.

When I was a boy in Fairfield, Connecticut, I would walk to his place for breakfast every morning. I left early, before my parents began their daily argument. My father was a gambler, and life in our house was at the mercy of his dark moods. So I'd escape to my uncle's childless apartment, which was always as quiet as a church.

I would sit at the dining-room table, surrounded by Aunt Ada's knickknacks and little boxes of violets, while Uncle Ben made our breakfast. (Aunt Ada always slept late, it seemed.) It was an elaborate ritual, and always the same—orange juice, two pieces of buttered toast, one soft-boiled egg and a cup of coffee (mine mostly milk). It was certainly not the usual breakfast for a child, but Uncle Ben made it sound like a king's feast.

He explained how he squeezed the oranges by hand in a cut-glass juicer, never grinding them too hard or there'd be too much pulp in the juice. The toast had to be a perfect shade of tan, he'd say, holding out a slice for me to see. Then he'd lay a pat of warm butter on top, let it melt and spread it evenly over the toast. The egg was cooked for exactly three minutes and brought to me in an eggcup. He showed me how to tap around the shell's circumference with the side of my spoon to remove the top half.

Uncle Ben had a way of singing the praises of the most mundane thing so that it became something of wonder to a child.

While we ate, for instance, he read the major-league baseball scores from the newspaper out loud. We were Yankee fans because the Yankees had many Italian Americans like us: Raschi, Berra, Rizzuto, Crosetti and, of course, Joltin' Joe DiMaggio. I clapped my hands softly at his mention of their success and dreamed of being a part of that someday.

After breakfast I helped do the dishes. When we finished, Uncle Ben would take a tiny porcelain Buddha out of Aunt Ada's china cabinet and let me rub its belly for good luck. Then we'd go play catch in his narrow driveway.

He'd lay a piece of folded cloth on the pavement as a plate and get down stiffly into his catcher's crouch, pinching the knee of each pant leg. Then I'd pitch to him. We made believe I faced the mighty Yankees. After each pitch, he would bounce out of his crouch and fire the ball back. "Attaboy, Paddy!" he'd say. "You got him!"

He was always tough on me, until I got behind in the count on Joltin' Joe and he saw my face flush with panic. Then he'd give me a break on a pitch even I knew was off

the plate. "Strike three!" he'd call, then fire the ball back so hard it stung my hand. I always pitched a perfect game with Uncle Ben.

Like many childless adults, he didn't have to feign having fun with children. He really did. Adults, with their neuroses and duplicities, made him nervous. Children, in their innocence, calmed him, which was why he jumped at the opportunity to be our town's Little League baseball coach when it was offered to him.

The job came open every couple of years because the coach was usually the father of one of the players.

He'd coach until his son graduated from Little League then he'd quit. It was assumed that Uncle Ben would coach for the two years I was eligible to play and then quit. But twenty years later, after I married and had children of my own, he was still our Little League coach.

Uncle Ben was harder on me than he was on the other players. We both knew this was a ruse to hide his obvious affection. On the field he called me Jordan, not Paddy, and he made me carry the heavy canvas bat bag from his car. At batting practice he grunted a little harder when he threw me his fastball and he never told me when his curve was coming, as he did for others.

I was the team's star pitcher, and no matter how hard he tried, my uncle could never really hide his pleasure when I was on the mound. It would be the final inning a one-run game, with a runner on third base and two out. He would pace back and forth, yelling encouragement, "Come on, Paddy! You can do it!" (I wasn't Jordan then) would get two strikes on the batter, and before I delivered I'd give my uncle a wink then get strike three. He would charge out to shake my hand.

Uncle Ben ran constant herd on us to act like men. remember the one time he ever really spoke harshly to me. It was before a game I was not scheduled to pitch. I was

three thousand fans. But I threw wildly on a bunt attempt early in the game, which let in what proved to be the only run. After the game we were presented trophies at home plate. When my name was announced, the crowd rose and gave me a standing ovation. My uncle walked out to the plate with his arm around my shoulder. I began to cry, and he was crying, too.

We drifted apart as I became a teenager. He still saw me as a child. I began to see my uncle as lovable but eccentric. He seemed fussy and enmeshed in the myriad details he felt were so important. His interests seemed trivial.

When I was eighteen, I signed a thirty-five-thousand-dollar bonus contract with the Milwaukee Braves and went away to the minor leagues. After three years of diminishing success, I was released by the farm club. I went home, depressed and confused by this first failure of my life.

My bride and I were living, temporarily, at my parents' house near the ballpark where I had had so many youthful successes. My parents had offered us the use of their house until, as my mother put it, "you get back on your feet."

But I couldn't get back on my feet. I spent most of each day lying on the bed in my old room, staring straight ahead. The sun came in through the window, illuminating in a dusty haze the mementos of my career arranged on the bureau: bronzed trophies from Little League, scuffed baseballs from notable high school successes. What had gone wrong?

I stared at those mementos for hours, not really seeing them, but rather lost in a kind of lassitude that made even the simplest tasks—dressing, reading the newspaper, going down to dinner, talking with my wife—seem superfluous.

Downstairs in the kitchen, I could hear whispering voices.

"What's wrong with him?" my mother said.

"I don't know," my wife answered, sobbing softly.

Then one day my uncle called. "Paddy, it's me, Uncle Ben," he said, as if I could ever forget his voice. "Why don't you come over tomorrow for breakfast?"

"I'll see," I said. I had no intention of going, but my mother insisted. "It will hurt him terribly if you don't."

It was just the way it had been when I was a child. The orange juice. The perfect toast. Uncle Ben showing it to me before he buttered it. "See," he said. "Tan." He wasn't trying to humor me; he was just transporting me back to that simple time of my childhood.

After we did the dishes he smiled and said, "I've got something for you." He went into the dining room and opened Aunt Ada's cabinet. Returning with her Buddha, he said, "Remember this, Paddy?"

I smiled. He held it out to me. I rubbed its belly for luck.

Maybe it was the Buddha. Maybe it was just seeing my uncle still take such pleasure in the little details of his life. But I was all right after that. It dawned on me that my life, far from being over, was just beginning. I had a wife. I was twenty-two years old, and there were so many things out there for me to do. I went back to college. Had children. Taught school. Became a writer. Filled my life with a host of things that give me pleasure.

Then, suddenly, my uncle was gone. I was stunned. I thought he'd always be there. And in a way he is.

I think a lot about my uncle these days, especially when I begin to feel sorry for myself. He never allowed himself to indulge in self-pity, even in the face of the one great disappointment of his life—not having a child of his own.

For Uncle Ben, happiness was never a given. It had to be worked at, created. He was a master at finding joy in life's details. He showed me how to take delight in small, everyday pleasures. Like perfect, buttered toast.

Pat Jordan

IN THE BLEACHERS   By Steve Moore

"Give it up, Johnson! We're bringing in
a new pitcher. Step off the mound!
Don't make me release the hounds!!"

Diapers and Diamonds

If you come to a fork in the road, take it.

Yogi Berra

Soon after his first child was born, Yogi Berra called fellow baseball player Jimmy Piersall, who has nine children, and asked for a few tips on changing diapers. "Yogi," explained Piersall, "you take a diaper and put it in the shape of a baseball diamond, with you at bat. Then fold second base down to home. Take the baby's bottom and put it on the pitcher's mound. Then pin first base and third to home plate."

"That's easy," said Berra. "I can do that."

"Wait a minute, Yogi," cautioned Piersall. "One thing about this game—when it starts to rain, there's no postponement."

Ron Reid

Life with Father

*Fatherhood is the single most creative, compli-
cated, fulfilling, frustrating, engrossing, enrich-
ing, depleting endeavor of a man's adult life.*

                                                    Kyle D. Pruett

One of my neighbors, a sincere young guy named Derek,
recently approached me for advice on a specialized aspect
of father-son relationships. That he should approach me
about any aspect of parenting is remarkable, considering
that Derek has actually met Graig, the nineteen-year-old
product of my own efforts in this area. But Derek's options
were limited: He was considering coaching his seven-year-
old, Chad, in Little League. And given the decade-long
record I compiled as a father-coach (I won a league title,
came in second once and coached several All-Star teams)
before hanging up my line-up card for good last season, he
wondered if I might have any words of wisdom.

There was a lot I could have said, and maybe should
have said, to Derek, but his request aroused mixed emotions. On the one hand, well, he did ask. On the other, he
was just so bright-eyed and eager that I didn't want to

make him feel unduly neurotic about something I knew he was going to undertake anyway. In the end I merely whittled down the insights of my lengthy service as my son's coach to these points:

First, this was not a decision to be made on impulse. Anyone considering this step should spend a summer at the ball field, observing such relationships up close and personal.

Second, there should be a special plea available to fathers who do bodily harm to their sons as a consequence of coaching them in youth sports—something along the lines of "assault with an explanation."

Derek began to laugh and then, noting that my face remained set and unsmiling, thanked me and walked away. I don't know what he made of me, but he is careful not to leave me alone with his son these days.

In their attempts to shed light on the father-son coaching relationship, sports psychologists invest a lot of time in constructing intricate behavioral models, most of which reduce to the fact that both man and boy lug much more than the equipment with them when they travel from the home to ball field.

Sometimes the spillover from home is unmistakable: I think of the day my frowning nine-year-old folded his arms over his chest and plopped down in the outfield in protest over my refusal to buy him a Slurpee before the game. More often the link between cause and effect is foggy. On one occasion, when Graig, normally a hard thrower, was fourteen, I yelled out to the mound that he didn't seem to have much on the ball. "Come on, dammit!" I shouted. "Chow [the family mutt] could hit that crap." He glared at me, and his pitches began arcing toward the plate in a high, defiant softball lob. I yanked him at once, he stormed into the dugout and it was only when we talked about things days later that I recognized the depths of the emotional morass I had carelessly wandered into. "You say something about everything I do," Graig sniffed. "With my homework, if the answers are right, you complain about the penmanship. When I mow the lawn, you always tell me I missed a spot. Why can't you ever just accept that I'm doing the best I can?"

It's true that a coach's son struggles with his father's shifting identities. And that's sad. But it is equally true that kids can be world-class manipulators. Sensing that their fathers, too, are far from comfortable with the situation, they respond with the unerring, I've-got-you-over-a-barrel instincts of, say, a woman you love very much who knows she has caught you doing something you hoped never to be caught doing.

And that's infuriating.

Typically, a coach's kid wants all the special rewards of having a coach who is also his father but is reluctant to accept any of the special burdens of having a father who is also his coach. His advantage-seeking is expressed in countless ways large and small—from demanding "just one more pitch" during batting practice to lobbying to be penciled in at a glamour position such as shortstop regardless of whether he can actually stop, oh, one out of every four ground balls.

Coaches' kids reject the notion that this favoritism should come at the cost of any added responsibility. Graig despised my constant reminders to "set a good example." His chronic complaint was that he wanted to be "a member of the team just like everyone else." (Except expecting to pitch regularly, bat third or fourth, and have the green light to steal at will even though the backstop would have beaten him in a foot race.)

The successful management of such schizophrenia requires of father-coaches an even-temperedness bordering on the divine. Further complicating matters is that we fathers are not quite sure how "professional" we want the on-field relationship with our sons to be. The identification between man and boy, after all, is never so close as on the athletic field, where the kids become walking advertisements for the potency of the father's testosterone. Any other child strikes out with the bases jammed, and you pat him on the fanny and say, "Tough break." The one time Graig watched a close pitch sail by for strike three in a championship game, stranding the tying run, I did not say, "Tough break." I meant to say it. Honest. I even formed the words. But something diabolical took hold of my larynx, and what I heard come out instead was, "How could you take a pitch that close with two strikes on you?" Then I kicked myself over it for the rest of the weekend.

Of course, my behavior toward Graig, like that of most father-coaches toward their sons, was marked by erratic cycles of indulgence and volatility. I would let him goad me, push me to the limit. I would look the other way as he cut up and did his best to undermine my authority over the team. All of this I would let slide until I would explode at him in a rage far out of proportion to the stimulus of the moment.

The worst of these eruptions came during the last year I coached Graig, when he was fifteen. We were having batting practice on a languorous afternoon in late May. Nobody felt like being there, yours truly included. It was too hot, too humid. But the team hadn't been hitting, and it struck me as a lousy time to be canceling a scheduled workout.

Wise guy that he is, Graig decided to liven things up. I would yell instructions to the batter, and from behind me I would hear my words repeated in this moronic voice that brought to mind Bullwinkle from "Rocky and His Friends."

It took awhile, but I finally got so fed up with the lame

echo from deep short that I whirled on the pitcher's mound and fired my best fastball in Graig's direction. It was an act I regretted at once, even before the ball had completely left my grip. But it was too late.

What happened next took a split second. And yet, amazingly, there was time enough for me to be aware of several things.

I was aware that around me, everything—everything— had ceased. There was no movement, no sound, no nothing.

I was aware of feeling more helpless than I had ever felt in my life.

And I was aware, in that terrifying instant before impact, that I could no longer see my son's mouth because it had been eclipsed by—and was about to merge with— the speeding ball in flight.

Graig was standing no more than thirty feet away. Had he not been looking directly at me and had he not been able to get his glove up in the nick of time, I might now be occupying the Bing Crosby chair at the College of Dubious Parenting.

As it developed, he made the catch cleanly and no damage was done. He just stood there for ten or fifteen seconds, holding the glove right where he had intercepted the ball, like a catcher giving the umpire a long look at a close pitch. His facial expression was a curious hybrid: half fear, half mirth. Several of the other kids, meanwhile, were staring at me with mouths agape, no doubt wondering what their psychotic coach might do for an encore.

I felt awful, ashamed. Above all, I was sickened by a thought that kept nagging at me for months afterward: What I had just done was not something you did to anybody's kid but your own. Graig had come within a whisker of being maimed, solely because he was the coach's kid.

Somehow we put that incident behind us and finished the season without trying to throttle one another. That winter Graig and I decided to go our separate ways. I would stay with our current team; he would graduate to "colt" ball, with a different coach. We both knew it was better this way.

I now ask myself whether I have a moral obligation to share these reminiscences with Derek. Should I tell him that when you are your son's coach, you are always your son's coach, even late at night and hours removed from the field? Should I tell Derek that as long as a son's coach remains his son's coach, the two of them will never be able to watch a ball game together in an unspoiled, purely recreational way? That the son's coach will find himself turning every play into an instructional video or an opportunity to critique the son's skills?

Maybe I should just tell Derek how much nicer it was for Graig and me after the breakup. In particular, I would tell him about the catch we had before the next season's tryouts. We threw freely, easily, without pressure. No longer were we coach and player. For the first time since Graig left kindergarten (kindergarten!), we were just a boy and his dad tossing a ball around in the sun.

Then I watched Graig go out and pound the horsehide, make graceful running catch after running catch and fire strikes to second base from the depths of the outfield. And you know what? Beaming on the sidelines, I thought, *I wouldn't mind having that kid on my team.*

Steve Salerno

Bringing Parents Up to Code

It exists for parents who are trying vicariously to recover an ability of their own that never really existed.

Bill Veeck

There's only one place in the galaxy where kids' sports is sane: Jupiter.

Jupiter, Florida, that is, where on February 15, the town's athletic association did something we should've done in America twenty years ago. It took the parents out behind the woodshed.

If you wanted your kid to play on one of the Jupiter association's zillion teams this year, you had to file into a minor-league baseball stadium, watch a video on sportsmanship and then vow not to insult, cuss at, holler at, spit upon, push, punch, body-slam or otherwise abuse a coach, referee, team mom, scorekeeper, fan, player or another parent.

You think it doesn't happen? In Port St. Lucie, Florida, a youth soccer coach head-butted a referee, breaking the ref's nose. In Wagoner, Oklahoma, a thirty-six-year-old coach started choking a fifteen-year-old umpire in a T-ball game for five- and six-year-olds. In Palm Beach Gardens, Florida, a baseball game for seven- and eight-year-olds ended in a parents' brawl. In Boca Raton, Florida, one of the managers in a baseball game for nine- and ten-year-olds mooned the opponents' parents.

And you thought pro sports was mayhem.

Jupiter parents had to sign the code of ethics, which included such pledges as "I will remember that the game is for youth—not adults" and "I will do my very best to make youth sports fun for my child." Break the code and they're banished from the association's games for as much as a year.

Problem was, that code didn't go nearly far enough. As a poor slob who has coached kids' sports for ten years and gone to more kids' games than Mr. and Mrs. Osmond combined, I would've made the parents sign this—in blood:

- I'll keep in mind that, in case I hadn't noticed, my kid isn't related to the Griffeys. There's probably no college scholarship on the line, to say nothing of a $116.5 million guaranteed contract with the Cincinnati Reds. In fact, right now my kid is filling the inside of his baseball glove with ants. He looks happy. I'll shut up.
- I won't dump my kid out of the Lexus twenty minutes late to practice and then honk the horn when I pick him up twenty minutes early, as though the coach is some kind of hourly nanny service. If my kid has to miss a game, I'll call the day before. It doesn't cost any more to be decent.
- I'll remember that this isn't the seventh game of the NBA Finals. This is the six-year-olds' YMCA Lil' Celtics finals, and by suppertime not one of these kids will remember the score. They *will* remember that I tried to ride the other coach bareback, and possibly

they'll remember the incident in the squad car, but not the score.

- I'll realize that the guy behind the umpire's mask, whom I've been calling "José Feliciano" and "Coco, the talking ape," is probably just a fifteen-year-old kid with a tube of Oxy 10 in his pocket, making twelve dollars the hard way. I'll shut up.

- I'll stop harrumphing out of the side of my mouth about how much the coach stinks, unless I want to give up my Tuesdays, Thursdays and Saturdays every week, call fifteen kids every time it rains and spend two hundred dollars every season on ice cream, catcher's throat guards and new seat covers. I'll shut up. (Oh, and once a year, I'll tell her thanks.)

- I won't rupture my larynx hollering nonstop directions. For one thing, my kid can't hear me. For two, because I'm shouting, he can't hear the coach, either. For three, I really have no idea what I'm talking about. Screaming at little Justin to "Tag up! Tag up!" when there are two outs is probably not very helpful. I'll shut up.

- Win or lose, I won't make the ride home the worst twenty minutes in my kid's life. "You played great" should about cover it every time. Then I'll shut up.

- One season a year, even if it kills me, I won't make my kid sign up for an organized sport. It's probably not necessary to have him play ninety-one hockey games in three leagues from September to June and then send him to Skating Camp, Slap Shot Camp and Orange Pylon Camp all summer. I'll try to remember that Be a Kid Camp isn't so terrible once in a while. Neither is Invent a Game Involving a Taped Sock, a Broom and Old Lady Winslow's Fence Camp, come to think of it.

- Most important, I promise I'll do everything in my power, no matter what, to remember to arrive at games with the single most important thing of all . . . the orange slices.

Rick Reilly

ADAM@HOME. ©*UNIVERSAL PRESS SYNDICATE. Reprinted with permission. All rights reserved.*

The Boys of Bummer

For the parents of a Little Leaguer, a baseball game is simply a nervous breakdown divided into innings.

Earl Wilson

It's Little League season again here in South Florida. I would estimate that this is the fifth Little League season we've had in the past year alone. That's the problem with all this nice weather: While most of the nation is protected for several months each year by a restful blanket of frozen slush, we subtropical parents are trapped in Year-Round Youth Sports Hell. The reason we have a high crime rate is that many parents are so busy providing transportation that they have to quit their jobs and support their families by robbing convenience stores on their way to practices, games, lessons, etc.

But at least our children are becoming well-rounded. That's what I tell myself while I watch my son stand out in left field, head down, examining subtropical insects while the ball rolls cheerfully past him and seven runners score (and if you don't think it's possible for seven runners to score on a single play, then you have never watched Little League baseball). I tell myself that if my son were not out there participating in sports, he would not be learning one of life's most important lessons, namely: "It doesn't matter whether you win or lose, because you are definitely going to lose."

My son's team always loses. This is because he is a Barry. We Barrys have a tradition of terrible sports luck dating back to my father, whose entire high school football career—this is true—consisted of a single play, which was blocking a punt with his nose. As a child, I played on an unbroken succession of losing baseball teams, although "played" is probably too strong a term. My primary role was to sit on the bench, emitting invisible but potent Loser Rays and joining with the other zero-motor-control bench-sitters in thinking up hilarious and highly creative insults to hurl at members of the other team. Let's say the opposing batter was named Frank. We'd yell: "Hey FRANK! What's your last name? FURTER?" Then we'd laugh so hard that we'd fall backward off the bench while Frank hit a triple, scoring twelve runs.

My son is a much better player than I was, but he's still a Barry, and consequently his team, the Red Sox, has never won a game. As the Red Sox's first-base coach, I've spent many hours analyzing our statistics, trying to find some clue as to what we're doing wrong, and the only thing I can come up with, far-fetched though it may sound, is that we never, ever, score any runs.

There's a good reason for this: The boys are not idiots. They do not wish to be struck by the ball. When they're batting, they look perfect—good stance, fierce glare at the pitcher, professional-style batting glove, etc.—until the pitcher actually pitches, at which point, no matter where the ball is going, the Red Sox batters twitch their bodies violently backward like startled squids, the difference being that a squid would have a better chance of hitting the baseball because it keeps its eyes open.

Frankly I don't blame the boys. This is exactly the hitting technique that I used in Little League on those rare occasions when I got to play. But now that I'm a first-base coach I have a whole new perspective on the game, namely the perspective of a person who will never have to get up to bat. So my job is to yell foolish advice to the batters. "Don't back up!" I yell. "He's not gonna hit you!" Every now and then a Red Sock, ignoring his common sense, will take me seriously and fail to leap backward, and of course when this happens it is always a bad pitch and the ball always hits the batter at 475 miles per hour. Then my job is to rush up and console the batter by telling him: "Legally, you cannot be forced to play organized baseball." I'm just kidding, of course. Far be it from me to bring down the republic. What I say is: "Rub it off! Attaboy! Okay!" And the boy, having learned the important life lesson that adults frequently spout gibberish, sniffles his way down to first base, while our next batter silently resolves to be in a different area code by the time the ball reaches home plate.

The other teams do not have this problem. This is because of the First Law of Little League Physics, which states: "The other team always has much larger kids." You parents have noticed this: Your child's team always consists of normal-sized children, and the other team is always sponsored by Earl's House of Steroids. We are constantly playing against huge mutant eight-year-olds who have more bodily hair than I do and drive themselves to the game. They can all hit the ball, and what is worse, when they get on base, they steal, and there's nothing we can do about it because our various catchers can't throw all the way to second base.

Our catchers can hardly walk once they get their equipment on, especially the protective cup, which is apparently not manufactured in a size small enough for eight-year-olds, because the one we have looks, next to our catchers, to be the size of a Coast Guard rescue vessel. Nevertheless I have seen signs of improvement. Recently several Red Sox, while leaping backward, have managed to hit solid foul balls, events which triggered jubilant celebrations among the long-suffering Red Sox parents, who joyously hurled convenience-store receipts into the air. I honestly think that we're getting better, and that despite the Barry luck, we could be in a position to challenge for the league championship, or at least score a run, in our next season. Which I think starts next month.

Dave Barry

"It's not necessary to yell, 'Ready or not, here it comes' before every pitch."

The Power of Motivation

People are always asking me: "Tommy, when did you first realize that you could motivate people."

I think I have always had the ability to motivate, but I remember one time in particular, early on in my minor-league coaching career for the Los Angeles Dodgers, when I had a situation that really tested my motivational skills.

I was coaching in the Pacific Coast League for Spokane. It was the bottom of the eighth inning and we were leading 3–2. Bobby O'Brien was pitching, and I knew that if we could just get this next batter out we could go on to win this game.

So I went out to the mound and I asked O'Brien a question.

"Bobby," I asked, "if the heavens came apart right now, and that great Dodger in the sky came down to get you, would you rather go as having gotten this final batter out, or would you rather face the Lord after having given up a hit to this guy?"

Bobby hardly hesitated. "I would rather get him out," he said.

"Okay then," I told him, "then that's how I want you to pitch—as if you were going to die getting this guy out."

I felt good having shared such an inspiring visual message with Bobby and I left the mound and started back toward the dugout. But before I even got there, O'Brien threw the next pitch, and gave up a hit. The other team scored two runs and we went on to lose the game 4–3.

After the game I called Bobby aside.

"What happened?" I asked him. "You said you wanted to get this guy out if it was the last thing you ever did."

"Skipper," he said, "you had me so afraid of dying, I couldn't concentrate on pitching."

Tommy Lasorda
As told to Ernie Witham

T-Ball and the Beaver

All kids need is a little help, a little hope and somebody who believes in them.

Earvin (Magic) Johnson

"Just call me Beaver. Everyone does. See why?"

With that he wrinkled up his face, displayed two extra large upper front teeth over his lower lip, flapped his arms, chirped like a bird and moved his posterior up and down.

So we called him "Beaver."

He was the least athletic member of our T-ball team—quite a distinction, for T-ball is populated by kids who are probably never going to be varsity players because they lack speed, coordination, strength or skill—or maybe all four, like Beaver. But no one was more lovable than the Beaver.

One of the goals of each season is to somehow help each kid—eight- and nine-year-old boys—have a moment when he is the hero, when his teammates mob him and praise his great feat on the diamond. It was going to be very hard to help the Beaver have his moment of glory.

Try as he would, the Beaver could not hit the ball off the tee very often, and when he did, the ball would dribble out to the pitcher, who would run and touch first base while an amazed Beaver stood and watched. Often the umpire—one of the dads recruited for the job—would give Beaver six strikes, usually in a futile attempt to help the Beaver hit the ball.

It bothered me to see the Beaver fail so often, and it hurt the whole team to watch. But it did not bother the Beaver. He always smiled and laughed after each disaster at the plate.

Beaver was no better in the outfield. Usually he and the closest outfielder teammate would be talking and laughing about who knows what. The Beaver was having a good time. Just being on the team was good enough.

The season was almost over. It was one of the last games. Then the miracle I prayed for happened. The Beaver accidentally hit the ball hard and just right after five strikes. The ball sailed over the heads of the shortstop and the left fielder, who were standing side by side, discussing which was worse—little brothers or sisters—and rolled out into left field.

Beaver just stood there in awe and utter amazement. All his coaches, teammates and fans, including me, yelled, "Run, Beaver. Go to first base. Yea, Beaver! Go, go, go!"

Beaver, totally overcome and utterly perplexed, stood motionless for a moment. Then he ran over to me and sat on the bench at my side.

"What are you doing here?" I asked. Beaver replied, "Everyone was yelling and screaming at me. I figured I was doing something wrong, so I ran over to be by you."

"Beaver, you did great. Now run over to first base where Mr. Johnson [one of the dads] is coaching."

Beaver got up and, with a gentle push from me, ran to first base. (The complexities of staying in the base path were for a future time.) The ball was still out in left field as a result of a badly executed relay.

When Beaver reached first base, Mr. Johnson told him to run to second base and gave him a gentle push in the right direction. He hollered at the Beaver as he ran toward second base, "Watch Mr. Andrews [the dad coaching third base] when you get to second base."

The throw to second base was wild and went out into right field. Mr. Andrews yelled to Beaver, "Come here, Beaver." Beaver ran to third base and stopped. The right fielder now had the ball. Another shout of encouragement and a gentle push from Mr. Andrews had Beaver running home. He beat the last wild throw of the play and scored! He just stood there, standing on home plate. He was smiling now.

His teammates, coaches, mothers and dads, and I ran to him and congratulated Beaver with unrestrained enthusiasm and utter joy. It was the kind of moment every kid should have at least once.

After the game Beaver taught us another lesson, in addition to facing adversity with a smile.

I said to him, "From now on we will call you Home-Run Ted."

"No," he said with a smile, "just call me Beaver." With that he wrinkled up his face, displayed two extra large upper front teeth over his lower lip, flapped his arms, chirped like a bird and moved his posterior up and down.

Beaver taught us that modesty in victory was a virtue as great as a happy disposition in adversity.

Amazing what we can learn from an eight-year-old in T-ball. In some thirty seasons of coaching kids' sports, T-ball and the Beaver was the greatest moment of all.

Judge Keith J. Leenhouts

$\overline{9}$

BOTTOM OF THE NINTH

You spend a good piece of your life gripping a baseball, and it turns out it was the other way around all the time.

Jim Bouton

Memories of My Hero

We can't all be heroes because someone has to sit on the curb and clap as they go by.

Will Rogers

During the endless summers of our youth, we would slide our baseball gloves onto the handlebars of our bikes and head to the neighborhood park, where we would play ball from sunrise to sunset.

We would arrange our bikes in the outfield to conform to the strange configuration of Yankee Stadium. We would make it ridiculously short in right, impossibly deep in center.

And then we would draw straws to see who got to be Mickey Mantle that day.

It was the early 1960s, a time when the Beatles invaded our shores and record stores, JFK inspired a nation to explore a New Frontier and baseball served as our national pastime instead of our national passé-time.

In those days, millions of us baby boomers wanted to be like Mick. He gripped our souls the way his powerful hands once gripped a Louisville Slugger.

We wanted to wear the regal New York Yankee pin-stripes with the No. 7 on the broad back, and roam the expansive, lush green outfield of the world's most famous ballpark. In our sandlot games, we would swing so hard from both sides of the plate in hopes of making baseballs get small in a hurry, just like the Mick. Some of us were so into Mantle we even imitated his gimpy-kneed home-run trot. Head down. Arms up.

One of the highlights of our youthful springs was rip-ping open a pack of baseball cards and finding a Mantle nestled between a Bill Tuttle and a Daddy Wags Wagner. We didn't need a price guide to tell us his card was valu-able. Our hearts told us so.

We kept scrapbooks of his heroics, pored over box scores in search of his name in the morning paper and sneaked transistor radios into classrooms to listen to the World Series exploits of the original Mr. October.

These eyes have had the privilege of seeing many sports icons perform up close and personal. We have watched Michael Jordan defy the laws of gravity, Joe Montana turn a pressure-packed Super Bowl into a leisurely backyard game of pitch and catch, and the Golden Bear drain a 60-foot birdie putt during a U.S. Open.

But none of those athletes, none of those moments, ever thrilled us the way Mickey taking batting practice did during the summer of '66. We were only eleven at the time, but the impression is indelible. It was our first trip to the House That Ruth Built and Mantle Renovated. And as we watched in awed amazement while the blond-haired, blue-eyed, biceps-bulging Mantle muscled batting prac-tice offerings into the clouds, we couldn't help but notice a different sound to the balls he hit. It was an explosion rather than a crack of the bat. White ash against horsehide never sounded so good.

All these memories came rushing back recently when

the idol of our youth fought a courageous but losing battle against liver cancer. Mantle's life, by his own admission, was flawed. He had endured considerable tragedy—some of it beyond his control, some of it self-induced. But he never sought pity, never blamed anyone but himself. And those of us who worshipped him unconditionally in our youth came to admire him even more during the final eighteen months of his life.

As the most gifted natural athlete ever to play the game, Mantle had often saved his best for the late innings. And so it was with his life.

He talked with amazing candor and poignancy about his forty-two-year struggle with alcoholism in hopes that others wouldn't follow the same path. He attempted to reconcile differences with his family, to be the father he rarely was when his boys were young.

And in a gesture more powerful than any of the 536 home runs he blasted during his eighteen-year Hall of Fame career, he threw his name and energies behind a national organ and tissue donor campaign. The liver transplant that prolonged his life so moved Mantle that he insisted on doing all he could to raise public awareness about the importance of organ and tissue donations.

Hemingway described courage as "grace under pressure," and in the final weeks of Mantle's life he embodied that definition. His doctors said he was, in many ways, the most remarkable patient they had ever seen. His bravery was so stark and real that even those used to seeing people in dire circumstances were touched by his example. Organ donations rose dramatically all across America. The Mick had homered again.

Scott Pitoniak

Giant Killer!

It is always better to proceed on the basis of a recognition of what is, rather than what ought to be.

Stewart Alsop

I wanted to warn them. I really did. But no one had ever warned me. Besides, they were big, strong football players . . . and she was just a little girl.

It was a charity softball game in the early 1990s and O. J. Anderson and other members of the New York/New Jersey Giants football team were playing to the crowd. When Grace stepped up to the plate, Anderson ordered all the infielders to get down on their knees.

In chess one might call this knights off, giving an apparent inferior opponent an advantage to even the game. In softball, however, this was nothing but male chauvinism.

Being raised in a matriarchal household, I thought I knew better. Being a sportswriter who often covered women's games, I thought I knew better. It turns out, however, that I didn't know Grace. Neither did the Giants.

On our first real date, Grace and I decided to go to

Grand Slam USA, which offers miniature golf, arcade games and batting cages all under one roof. Still in that awkward stage where you want to talk but are afraid of what you might say, this seemed like an ideal place to let actions speak louder than words. And my greatest action during the night was going to dump.

Whatever we played—wherever we played it—I was going to lose. I thought this was what gentlemen did.

As the night dragged on, I did lose. Not that I could have done much to prevent the inevitable.

Grace sank a hole-in-one on her first swing in miniature golf. She fired the puck off my hand, drawing blood in an air hockey game. She won at pool.

She held off alien invasion after alien invasion in the arcade. Then she suggested we try the batting cages.

On her insistence, I went first. Not competing directly against her, I decided to swing away. Unfortunately, as much as I love baseball, this was never my game. More often than not, I heard that sickening thud of the ball hitting the padding behind me. I choked up on the bat and managed to slap a ball here, foul one off there. Mercifully, it was soon over.

"Boy, that was quicker than I thought," I said as I tried not to stare up at the huge SLOW sign connected to the battling cage that I had just left. "You want me to tell them to change the cage to softball for you?"

Grace pulled on her batting helmet and shook her head no. "I'll just try this one." She then stepped into the cage marked FAST and put in her tokens.

While preparing for my turn at bat, I went through all the motions. I stretched. I took my practice swings. I tugged at the back of my shirt. I may have even absent-mindedly even tried to knock dirt out of my sneakers with the barrel of my bat. Grace did none of this. She dropped her bat over her shoulder like a jacket and stood straight up and motionless as if waiting for a bus.

Perhaps O. J. Anderson was thinking the same thing I thought the first time I saw Grace stand next to the plate. She was fundamentally wrong. I expected her to swing and miss. O. J. Anderson expected her to swing and miss.

She didn't.

Once the pitch was released, Grace dropped her bat through the strike zone like a sledgehammer. The bat dropped quicker than my jaw as she smacked liner after liner back up the middle.

Against the Giants, she went down the third base line at Gary Taylor, who was a little more vocal than all his teammates about how he felt a girl would play.

The ball hit two feet in front of Taylor and kicked up dirt into his face. He got even dirtier as he dove into the ground to get away from the sharp bounce coming right at him.

The Giants wanted their laugh. Well, they got it. In fairness to most of the team, however, they seemed happier that the joke was now on Taylor.

Taylor, much the same as myself, also took it well after a moment or two of adjustment.

Stepping out of the batting cage Grace must have looked into a stunned face. "Didn't I tell you I went to college on a softball scholarship? I'm sorry. I thought I did. Are you mad?"

Grace and I have been married eight years now. We argue about money and household chores. From time to time, we get mad at each other. This anger is never manifested out of jealousy of the other one's strengths, though. Grace's ridiculous-looking—but amazingly effective—swing has always been a source of pride for me. It's also been a source of humor. There's nothing quite as funny as watching a guy playing the outfield wave for all his teammates only to have to turn around and chase a ball that flew fifty to one hundred feet over his head.

A part of me wanted to warn these guys. A part of me wanted to warn the Giants. It is a very small part. The rest understands the best way to learn a lesson is firsthand.

Later in the charity game against the Giants, Anderson spotted who was coming to the plate before his team-mates and once again ordered the infielders down to the ground. Taylor obediently dropped to his knees before looking up and spotting Grace at the plate.

Quicker than most receivers in the open field, Taylor jumped up to his feet and started to laugh. "You jerk! You jerk!" he yelled at Anderson. "If I stay down there, she's going to kill me."

I wanted to warn them. I really did. But hey, she's just a little girl.

What could she possibly do against all those big, strong football players?

Kyle Moylan

A Cup for the Coach

Our next-door neighbor was the coach of my oldest son's team. He frequently took the team "back to the field for practices." On one such occasion it was a warm spring day, and the boys were at practice. I was busy doing my "motherly chores" when I heard a knock at the back door. Upon answering the door I found two boys from the team. They said Mr. P., the coach, needed a cup. I immediately went to one of my boys' rooms and got a cup. The boys ran back to the field with it. A few minutes later and another knock at the back door. The same players were there. I opened the door and the boys proclaimed Mr. P. didn't need an athletic cup, he needed a drinking cup! Oh the mind-set of the mother of boys!

Joanne P. Brady

Back When

Family life is the basis for a strong community and a great nation.

Bing Crosby

It was an American tradition—a real, honest-to-goodness game of sandlot baseball—and it was being revived. Gone were the uniforms and the uniformed children, identical in age and size. Gone were the tension-ridden parents overseeing the nerve-racking games. Gone were the agitated umpires, managers, assistant managers and assistant-assistant managers. Gone were the scheduled "time-outs" while harried officials consulted section B of article 2 of part 1 of the ever-so-official rule book.

It was wonderful! We held an old-time, Saturday afternoon softball game. We had invited twenty friends and neighbors to come; twenty-five showed up, hesitantly eager to play. Just minutes after the game began a carload of strangers slowed to watch, and then asked if they could join the fun. The players were men and women, boys and girls, ranging in age from eight to sixty-eight.

"You're out!"

"No, I'm not!"

"I said you're out!"

"You don't know what you're talking about!"

It was good old-fashioned democracy in action.

"I don't see too well without my glasses," explained the guy who had been my neighbor for ten years and whose conversation had consisted of tight-lipped greetings. "You take first," he said to my son, "and I'll go way out in the field so I won't mess up an important play." It was teamwork because the individual wanted to do what was best for the team, not because some coach was shoving "teamwork" down his throat. When one oldster got tired, he sent a youngster in to relieve him, while he sat on a haystack and sipped some refreshment. Nobody kept score. Everybody kept score. Nobody cared what inning it was, and the game ended when there was no one left who wasn't too tired to play. Best of all, everybody had a grand time and went away wanting to do it again.

I have silently watched progress replace country roads with freeways and corner grocery stores with sterile supermarkets. But something in me hesitated to accept progress when organized Little League games started replacing spontaneous neighborhood softball games.

It is not just nostalgia. It is a memory revived and brought to life for a gathering of friends and family. But I feel just a little sad that a scene so interwoven with my childhood and the childhoods of so many Americans has become a novelty in this country. What happened to that empty lot that used to be on everybody's block?

Audrey Curran

Coming Out of Retirement

You can't help getting older, but you don't have to get old.

George Burns

The baseball glove had been in hibernation for nearly a decade, collecting dust rather than line drives, on a bookshelf next to Hemingway's *A Farewell to Arms*. Occasionally, the man would grab the old Wilson A2000 and pound a fist or a ball into it. Although the glove had grown hard and crusty from years of neglect, there was still something special about it.

Each time the man put it on, a smile would crease his face and pleasant memories would come rushing back. He would recall all those boyhood games at the park down the street during summer vacations when he and his neighborhood friends would play ball from sunrise to sunset, breaking only for lunch and dinner. He would replay the Little League games and the high school games and the Legion games and the beer-league softball games.

Then the phone would ring or one of his kids would scream, and reality would return and the man would place his glove and his memories back on the shelf.

A few weeks ago, an acquaintance asked the man if he would like to play on a softball team. The man hesitated at first. There was a time when he couldn't get enough of the game. He'd play in a couple of leagues during the week, then participate in tournaments on the weekends. But that was when he was twenty-something rather than thirty-something approaching the big four-oh.

That was when his back didn't ache and the reading on the bathroom scale didn't depress him and he could make out the bottom line of the eye chart without the aid of contact lenses.

He wondered if his fragile male ego would be able to handle the humiliation he might feel if a ground ball zipped through his legs or if he swung with all his might and popped feebly to the catcher.

After rounding up all the reasons that he shouldn't come out of retirement, he forked over his ten-dollar registration fee and scrawled his name on the softball sign-up sheet. *What the heck?* he thought, *there are worse things in life than letting a ball roll under your glove.*

The man showed up at practice a week ago, left hand comfortably encased in the A2000, feet stuffed into baseball spikes that over time had become two sizes too small. He stretched a bit, then began playing catch. His arm felt good, real good.

A coach grabbed a bat to hit some infield balls. The man settled in at third base. He spit in his glove and readied himself on the balls of his feet.

"You and me, baby. You and me," he told the pocket of the A2000. The coach meant to hit a grounder, but instead whacked a line drive and the man ranged a few steps to his right and backhanded the ball. He threw to first just for the heck of it. The ball made a loud pop in the first baseman's mitt. "What an arm," bellowed one of the players. "What an arm."

A hard grounder followed. It bounced off the man's chest. He retrieved it and let loose with a throw that Manute Bol couldn't have pulled back to Earth. "What an arm," came the bellow again. The man smiled.

Later, during a practice game, the man blooped a Texas Leaguer just beyond the shortstop's reach. He dug for first, feeling as if he were lugging Cecil Fielder on his back. When the outfielder bobbled the ball, the man instinctively began digging for second. Halfway there, he felt something pull in his right leg. He grabbed his hamstring and limped safely into second. He gimped around for the rest of the practice, but never, for a minute, considered taking a break. It had been years since he had hurt so bad and felt so good.

His wife shook her head when he limped through the door. There was dried blood on his left knee and a grotesque, purplish bruise on his right hand, the result of foolishly trying to field a bad hop bare-handed.

"Honestly," she said, examining her disheveled husband. "Some people never grow up."

The man grinned, then walked gingerly over to the shelf and placed the A2000 in its old spot, next to Hemingway's classic.

"Retirement's over," he said to the glove. "See you in a week."

Scott Pitoniak

A Childhood Memory

Baseball, to me, is still the national pastime because it is a summer game. I feel that almost all Americans are summer people, that summer is what they think of their childhood. I think it stirs up an incredible emotion within people.

Steve Busby

When I write a story, I'm rarely thinking of the reader. It's not that I don't care what they reader thinks. I do. But first and foremost, I'm concerned with telling a good story. In the process, I oftentimes forget, or rather don't realize, what impact my words have on a reader.

That point hit home at the 2000 All-Star Game in Atlanta.

Major League Baseball sponsored a Wiffle ball tournament, and it prompted me to write a story on the seemingly forgotten game.

I talked to a childhood friend, who had joined me in countless Wiffle Ball games in my backyard. I talked to a coworker, the baseball editor at *USATODAY.com*. And finally, at the All-Star Game, I went from player to player asking if he ever played Wiffle ball and if he would mind sharing some of those memories.

The article generated a lot of feedback, more than I imagined. The e-mails reached my in box from places around the world. Obviously, I helped stir a whirlwind of emotions that I had no idea existed.

Wiffle ball, a primitive form of baseball, is a game for everyone. All you need is two people, the long skinny plastic yellow bat and the hole-filled white plastic ball.

You could play most anywhere, in the strangest of field dimensions. The peculiarities of a Wiffle ball diamond enhanced the affection you had for the game. I wilted away several summer days playing Wiffle ball, mostly with my friend Steve Boudrie.

We used to play in my backyard. We had standings, a schedule and eventually play-offs and a World Series. You were Nolan Ryan, Reggie Jackson and George Brett all in the same afternoon.

A three-section lawn chair determined balls and strikes, the middle section being the strike zone. A hit past the pitcher was a single. A hit past the tree in the backyard was a double. Off the fence in the air was a triple and over the fence was a homer. Anything not hit past the pitcher was an out, and anything you caught in the air was an out.

Nothing was better than hitting an opposite-handed homer or striking out a batter. Nothing was worse than striking out with two outs and ghost runners on second and third, or having the tree block the ball from sailing over the fence, or watching a third strike barely tick the lawn chair.

Boy, did my mom get upset when foul balls regularly tinked off the house's siding. Boy, did old man Orick get peeved when we had to go trudging through his garden to get a foul ball. I remember this quote from him: "I'll beat you with a hoe handle until you piss your pants if you don't get outta that garden." I hopped back over the fence into my yard in record speed, laughing so hard I nearly wet myself.

"Wiffle ball was great because we could play with just two people," Boudrie told me in an e-mail. "It involved our imagination. The games allowed us to use our creativity, imagining we were certain players, following the line-ups, utilizing the dimensions of the 'diamonds' that we played on, such as a short right-field porch."

Steve Gardner, the baseball editor at *USATODAY.com*, was no stranger to the game.

"First of all, it was a great neighborhood game for all ages, but it was even better one-on-one," he said. "My brother and I used to assume the identities of our favorite major-league teams and stage a World Series game—usually complete with the requisite down-to-the-wire drama.

"To maximize the pitcher-batter concentration we had my mom's '74 Ford Pinto parked right on the street behind home plate. It was great for blocking just about every pitch the batter let pass. As an added bonus the door panel was just about equivalent to a batter's strike zone. The batter watches it go by, and it hits the door— called strike. Hits the window—ball high. Goes under the car or bounces—ball low."

San Francisco Giants second baseman Jeff Kent busted out in laughter when asked about Wiffle ball memories.

"We used to put duct tape on the ball so we could throw it faster," Kent said. "Someone once threw a sinker or slider and it was coming down the middle of the plate. The next thing I know the ball breaks and drills me in the face. I didn't like playing much after that."

Boston Red Sox reliever Derek Lowe recalled his Wiffle ball days with a fondness he carries with him when he pitches today.

"We played in an alley behind my buddy's house," he said. "The fence wasn't even a hundred feet. There was a garage in left field that we had to hit it over for a home run. That's when the game was fun. I apply that attitude to baseball today. It hurt me when I was younger in the minors because people thought I was lackadaisical. But I was just having fun. It's helped me in the big leagues. As a reliever, you're in some pretty intense situations, and those days have helped me find a way to settle down."

The article ran, and the e-mails flooded my inbox.

Then there was an e-mail from David J. Girman, and he made me realize how important Wiffle ball was to someone else. This is what he wrote:

"I just wanted to thank you for bringing me back to my backyard, probably twenty years. My brother and I used to play every day. We also had the lawn chair as the strike zone, with an old fence post as first base, the center pole of a swing set as second, and a cherry tree as third (all for ghost runners, of course). . . . You see, my brother died from brain cancer in 1987 (at the age of twenty). I am starting my own family now with a new wife, I adopted her daughter, and we are pregnant with our first. I think we are having a boy and naturally I will name him after my best friend, who just happened to be my brother. There are a lot of things I wish for, a lot of things I wish that he could have seen, and many of those things are sports-related. Things like the talent that K. Griffey Jr. has, or just how B. Sanders could see behind him, or how fast Michael Johnson can run so easily and how M. Jordan ascended into superhuman on the court. There are times still when I see something and I look over to share it with him (just last night when Sosa hit his second five-hundred-footer) and they are some of the saddest moments that I spend alone. At the same time they are bringing me back to my favorite days when my brother and I would play ball all day long until we heard our mother yelling for Joey and David to come home."

Baseball is not life and death. But in life and in death, we remember the game, and we remember those who shared the game with us.

Wiffle ball might not be traditional nine-on-nine baseball with hard ball, wood bat, spikes, gloves and umpires. But we invoked the images of real players and expanded the boundaries of imagination in the name of sport, creating memories and friendships that are tied to baseball. Those are days I'll never forget.

When I was at the grocery store the other day, I saw two guys buying a Wiffle ball and bat. I should probably do the same sometime soon.

Jeff Zillgitt

Frank and Ernest

FRANK & ERNEST ©*NEA. Reprinted by permission.*

So Many Things to Love About America's Game

It's opening day, and I love baseball.

I love baseball stadiums, especially old ones in old parts of town.

I love baseball cards—for the right reasons, not for the money.

I love the fact that sixty feet, six inches, three strikes, nine innings and ninety feet are still perfect after all these years.

I love the echo of baseballs being hit during batting practice in any empty stadium.

I love watching windbreaker-clad pitchers run wind sprints on the outfield warning track during exhibition games.

I love the fact that Choo Choo Coleman, Pee Wee Reese and Cool Papa Bell answered to those names. As adults. In public.

I love the scent of freshly cooked popcorn in a stadium just about to open.

I love a beautifully dragged infield, and a pitcher's mound carved just so with the resin bag in back.

I love the ivy at Wrigley, the Green Monster at Fenway, the subway that practically drops you off at home plate at Montreal's Olympic Stadium.

I love the Baseball Hall of Fame.

I love the fact that the Baseball Hall of Fame is located in charming little Cooperstown, New York, even though the myth of baseball being invented in Cooperstown was exposed long ago.

I love the minor leagues.

I love the Little League World Series and the jewel of a miniature diamond in Williamsport, Pennsylvania.

I love finding a game on the radio when driving a lonely stretch of highway late at night.

I love the fact that Yogi Berra didn't say half the funny stuff he's credited with saying, but the stories are just too good to let go.

I love the fact that a grizzled sportswriter can still cherish the memory of Willie Davis, thirty-eight years after he last saw him play in person.

I love batboys, ball girls and P.A. announcers with pizzazz and a clue.

I love shagging fly balls. Still.

I love seeing kids' faces light up when a ballplayer says anything to them. Anything at all.

I love watching men so incredibly gifted that they can swing a stick at a tiny, speeding, rock-hard sphere and make it fly great distances.

I love watching second basemen fly over sliding base runners to complete the double play.

I love bullpen cars and foul poles that are in fair territory and dugouts that are truly dug out of the earth.

I love a deserted clubhouse decorated with freshly laundered uniforms hanging in cubicles filled with the working tools of ballplayers.

I love Edgar Martinez's swing.

I love Randy Johnson's fastball.

I love Junior Griffey's smile.

I love a center fielder flagging down a fly in the gap, a shortstop coming up throwing from the hole, a blurry-fast relay from the outfield that nips a sliding runner at the plate.

I love meal money, tips for the clubhouse attendants and visiting players who take the time to say something to put the batboy at ease.

I love *Bull Durham, Major League* and *A League of Their Own* because they captured on film the incredible joy and agonizing pain of trying to play a game for a living.

I love that Harry Caray was loved by fans because he loved them, the Cubs and baseball. Not necessarily in that order.

I love bratwurst with Special Stadium Sauce at County Stadium in Milwaukee.

I love crab cakes at Camden Yard in Baltimore—I'm sure of it, though I've never eaten crab cakes and never been to Baltimore.

I love keeping a scorecard.

I love the seventh-inning stretch.

I love drinking a cold beer in a distant seat in a minor-league stadium I've never seen before.

I love Dave Niehaus and Grand Salami Time.

I love the fact that now-famous millionaires like Ken Griffey Jr. (Bellingham, Washington), Mike Piazza (Salem, Oregon) and Cecil Fielder (Bune, Montana) made their professional debuts nearby not so many years ago, and many of us were lucky enough to see them and realize we were witnessing something very, very special.

Howie Stalwick

Still Dangerous

Cobb lived off the field as though he wished to live forever. He lived on the field as though it was his last day.

Branch Rickey

Ty Cobb is remembered as one of baseball's all-time ferocious competitors. He owns the highest lifetime batting average in the history of the majors. Always controversial, the Georgia Peach was a legend in his own time, and his peculiar mystique seems to grow with each passing decade.

Cobb was a man driven to succeed. And while Ty's confrontational style won him few friends, it did win him respect. Cobb was a force to be reckoned with, and everyone in baseball knew it . . . not least of all Cobb himself.

Two players dominated baseball in the early twentieth century: Ty Cobb and Babe Ruth. The two men couldn't have been further apart, both in their approach to the game and in their unique personalities. Always in excellent physical shape, the fanatical Cobb was a percentage man, a baseball purist. Cobb would get on base any way he could . . . by a walk, getting hit by a pitch, bunting or punching line drives through the holes. And once on base he became a terror—stealing bases, heckling opponents and breaking up potential double plays with his infamously sharpened spikes. The Georgia Peach was definitely "old school."

Ruth, of course, changed the game forever with his emphasis on the long ball. In an era when Frank "Home Run" Baker had led the majors with twelve round-trippers, Ruth came along to hit forty, fifty and eventually even sixty. Of course, the Babe also led the league in strikeouts. But his titanic blasts captured the imagination of an entire generation. Coupled with his proclivity for beer, hot dogs and practical jokes, Ruth's bigger-than-life persona seemed the embodiment of excess . . . the perfect marketing package for the Roaring Twenties. Ruth was definitely not old school.

Inevitably, as the fans came to love the Babe, Cobb came to loathe him. He outwardly showed contempt for Ruth's performance. Frustrated by the tremendous attention Ruth received, Cobb took his explosive anger out on opponents. He scratched for even more hits, stole more bases and piloted his Detroit Tigers to even more wins. Once, to prove his point that Ruth's home runs were not a terribly difficult feat, Cobb told his teammates to pay close attention to his at bats in an upcoming two-game series with the Browns. On the first day Cobb changed his grip, his stance and his signature style. Swinging for the fences in imitation of Ruth, Cobb treated his Tigers to an awesome display of the long ball, belting three Ruthian blasts to the astonishment of many in attendance. The following day Cobb crushed two additional homers as an exclamation point, then returned to his "old school" ways. Obviously, there was no doubt in Cobb's mind who the greatest player of the day was: Tyrus Raymond Cobb.

Several decades after his retirement, Cobb's competitive fires still burned. When he was invited to participate in an "old-timers" exhibition before a regularly scheduled major-league game, Cobb gladly accepted. Although his fellow old-timers jogged the bases, showboated and basically clowned around, Cobb would have none of that nonsense. He was strictly business, just like the Ty Cobb of old. Despite being one of the most senior players on the field, the Georgia Peach charged after fly balls, smashed line drives and even stole bases. Not surprisingly, Cobb was named the event's MVP. Afterwards, as a special guest of honor, Cobb was invited up to the broadcast booth for an on-air interview. The subject of Cobb's gaudy lifetime .367 batting average was soon introduced.

"Ty, let's talk about your lifetime average and all the changes that baseball has seen since you played," segued the announcer. "Of course, it's a totally new era today and an entirely different game. We have new rules, new ballparks and a new strike zone. The players are bigger and faster. We've seen the rise of the great black and Latin American players, plus the emergence of the relief pitcher as a specialty position. Ty, when you consider all these changes over the years, tell us, what kind of batting average do you think Ty Cobb would carry if he were playing today?"

"Oh, I don't know," Cobb shrugged. "That's a hard question to answer. Anything I say would just be a guess."

"Of course," replied the announcer. "But in your opinion, what would you be batting if you were playing in the major leagues today?"

The Hall of Famer rubbed his chin and pondered for a moment.

"Well," said Ty, "maybe .270 or .275."

The announcer was stunned. "Mr. Cobb, let me make sure I understand you correctly. You're saying that the great Ty Cobb, the man who once routinely hit over .400, would only hit for .270 or .275 if playing today?"

"It's just a guess. But .275 seems about right to me," Cobb confirmed.

"Well, I'm amazed, Mr. Cobb," the announcer confessed. "I wouldn't have guessed that. Why do you suppose your average would be so low?"

The Georgia Peach frowned and shook his head. "Listen, young fella," he snapped. "You saw me play out here tonight. Look at me . . . let's face it, I'm past seventy years old now. My wheels aren't so good anymore and I can't get down the first-base line like I used to. You wait till you're seventy and see if *you* can still hit .400. To tell you the truth, I don't think .275 would be all that bad for a man my age!"

Jack Myers

Full Circle

Baseball, it has been said, is a game of inches. But even more, it is a game of innocence. It is a child holding tightly to his father's hand as he is taken to his first big-league ball game. Some twenty years later the scene is repeated— the child, now a man, has his own hand clasped just as tightly by his son as they approach the ballpark together for the first time.

The father, as his father before him, knows full well that baseball is as much business as sport. He also knows that the world is not just and that life is not fair. But, given the slightest encouragement, mind and heart keep to their separate orbits. As father and son pass through the turn-stiles, walk side by side through the damp passageways under the stadium and then suddenly emerge into the dazzling brightness—the vast green playing field laid out like a magic carpet before them—they share the excite-ment that today is something very special for both of them. The parent passes on the wonder and awe of his own youth to his children, and in so doing renews it within himself.

Lawrence S. Ritter

More Chicken Soup?

Many of the stories and poems you have read in this book were submitted by readers like you who had read earlier *Chicken Soup for the Soul* books. We publish at least five or six *Chicken Soup for the Soul* books every year. We invite you to contribute a story to one of these future volumes.

Stories may be up to twelve hundred words and must uplift or inspire. You may submit an original piece, something you have read or your favorite quotation from your refrigerator door.

To obtain a copy of our submission guidelines and a listing of upcoming *Chicken Soup* books, please write, fax or check our Web site.

Please send your submissions to:

Chicken Soup for the Soul
P.O. Box 30880
Santa Barbara, CA 93130
fax: 805-563-2945
Web site: *www.chickensoup.com*

Just send a copy of your stories and other pieces to the above address.

We will be sure that both you and the author are credited for your submission.

For information about speaking engagements, other books, audiotapes, workshops and training programs, please contact any of our authors directly.

Supporting Others

Tommy and Jo Lasorda's son "Spunky" (Tommy Jr.) passed away in 1991. In his memory, Tommy and his wife wanted to fulfill their dream of helping people to better their lives. They accomplished this by establishing the Thomas Lasorda Jr. Field House. This facility, located in Yorba Linda, California, includes a large gymnasium and multipurpose room. It was completed on November 2, 1996, and was rededicated the Thomas Lasorda Jr. Field House on September 7, 1997. The City of Yorba Linda participated in the construction of the facility, and continues to give in order to maintain a quality center and program. The center, which is also used by the Placentia Yorba Linda School District, provides a place for children of all ages to learn strong moral values while teaching them skills in athletics, music, arts and crafts, drama and much more.

It is the goal of the Foundation that all young people are actively involved in all that the facility has to offer. This will help prepare these young people for the future in an atmosphere where they can learn to have fun and spend time with people who care about them.

For more information, or to find out how to get involved in this ongoing and fulfilling commitment please fax or write to:

Tommy Lasorda Jr. Memorial Foundation
c/o I.A.R.
156 N. La Brea Avenue
Los Angeles, CA 90036
phone: (323) 937-0327
fax: (323) 937-0329

Who Is Jack Canfield?

Jack Canfield is one of America's leading experts in the development of human potential and personal effectiveness. He is both a dynamic, entertaining speaker and a highly sought-after trainer. Jack has a wonderful ability to inform and inspire audiences toward increased levels of self-esteem and peak performance.

He is the author and narrator of several bestselling audio- and videocassette programs, including *Self-Esteem and Peak Performance, How to Build High Self-Esteem, Self-Esteem in the Classroom* and *Chicken Soup for the Soul—Live.* He is regularly seen on television shows such as *Good Morning America, 20/20* and *NBC Nightly News.* Jack has coauthored numerous books, including the *Chicken Soup for the Soul* series, *Dare to Win, The Aladdin Factor, 100 Ways to Build Self-Concept in the Classroom, Heart at Work* and *The Power of Focus.*

Jack is a regularly featured speaker for professional associations, school districts, government agencies, churches, hospitals, sales organizations and corporations. His clients have included the American Dental Association, the American Management Association, AT&T, Campbell's Soup, Clairol, Domino's Pizza, GE, ITT, Hartford Insurance, Johnson & Johnson, the Million Dollar Roundtable, NCR, New England Telephone, Re/Max, Scott Paper, TRW and Virgin Records.

Jack conducts an annual eight-day Training of Trainers program in the areas of self-esteem and peak performance. It attracts educators, counselors, parenting trainers, corporate trainers, professional speakers, ministers and others interested in developing their speaking and seminar-leading skills.

For further information about Jack's books, tapes and training programs, or to schedule him for a presentation, please contact:

Self-Esteem Seminars
P.O. Box 30880
Santa Barbara, CA 93130
phone: 805-563-2935 • fax: 805-563-2945
Web site: *www.chickensoup.com*

Who Is Mark Victor Hansen?

Mark Victor Hansen is a professional speaker who in the last twenty years has made more than four thousand presentations to more than two million people in thirty-two countries. His presentations cover sales excellence and strategies; personal empowerment and development; and how to triple your income and double your time off.

Mark has spent a lifetime dedicated to his mission of making a profound and positive difference in people's lives. Throughout his career, he has inspired hundreds of thousands of people to create a more powerful and purposeful future for themselves while stimulating the sale of billions of dollars worth of goods and services.

Mark is a prolific writer and has authored *Future Diary, How to Achieve Total Prosperity* and *The Miracle of Tithing*. He is coauthor of the *Chicken Soup for the Soul* series, *Dare to Win* and *The Aladdin Factor* (all with Jack Canfield), and *The Master Motivator* (with Joe Batten).

Mark has also produced a complete library of personal-empowerment audio and videocassette programs that have enabled his listeners to recognize and use their innate abilities in their business and personal lives. His message has made him a popular television and radio personality, with appearances on ABC, NBC, CBS, HBO, PBS and CNN. He has also appeared on the cover of numerous magazines, including *Success, Entrepreneur* and *Changes.*

Mark is a big man with a heart and spirit to match—an inspiration to all who seek to better themselves.

For further information about Mark, write:

MVH & Associates
P.O. Box 7665
Newport Beach, CA 92658
phone: 714-759-9304 or 800-433-2314
fax: 714-722-6912
Web site: *www.chickensoup.com*

Who Are Mark and Chrissy Donnelly?

Mark and Chrissy Donnelly are a dynamic married couple working closely together as coauthors, marketers and speakers.

They are the coauthors of the #1 *New York Times* bestsellers *Chicken Soup for the Couple's Soul, Chicken Soup for the Golfer's Soul, Chicken Soup for the Sports Fan's Soul* and *Chicken Soup for the Father's Soul.* They are also at work on several other upcoming books, among them *Chicken Soup for the Friend's Soul, Chicken Soup for the Romantic Soul,* as well as *Chicken Soup for the Golfer's Soul 2.*

As cofounders of the Donnelly Marketing Group, they develop and implement innovative marketing and promotional strategies that help elevate and expand the *Chicken Soup for the Soul* message to millions of people around the world.

Mark grew up in Portland, Oregon, and unbeknownst to him, attended the same high school as Chrissy. He went on to graduate from the University of Arizona, where he was president of his fraternity, Alpha Tau Omega. He served as vice president of marketing for his family's business, Contact Lumber, and after eleven years resigned from day-to-day responsibilities to focus on his current endeavors.

Chrissy, COO of the Donnelly Marketing Group, also grew up in Portland, Oregon, and graduated from Portland State University. As a CPA, she embarked on a six-year career with Price Waterhouse.

Mark and Chrissy enjoy many hobbies together including golf, hiking, skiing, traveling, hip-hop aerobics and spending time with friends. Mark and Chrissy live in Paradise Valley, Arizona, and can be reached at:

Donnelly Marketing Group, LLC
2425 E. Camelback Road, Suite 515
Phoenix, AZ 85016
phone: 602-508-8956 fax: 602-508-8912
e-mail: *chickensoup@home.com*

Who Is Tommy Lasorda?

Regarded by many as baseball's most popular ambassador, Tommy Lasorda will begin his fifty-second season in the Dodgers organization and fifth as vice president. He was named vice president on July 29, 1996 after retiring as manager, a position he held for the previous twenty seasons. Lasorda assumed all player personnel responsibilities when he was named the Dodgers' interim general manager on June 22, 1998. He relinquished his general manager duties when he was promoted to senior vice president on September 11, 1998.

In his current front-office capacity, Lasorda spends much of his time scouting, evaluating and teaching minor-league players as well as spreading baseball goodwill to thousands as he makes more than 100 speeches and appearances to various charities, private groups and military personnel each year.

In 1997, Lasorda was elected to the National Baseball Hall of Fame by the Veterans Committee in his first year of eligibility. He was the fourteenth manager and fifteenth Dodger inducted into the Hall of Fame. Lasorda's uniform number (2) was retired by the Dodgers on August 15, 1997 and the main street that leads to the entrance of Dodgertown in Vero Beach, Florida, was renamed Tommy Lasorda Lane on March 5, 1997. Lasorda also threw out the first pitch in Game 7 of the 1997 World Series.

Lasorda compiled a 1,599-1,439 record and won two World Championships, four National League pennants and eight division titles in an extraordinary twenty-year career as the Dodgers manager. He ranks thirteenth with 1,599 wins and twelveth with 3,038 games managed in major league history. Lasorda's sixteen wins in 30 National League Championship Series games managed were the most of any manager at the time of his retirement in 1996. Atlanta's Bobby Cox now holds the record with twenty-six wins in forty-nine games managed. His sixty-one post-season games managed rank third all-time behind Cox and Casey Stengel. Lasorda posted a 3-1 record as the National League manager in four All-Star Games. He joined St. Louis' Gabby Street (1930-31) as the only other manager in National League history to win league titles in his first two seasons when he led the Dodgers to titles in 1977-78. Lasorda also managed nine of the Dodgers' sixteen Rookies of the Year, more than any other big league skipper in history. He also managed six current major league managers during their playing days: Texas' Johnny Oates, Anaheim's Mike Scioscia, San Francisco's Dusty Baker, Detroit's Phil Garner, Milwaukee's Davey Lopes and the New York Mets' Bobby Valentine.

Prior to replacing Hall of Famer Walter Alston as manager on September 29, 1976, Lasorda spent four seasons in Los Angeles on Alston's coaching staff from 1973-76. He spent eight seasons as a manager in the Dodgers' minor league system at Pocatello (1965), Ogden (1966-68), Spokane (1969-71) and Albuquerque (1972). Lasorda also spent four years as a Dodgers scout after retiring as a player following the 1960 season. An astounding seventy-five players Lasorda managed in the minor leagues went on to play in the majors.

As a player, Lasorda compiled a 0-4 record and 6.52 ERA as a left-handed pitcher in parts of three major league seasons with the Brooklyn Dodgers (1954-55) and Kansas City Athletics (1956). In all, he spent sixteen seasons in the minor leagues from 1945-60, including a two-year stint in the military from 1946-47.

Lasorda has won numerous awards throughout his career, including being named Minor League Manager of the Year by *The Sporting News* in 1970, Manager of the Year by UPI and AP in 1977, Manager of the Year by AP in 1981 and National League Manager of the Year by Baseball America and Co-Manager of the Year by *The Sporting News* in 1988. He was the recipient of the Association of Professional Baseball Players of America's inaugural Milton Richman Memorial Award with Sparky Anderson in 1987, the BBWAA Philadelphia Chapter's Humanitarian Award in 1993, Los Angeles Junior Chamber of Commerce's Award of Merit in 1997, Touchdown Club of Columbus' Baseball Ambassador of the Year in 1997, Arete's Courage in Sports Award in 1997 and was honored by the President of the Dominican Republic in 1997 for his dedication to the game of baseball throughout his career.

Lasorda has been a spokesperson for the American Heart Association and has received honorary doctorate degrees from

Pepperdine University, St. Thomas University and the University of Phoenix.

Lasorda and his wife, Jo, reside in Fullerton, California. They will celebrate their fifty-second wedding anniversary on April 14, 2001.

Contributors

Several of the stories in this book were taken from previously published sources, such as books, magazines and newspapers. These sources are acknowledged in the permissions section. If you would like to contact any of the contributors for information about their writing, or would like to invite them to speak in your community, look for contact information included in their biography.

The remainder of the stories were submitted by readers of our previous *Chicken Soup for the Soul* books who responded to our requests for stories. We have also included information about them.

R. Gregory Alonzo, heralded as the definitive speaker on success, has achieved national acclaim for his work on prosperity consciousness and lifestyle fulfillment. Honored in 1992 by his peers as Speaker of the Year ,he is the author of *Say Yes to Success.* He makes his home in Carlsbad, California. He can be reached at 2943 Cottonwood St., #11, Orange, CA 92865 or (714) 936-3863.

Dom Amore, thirty-nine, has covered sports for Connecticut newspapers since 1982. He has covered the NFL and Major League Baseball for the *Hartford Courant* since 1992, including seven Super Bowls and three World Series. He authored *Return to the Final 4,* a chronicle of the University of Connecticut women's basketball teams 1995–1996 season. He is single and lives in Branford, Connecticut.

Phil Arvia is a sports columnist for the *Daily Southtown* in Chicago's south suburbs. A lifelong White Sox fan, in three years as Sox beat writer and seven years as a columnist, he has been guilty only once of cheering in the press box. Blame Ozzie Guillen.

Dave Barry is a humor columnist for the *Miami Herald.* His column appears in more than 500 newspapers in the United States and abroad. In 1988 he won the Pulitzer Prize for commentary. Many people are still trying to figure out how this happened. Dave lives in Miami, Florida, with his wife, Michelle, a sportswriter. He has a son, Rob, and a daughter, Sophie, neither of whom thinks he's funny.

Bob Batz, a Michigan native, has been writing for newspapers for forty-three years, the last thirty-two at the *Dayton* (Ohio) *Daily News.* Batz's writing awards include a Pulitzer Prize nomination for a series on Alzheimer's disease, which he turned into a stage play called *Long Goodbyes.* You can reach him at *bob_batz@coxohio.com.*

Hal Bock has written sports in New York for forty years, covering thirteen Olympic games and more than twenty-five World Series and Super Bowls.

Joanne P. Brady is a former private schoolteacher. She is the wife of a great husband, Tom. Mrs. Brady's most important job, thus far, is her role as the mother of Paul, Craig, Ross and Erin (the Brady Bunch without Alice). Missy, her daughter-in-law, and Paul recently presented her with beautiful Halle Rebecca, her first grandchild. She is presently working as an administrative assistant in an elementary school. She can be reached at *Jobradync@aol.com*.

James Breig is a native of Cleveland whose older siblings grew up in Pittsburgh. Naturally, he became a Yankees fan. An editor and writer, he lives in upstate New York and regularly contributes to such magazines as *Colonial Williamsburg Journal*. He now plays ball with his grandchildren.

Mike Bryan, a native Texan, is the author of two books with Keith Hernandez and one with Kirby Puckett. His other books include *Baseball Lives, Chapter and Verse, Dogleg Madness,* and most recently, *Uneasy Rider.* He lives in New York City.

Steve Carlson has had a varied career as a journalist, congressional staffer and radio personality. He currently runs a small book publishing company, Upper Access Books. His Web site is: *www.upperaccess.com*.

Dave Carpenter has been a full-time cartoonist since 1981. His cartoons have appeared in a number of publications, including *Harvard Business Review, Barron's, Reader's Digest, Wall Street Journal, USA Weekend, Saturday Evening Post, Better Homes and Gardens, Good Housekeeping* as well as a number of other publications. Dave can be reached at *davecarp@ncn.net*.

Rick Carson says, "When it comes to gremlin taming, he wrote the book." His several publications include two HarperCollins books. His first book, *Taming Your Gremlin,* has been on the stands for eighteen years, and has spawned translations in Portuguese, Japanese and French. He is founder of the Gremlin Taming Institute *(tamingyourgremlin.com)*.

Anne Carter is a retired teacher born and raised in New York City. Today she enjoys the "snowbird" life with her husband and precious feline. Anne loves time spent with grandchildren, traveling and writing. An avid animal lover, she plans to chronicle inspirational stories about her loved ones and pets. You can contact Anne at *carteracdc@webtv.net*.

Dan Connolly covers the Baltimore Orioles for the *York* (PA) *Daily Record.* The 1991 Elizabethtown College graduate has worked for Pennsylvania-based newspapers in York, Williamsport, Kennett Square and Coatesville. He lives in York with his wife, Karen and son, Alex. Reach Dan at *dconnolly@ydr.com* or *kdaconno@aol.com*.

Carol Costa is an award-winning playwright and the published author of three novels, a short story collection, and many magazine and newspaper articles.

Her plays have been produced in New York and in regional theaters across the country. She has also written two nonfiction books published by Pearson Education.

Clark Cothern has authored *At the Heart of Every Great Father* and *Detours: Sometimes Rough Roads Lead to Right Places*, both published by Multnomah. Clark pastors the Trinity Baptist Church in Adrian, Michigan. He is in demand as a public speaker. Reach him at *revwrite@aol.com*. See his Web site at *www.createdforapurpose.org*.

Robert W. Creamer is the author of a shelf of fine baseball books, including *Babe: The Legend Comes to Life*, and the following Bison Books: *Stengel: His Life and Times*, *Jocko* (with Jocko Conlan) and *Rhubarb in the Catbird Seat* (with Red Barber).

Audrey Curran author of two syndicated columns, "Curran Events," a (sophisticated Erma Bombeck) and "Headlines" (popular psychological issues), contributes articles to major publications and appears on talk shows. A licensed psychologist in private practice, a college psychology department chair and a forensics psychologist, she is currently working on a book.

Clive Cussler, acclaimed as America's grandmaster of adventure, has twenty international bestsellers to his credit, including *Raise the Titanic* and his latest *Valhalla Rising*. He has sold more than 120 million books in forty languages in more than 110 countries. All have made *The New York Times* list as well as other bestseller lists around the world.

Gary D'Amato is an award-winning sportswriter for the *Milwaukee* (Wisconsin) *Journal Sentinel*. He has written two books—*Mudbaths and Bloodbaths: The Inside Story of the Bears-Packers Rivalry* and *The Packer Tapes: My 32 Years with the Green Bay Packers*—with Domenic Gentile. D'Amato's work also has appeared in *Chicken Soup for the Golfer's Soul* and *Chicken Soup for the Sports Fan's Soul*. Contact him at *gdamato@onwis.com*.

Ken Daley covered the Dodgers for the *Los Angeles Daily News* from 1990–1995, and has been the national baseball writer for the *Dallas Morning News* since 1995. He has contributed to several publications, including *USA Today*, *Baseball America*, *Sports Illustrated* and *Maxim*. He lives in Dallas with wife Jennifer and daughter Eileen, whose softball team he coaches each summer.

Paul Della Valle is the publisher of The Lancaster Times, Inc., a small newspaper company in central Massachusetts. He has been named New England's Press Association Columnist of the Year three times and has published two books, *Welcome to Your Midlife Crisis* and *My Favorite Column of Yours Is the One Your Wife Wrote*. He is a diehard Boston Red Sox fan.

Harry Del Grande grew up in San Francisco North Beach area, where his love for sports developed as he played and coached in the neighborhood organizations. As the father of four sons, he became known as "Mr. Coach." Most of his leisure time was spent with the youth of the area.

Michael J. Feigum, a USAF veteran, has been writing sports on and off for the last twenty years. Mike, his wife, Barbara, and son, Michael, reside and work at Bethany Children's Home, Womelsdorf, Pennsylvania. Mike is currently the sports/outdoor columnist for the *West Berks Crier,* in Robesonia, Pennsylvania.

Michael Finley is a poet, novelist and business writer living in St. Paul. He has coached youth baseball for almost ten years. For more of his writings, visit his Web site at *www.mfinley.com.* Or write him at *mike@mfinley.com.*

David Fisher has coauthored several bestsellers, among them *Gracie* and *All My Best Friends,* with George Burns, and *The Empire Strikes Back,* with Ron Luciano. He brakes for lawyers, most of the time.

Jeffrey Flanagan has been a baseball writer/columnist for the *Kansas City Star* since 1989. He has also worked at the *Decatur* (Ill.) *Herald & Review, Portsmouth* (N.H.) *Herald,* and *Arizona Republic.* He is a native of Oshkosh, Wisconsin, and a graduate of University of Minnesota. He bats and throws right-handed and lives in Westwood, Kansas.

Ken Gire wrote Bible study guides for *Insight for Living* for four years. He is a graduate of TCU and Dallas Theological Seminary. He has written eleven books and two unproduced screenplays. Two of his books have won Gold Medallion Awards, one was voted "Book of the Year" by *Campus Life,* and two more have been honored as C. S. Lewis Honor Books. He and his wife, Judy, live in Monument, Colorado, with their four children: Gretchen, Kelly, Rachel, and Stephen.

Ellen Goodman has been with the *Boston Globe,* where she is an associate editor as well as a columnist, since 1967. In 1980, she won the Pulitzer Prize for distinguished commentary. Her book on social change, *Turning Points,* was published in 1979. Five collections of her columns have also been published: *Close to Home, At Large, Keeping in Touch, Making Sense,* and *Value Judgments.* Born in 1941, she lives with her husband in Brookline.

Bill Goldberg was raised in the Bronx, New York. In the shadows of Yankee Stadium and the once upon a time Polo Grounds, he worked his way through high school and college as a lifeguard in the neighborhoods of New York City. Graduate school took him out to Los Angeles, where he developed and still owns an art corporation. He is also the founder of International Athletic Representation, a firm representing the likes of Tommy Lasorda.

Bob Greene is a syndicated columnist for the *Chicago Tribune;* his columns can be read at *www.chicagotribune.com/greene.* As a magazine writer, he has been lead columnist for *Life* and *Esquire;* as a broadcast journalist, he has served as contributing correspondent for ABC News *Nightline,* and his news commentaries can be seen on television superstation WGN. His bestselling books include *Duty: A Father, His Son,* and *The Man Who Won the War, Be True to Your School, Hang Time: Days and Dreams with Michael Jordan* and, with his sister, D. G. Fulford, *To Our Children's Children: Preserving Family Histories for Generations to Come.*

Joe Haakenson began covering Major League Baseball in 1989, serving as a newspaper beat writer following the Angels and Dodgers. He has covered World Series games, All-Star games and has interviewed baseball legends like Mark McGwire, Cal Ripken Jr. and Nolan Ryan. Born, raised and living in Southern California, he can be reached at *Jhaak922@aol.com*.

Sharon Shearer Harsh is a graduate of Penn State University. She is the founder and president of Loss-Pro Services, Inc., a firm specializing in safety, loss prevention and traffic control for the utility industry. She resides in Acme, Pennsylvania, with her husband Jim and daughter Josie Marie.

Orel Hershiser has reached the pinnacle as a baseball player: MVP of two League Championship series and the MVP of the World Series; *Sports Illustrated* "Sportsman of the Year;" and the unanimous winner of the Cy Young Award. He also holds the record for the most consecutive innings pitched without yielding a single run—fifty-nine scoreless innings. But in spite of these achievements, Orel Hershiser may be best known for his strong character, his clear example of right living, and his esteem for traditional family values. This story was adapted from his new book, *Between the Lines: Nine Principles to Live By*, published in 2001 by Time Warner Books.

Bunny Hoest is one of the most widely read cartoonists today, reaching nearly 200 million diverse readers every week. She has produced "The Lockhorns," "Agatha Crumm," "What a Guy!" and "Hunny Bunny's Short Tale," distributed internationally by King Features, as well as "Laugh Parade" featuring Howard Huge for *Parade*. Known as "The Cartoon Lady," this dynamic and versatile talent has twenty-five bestselling anthologies and a host of exciting projects in the works.

Ted Janse received a journalism degree from the University of Pennsylvania and enjoys freelance writing. After a career selling printing, he is now enjoying retirement and watching the Red Sox spring training in Florida. He and his wife, Joan, enjoy gardening and spending time with their three daughters, Cheryl, Linda and Allison. His email address is: *e.janse@worldnet.att.net*.

Pat Jordan played professional baseball in the Milwaukee Braves organization from 1959 to 1962. His experiences resulted in the memoirs *A False Spring* and *A Nice Tuesday*, both called classics in their field. He has also written nine other books, among them the novels *The Cheat* and *AKA Sheila Doyle*, and hundreds of magazine articles for publications including *The New Yorker* and *The New York Times* Magazine.

Richard Justice received a bachelor of journalism degree from the University of Texas in 1976. A native of Waxahachie, Texas, he is a sportswriter for the *Houston Chronicle*. He has also worked for the *Washington Post, Baltimore Sun, Austin American-Stateman* and can be reached at *Richard.justice@chron.com*.

Bil Keane draws the internationally syndicated cartoon "The Family Circus," which appears in more than fifteen hundred newspapers. Created in 1960, it is based on Keane's own family: his wife, Thel, and their five children. Now nine grandchildren provide most of the inspiration.

Jeff Kidd is the sports editor for the *Beaufort (S.C.) Gazette*. He has written professionally for fourteen years, starting as a correspondent for South Carolina's largest daily newspaper, the *State*. Kidd's work has been recognized by the South Carolina Press Association eighteen times. He is also the author of a self-published baseball book, *The Total Hitter*.

Ralph Kiner, the Pittsburgh Pirate outfielder, led the National League in homeruns in each of his first seven years in the big leagues. Kiner's name is synonymous with the Pirates all-time offensive records along with Willie Stargell. As Willie was the greatest offensive threat from the left side of the plate, Kiner was their greatest threat from the right of the plate. His ten-year career statistics speak for themselves: twice he hit over fifty home runs, drove in one hundred or more runs six times, ranked first in slugging percentage three times, and averaged over one hundred walks. In 1949 his 127 RBI was tops in the league. Kiner's shortened career was complete in 1975 with his selection into the Hall of Fame.

Judge Keith J. Leenhouts is a pioneer in the court volunteer movement involving some seven million volunteers since 1959 research confirmed that repeat crime was reduced eleven and one-half times (not percent). One hundred probationers had twenty-three repeat convictions in a court using volunteers over five years. A court not using volunteers had 270. For free information write: 830 Normandy, Royal Oak, Michigan, 48073 or *www.courtmentor.org* or *www.olemiss.edu/depts/mje*.

Doug Lesmerises lives in Wilmington, Delaware, with his wife, Katie. He grew up in Palmyra, Pennsylvania, and graduated from Northwestern University in 1995. He has covered baseball and the Philadelphia Phillies since 1998. He hopes to write a whole book someday and hopes you read it.

Lois J. Mannon holds a bachelor of science degree and works at University Hospital in New York. She is currently finishing a novel, a murder mystery that further explores the relationships between fathers and sons. Lois enjoys horseback riding, shooting sports and baseball games. Please reach her at *Lois.mannon@med.nyu.edu*.

Mickey Mantle played for the New York Yankees, leading the team to twelve World Series between 1951 and 1968.

John McNamara received his degree in journalism from the University of Maryland in 1983. He works as a sportswriter/editor for the *Annapolis Capital* newspaper in Annapolis, Maryland, and recently coauthored a book about Cole Field House. Please contact him at *jmcnamara@capitalgazette.com*.

Steve Minnick lives in Utah with his wife Leanna. Writing is a lifelong avocation for Steve whose work has appeared in *Chicken Soup for the Golfer's Soul* among other articles, stories and screenplays. He says, "Second only to the writing itself, my greatest joy is the feeling of support and encouragement I receive from my wife, our children and some very good friends."

Kenneth Montgomery lives in Columbus, Mississippi, where he has been the owner of a bail-bonding agency for over twenty-one years. Very active in his church, he still finds time to do volunteer work at the local high school and coach in the park league. His favorite activities are family time, camping, and tailgating at Alabama football games. Keith is married to a beautiful lady named Anna and they have two children together: Heather, a nail technician and Jason, a park ranger.

Steven Moore splits his time between sitting in a chair writing and sitting on a tractor farming sheep, pigs and chickens with his family. A version of this story also appears in his upcoming novel about a city forklift driver's personal discovery through rural stories and myths. He can be reached through Chicken Soup for the Soul Enterprises, Inc.

David E. Morine is the author of *Good Dirt: Confessions of Conservationist, The Class Choregus* and most recently, *Vactionland: A Half Century Summering in Maine.* When Dave's not writing, he spends his time helping local conservation organizations save land.

Kyle Moylan is a graduate of Trenton State College. He is married and works as a sports editor for the Princeton Packet Group. Kyle collects sports memorabilia and enjoys writing. He can be reached at *DomAnnNick@aol.com.*

Earl T. Musick's humor has appeared in over one thousand newspapers, magazines and publications. Earl has worked with the Walt Disney Company, Christian Broadcasting Network and many others. Earl lives in Ohio with his beautiful wife, Debbie, and their two sons, Matthew and Mark. Please contact Earl at *www.musicktoons.com.*

Jack Myers pitched in amateur baseball for nearly a decade. He writes technical manuals and lives in Wayne, Pennsylvania, with wife, Joan, and their three cats. Jack also writes juvenile fiction. His basketball thriller, *Dr. Dunkenstein,* is represented by Dystel Literary Agency. Jack can be reached at *jackmyers@peoplepc.com.*

Michael O'Connor was eight years old when he attended his first Major league baseball game, but he had already developed a respect for the sport that bordered on the sacred. He and his wife now head a national touring music ministry called Improbable People. They live in Southern California with their two daughters.

Mary Owen is an award-winning journalist who freelances, teaches seminars and hosts speaking engagements nationally and internationally. She is the editor of the *Stayton* (Oregon) *Mail.* Once a full-time missionary, she travels on assignment and teaches journalism for youth with a mission. Contact her at *mmowrite@home.com.* Or write to: P.O. Box 165, Turner, OR 97392.

Daniel Paisner has collaborated on several *New York Times* bestsellers. He is also the author of the novel *Orbit* and several works of nonfiction. He has written for the *New York Times Magazine* and *Entertainment Weekly*. A lifelong baseball fan, he lives with his wife and three children—and his own prized collectible, a baseball signed by Brooklyn Dodger great Gil Hodges.

Scott Pitoniak is a nationally honored sports columnist and writes often about the human side of sports. Scott was born in Rome, New York, and graduated with honors from Syracuse University in 1977. He cherishes his time with his wife, Susan, and their children, Amy and Christopher. Please contact him at *spitoniak@democratandchronicle.com*.

Linda Poynter is a wife, mother and dental hygienist in New Richmond, Ohio. She spends her spare time with her horse, dogs and cats, and enjoys boating with her husband. Linda is an avid fan of baseball, especially the Cincinnati Reds.

Darrel Radford has been a professional journalist in Henry County, Indiana, for more than twenty-five years. He has authored one book, *New Castle: A Pictorial History*, which was first published in 1992 and is now almost sold out of its second printing. You may reach him at *radford@kiva.net*.

Dan Raley has been a sportswriter at the *Seattle Post-Intelligencer* for twenty-two years. He realized a childhood dream by working for his hometown paper. His two daughters are avid readers of *Chicken Soup* books. Please him reach at *Danraley@seattle-pi.com*.

Ron Reid, who has been a sports staffwriter for the *Philadelphia Inquirer* the past twenty years, wrote for *Sports Illustrated* from 1972 to 1980. He is a University of Michigan graduate and a three-time winner of the Jesse Abramson Award presented by the Track and Field Writers of America. Reid, sixty-six, the father of four, has two grandsons.

Rick Reilly is a six-time National Sportswriter of the Year and the popular back-page columnist for *Sports Illustrated*, the first signed, weekly opinion column in the magazine's history. His collection of columns, *The Life of Reilly* (Total Sports) is a national bestseller. He lives in Denver with his wife, three kids, and a golf game that keeps him from concentrating on anything very important.

Robert Remler received his bachelor of arts from Boston University in 1977 and a degree from the Culinary Institute of America in 1984. Robert is the health editor for a weekly newspaper on Long Island. He plans to write a novel about a jazz musician. Please reach him at *Rremler@aol.com*.

Cal Ripken Jr. was born in Havre de Grace, Maryland. He now lives outside of Baltimore with his wife and two children, and plays baseball—every day—for the Baltimore Orioles.

Lawrence S. Ritter's *The Glory of Their Times* remains the seminal oral history of the game. He was a professor of finance at New York University for over thirty years. Mr. Ritter is the author of numerous books on baseball and sports including *The Babe: The Game That Ruth Built, A Life in Pictures, The Story of Baseball* and *Lost Ballparks.* He is also coauthor of a novel.

Ken Rosenthal became a senior baseball writer at the *Sporting News* in August 2000. Prior to that, he worked thirteen years at the (Baltimore) *Sun*, the first four as an *Orioles* beat writer and the next nine as a general sports columnist. He is as 1984 graduate of the University of Pennsylvania.

Philip Ross, a Manhattan psychotherapist in private practice, has been writing for a general audience for nearly forty years. No matter what he's writing, a certain baseball autographed in 1983 is prominently displayed in his office. Phil lives with Barbara Coffino, mother of writer/public defender Michael Coffino, and can be reached at: *ipiprossi@aol.com.*

Mike Royko was born in Chicago in 1932 and for much of his youth lived in the flat above his family's tavern on Milwaukee Avenue. Not only did he become the most widely read columnist in Chicago history, but his column was syndicated in more than six hundred newspapers across the country. He was also the author of the classic account of city machine politics, *Boss.* Mike Royko's last column in the *Chicago Tribune* appeared in March 1997, a month before his death. His memorial service was held on a sunny day in Wrigley Field.

Alan Schwarz is the senior writer of *Baseball America Magazine* and a regular contributor to *ESPN Magazine*, the *New York Times* and many other publications. He lives in New York.

Peggy Spence received her bachelor of science with honors from Delta State University (Mississippi) and master of education from the University of Arizona. She is an educational consultant and children's book writer. She and her husband reside in Arizona's eastern mountains where they enjoy camping, fishing and the great outdoors.

Howie Stalwick is sports editor of the *Coeur d'Alene* (Idaho) *Press Daily* newspaper. A native of Spokane, Washington, he graduated from Eastern Washington University in 1977. Howie and Jennifer are the extremely proud parents of teenagers, Cheyanne (a college softball player) and Shanna (a college volleyball and track and field prospective).

Jayson Stark is currently a baseball columnist for *ESPN.com* and analyst on "Baseball Tonight" on ESPN TV. He formerly spent twenty years as a baseball writer and baseball columnist at the *Philadelphia Inquirer.* His work has appeared in *ESPN Magazine, Baseball America, "Sport" Magazine* and many other publications. His work has also appeared in two anthology books, *The Phillies Reader* and *Worst to First.* He lives in the Philadelphia area with wife, Lisa, and their three children, Steven, Jessica and Hali.

Mark Stodghill is legal affairs reporter for the *Duluth News Tribune.* He is an Air Force veteran who served a year in Vietnam and a year in Korea. He was a starter on the baseball and basketball teams at Macalester College in St. Paul, Minnesota. His claim to fame in college is pitching two complete games of a baseball header—and losing both. An avid marathoner and ultramarathoner, Mark has run 125 races of between 26.2 and 100 miles. The cracks he hears these days come from his sore knees, not from the bats of baseball sluggers. Please reach him at *Duluth News Tribune,* 424 West First Street, Duluth, MN 55802; e-mail *mstodghill@duluthnews.com.*

Andy Strasberg, is a native New Yorker, completed college and graduated cum laude from Long Island University. He realized a lifelong dream of working in Major League Baseball when he began a career with the San Diego Padres in 1975 that lasted twenty-two years. Since 1997, Andy has opened ACME (All-Star Corporate Marketing Enterprises) Marketing and has, with his staff, provided valuable service to a diverse group of clients. Andy frequently is a guest lecturer of sports marketing symposiums and is a recognized innovator in creative marketing.

William G. Tapply has lived his entire life in eastern Massachusetts and has suffered with the Red Sox the entire time. He retired from competitive softball last year only because he didn't want to be the only sixty-year-old infielder in the league. When he's not at Fenway Park, he writes mystery novels and fly-fishing stories and teaches college writing courses. He invites visitors to his Web site at *www.williamgtapply.com.*

Patrick Thomson received his bachelor of arts in speech communication from Cal State University, Northridge. He is a freelance writer and speaker living in Irvine, California. He and his wife, Geri, enjoy racquetball, movies, theater, bike riding and traveling to see their three married sons and three grandchildren. He can be contacted at (949) 559-4460.

Denise Turner is an editor at the *Times-News* in Twin Falls, Idaho. A graduate of Southern Illinois University, she wrote two books for Words books. Husband Revis is a college counselor. Daughter Becky just graduated magna cum laude from Boise State University. Son Steve is a high school baseball pitcher. Contact Denise at 1880 Falls Ave. E., Twin Falls, Idaho, 83301. Phone: (208) 734-7029. E-mail her at *denise@magicvalley.com.*

Don Wade is a columnist and feature writer for the *Memphis Commercial Appeal.* His work has been published on *ESPN.com* and in many newspapers across the country. Don and his wife Deb have three sons: Stephen, Matthew and Jonathon. You can reach Don at *dwadeinMemphis@aol.com.*

Dale Wannen received his bachelor of arts in economics from Rowan University in 1998. Currently he is a financial advisor for a major bank in southern New Jersey. In his spare time Dale involves himself in playing guitar, golfing and traveling. He plans on writing fiction novels. Contact him at 856-616-6805.

Ernie Witham writes a humor column called "Ernie's World" for the *Montecito*

Journal in Montecito, California. His humor has also been published in the *Los Angeles Times, Santa Barbara News-Press,* various magazines and a number of anthologies including five *Chicken Soup* books. He is available to lead humor workshops for any age group and can be reached at *ernie@ernieswebsite.com.*

Woody Woodburn is a sports columnist for the *Daily Breeze* in Torrance (Calif.) and author of *The Pirate Collection* featuring his columns. He has won numerous writing awards from the Associated Press as well as a number (the number being zero) of Pulitzer Prizes. E-mail: *Woodycolum@aol.com.*

Stephen Yudelson graduated from Brooklyn College in 1976. He is currently a businessman in Norwalk, Connecticut. An avid softball player and coach, he remains a loyal Mets fan. He lives in Newtown, Connecticut, with his wife Holly and family, where he spends much time contemplating life from the front porch. E-mail him at *BntlySlg2@yahoo.com.*

Jeff Zillgitt was born April 4, 1970, and writes about sports for *USATODAY.com.* Zillgitt, who went to Michigan State University, enjoys fly-fishing, camping, hiking, reading, writing and music, especially jam bands, bluegrass, jazz, rock and roll and the blues. You can read his columns at *www.usatoday.com/sports/comment/zillgitt/index.htm.*

The Legend. Reprinted by permission of William G. Tapply. ©1981 William G. Tapply.

Living His Dream. Reprinted by permission of Daniel Raley. ©2001 Daniel Raley.

That's Why God Made Tall Infielders and *The Power of Motivation.* Reprinted by permission of Tommy Lasorda as told to Ernie Witham. ©2001 Tommy Lasorda as told to Ernie Witham.

The Heart of the Game. Reprinted by permission of Steve Minnick. ©2000 Steve Minnick.

My First Home Run. Reprinted by permission of Jeff Kidd. ©2000 Jeff Kidd.

One Hit Makes All the Difference. Reprinted by permission of Douglas L. Lesmerises. ©2000 Douglas L. Lesmerises. First appeared in *The Wilmington* (Delaware) *News Journal,* March 12, 2000.

Catch of a Lifetime. Reprinted by permission of R. Gregory Alonzo. ©2000 R. Gregory Alonzo.

The Foul Ball. Reprinted by permission of Gary D'Amato. ©2001 Gary D'Amato.

Hero for the Day. Reprinted by permission of Clive Cussler. ©2000 Clive Cussler.

Winning Isn't Everything. Reprinted by permission of Mary Owen. ©1999 Mary Owen.

Man of His Word. ©1988 Ralph Kiner, first published by *Reader's Digest.*

True Heroes Earn the Title. Reprinted by permission of Michael J. Feigum. ©2000 Michael J. Feigum.

Meeting My Favorite Player. Reprinted by permission of Carol Costa. ©1999 Carol Costa.

A True Hero. Reprinted by permission of Joseph Haakenson. ©2000 Joseph Haakenson.

The Day I Met The Splendid Splinter. Reprinted by permission of Ted Janse. ©2001 Ted Janse.

Hero of the Game. Reprinted by permission of Dan Connolly. ©2000 Dan Connolly. First appeared in *The York* (PA) *Dispatch/York Sunday News.*

The Last Game. Reprinted by permission of Linda Poynter. ©2001 Linda Poynter.

One Man, Alone. Reprinted by permission of Hal Bock. ©2001 Hal Bock.

A Batboy Looks Back. Reprinted by permission of Mark Stodghill. ©1996 Mark Stodghill. Appeared in the *Minnesota Monthly* magazine, April 1996.

Who's on First? From *Strike Two* by Ron Luciano and David Fisher, ©1984 by Ron Luciano and David Fisher. Used by permission of Bantam Books, a division of Random House, Inc.

A Childhood Memory. Reprinted by permission of Jeffrey Zillgitt. ©2001 Jeffrey Zillgitt.

So Many Things to Love About America's Game. Reprinted by permission of Howie Stalwick. ©1998 Howie Stalwick.

Still Dangerous. Reprinted by permission of John G. Myers. ©2001 John G. Myers.

Full Circle. From *Full Circle* by Lawrence S. Ritter from *Baseball for the Love Of It.* ©1982 Anthony J. Connor.

Get Inside the Game

ML

Also Available:

Available Now!